PUBLIC SERVICE

THE HUMAN SIDE OF GOVERNMENT

John W. Macy, Jr.

1817

HARPER & ROW, PUBLISHERS

NEW YORK, EVANSTON
SAN FRANCISCO
LONDON

FIRST EDITION

STANDARD BOOK NUMBER: 06–0127694

LIBRARY OF CONGRESS CATALOG CARD NUMBER: 70–123950

Contents

	Introduction	*vii*
1.	Dimensions of American Public Service	1
2.	The Anatomy of Merit	13
3.	Public Service by Contract	27
4.	The Meaning of Public Careers	39
5.	Government Seeks the College Talent	49
6.	Making Equal Opportunity a Reality	65
7.	"Every Day Is Ladies' Day"	83
8.	Emphasizing Ability, Not Disability	95
9.	Public Employment as an Instrument of Social Change	111
10.	Labor-Management Relations in the Public Service	119
11.	Balancing of Rights and Responsibilities in Public Employment	145
12.	The Public Servant and Prohibited Political Activity	157
13.	Training and Education for Public Service	171
14.	Intergovernmental Cooperation in Public Service Development	185
15.	Pay Isn't Everything	195

16. The Quest for Leadership in Public Service   215
17. The American Public Servant Beyond the Borders   233
18. Performance in the Fish Bowl with the Spotlight on It   249
19. The Impact of the Computer in Public Service   257
20. Incentive for Improved Performance in Public Service   265
21. The International Dimension of Civil Service   273
22. Futures in Public Service   285

    Index   295

Introduction

The most rapidly growing segment of the American work force is public employment. The creation and expansion of public programs by government at all levels—federal, state, county, and municipal—have heightened the public demand for men and women who possess the total spectrum of American skills. These government programs, and their manpower requirements, are increasingly in competition with private employers for the highly educated professionals. The public payroll totals are rising rapidly and constitute an ever larger portion of public budgets. The ability of the nation to solve its most critical problems—education, law and order, environmental decay, urban blight—rests squarely upon the ability of the public services of the country to attract, retain, motivate, and utilize human talent. Recent program authorizations by Congress, state legislatures, and city councils may have been totally frustrated through the inability of governmental institutions to train and assign an adequate supply of professionals to plan and deliver these authorized services to the public.

With the expansion of government functions and the quantum leap in the number of public employees, labor-management relations in the public sector have emerged as a complex of critical problems of national significance. The strike of the sanitation workers in Memphis early in 1968 became the backdrop for the assassination of Martin Luther King,

Jr. The teachers' strike in New York City that fall triggered intergroup hostility and led to erosion of the city's school system. Hospital workers in San Francisco and Charleston, transit workers in Washington and New York City, firemen in Atlanta, have all resorted to unauthorized wildcat strikes in the past few years to dramatize their grievances against their public employers in this age of confrontation. Throughout the federal service, growing union restiveness has exploded in the first massive strikes among postal workers and air-traffic controllers in the face of a statutory no-strike provision.

Because of its size, government as employer faces in magnified form all the special employment problems in our changing society. Not only are these problems magnified, they must be presented, and their solutions sought, in the full spotlight of public accountability. There must be means for assuring the existence of equal opportunity as a reality, not just as a policy statement. The public employer should be looked to for leadership in developing new job patterns for the undereducated and underemployed. The special experience associated with summer employment for those on vacation from school should be nurtured by the managers in government. The therapy of work for the mentally restored, the mentally retarded, and the physically disabled must become a feature of employment pace-setting by government.

But do these special actions for special groups create an incompatibility with traditional procedures of merit selection and advancement? The customary measures of relative ability found in tests or in application ratings may exclude individuals whose potential ability is great but whose test-taking skill is limited. In view of the contemporary concern about cultural bias in our society, the possible presence of such bias in these standard measures becomes a tantalizing issue for administrative evaluation. If a meritocracy has been created in government through nearly a century of civil service, the validity of the process by which individuals enter such a group in contemporary society must be subjected to question in the light of changing conditions.

A distinguishing feature of public employment has been the forfeiture of certain rights that still accrue to workers outside of government. Denial of the right to strike, limitations on political activity, execution of oaths of allegiance, susceptibility to background investigation, and other restraints on freedom are increasingly being examined and reassessed. There are those who would challenge the time-honored cliché that "government employment is a privilege and not a right."

The terms "civil service" and "public careers" have become almost synonymous. And yet the vast majority of civil servants remain in government employ for relatively limited periods. In a highly mobile society the concept of a career with a single employer, even an employer as expansive in its opportunities as the national government, must be probed for justification. In a society that seeks to be open, should careers such as those in the Foreign Service or the regular military service be closed to entry at more mature levels? Advocates of self-renewal favor life careers of work that include the stimulus of organizational and professional change. Such renewal may be injected into government service through a variety of public and private experiences for those with the potential for significant leadership.

But what of leadership in the public realm? Where should it come from? Systems have been devised for the early detection of leadership candidates, for the training of the most promising, for their movement across organizational lines, and ultimately for their preparation to enter high responsibility. Nevertheless the top leaders, those appointed by the President himself and by other executive officers, are all too frequently selected without consideration of professional qualifications and preparation.

There is an urgent need for these and other issues relating to public employment to receive better-informed attention on the part of the American people. There is a need to shatter the myths and junk the stereotypes that symbolize public employment to many Americans. The prestige of public employment has never been particularly high. But the critical importance of government in the life and the future of the nation calls not for just sympathetic recognition of the abilities of those who work for all the people but also for a better knowledge of those people and the conditions at the public places of their employment. Perhaps broader knowledge may even move the citizen toward greater participation in government.

The purpose of this book is to present and discuss public service from the vantage point of a longtime practitioner in public personnel management. These are the retrospective observations of a government civil servant who was privileged to serve in the top federal personnel management post, the chairmanship of the Civil Service Commission, throughout the Kennedy and Johnson administrations. Most dissertations on public policy issues, most histories of government action, and most reporters of day-to-day government activities give scant coverage to the role of these subjects in the lives of millions of Americans. A few scholars have reviewed these problem areas from their observation towers in academia but not from within the high-pressure atmosphere of government operations, where the luxury of research and analysis is not always available. The significance of these issues has been highlighted through my own experiences and through actual problem-solving. This is not to say that the volume specifies final solutions and everlasting answers. In many instances the solutions arrived at prompted a new line of questioning and opened up policy issues as yet unexplored. Some of the solutions were judged to be deficient or inadequate through the test of governmental operations. Many of the issues were far short of solution at the watershed of administrations on January 20, 1969, when the author ceased to be a practitioner.

This volume is not intended to be an authoritative text or a comprehensive history of the civil service. It is neither a puff piece nor an apology for actions taken, decisions made, or declarations offered. Although the views are personal, there is an effort to present more than the personal view. Certain observations may seem critical to the point of self-injury, but there is throughout the volume an earnest endeavor to chart a course toward a better and more responsive public service. This endeavor is motivated by a lifelong enthusiasm for public service and by gratitude for a rewarding participation in the human side of government.

J.W.M., JR.

Washington, D.C.
February 15, 1971

PUBLIC SERVICE

Dimensions
of American

1   # Public Service

As America prepares to commemorate two centuries of national development, 11 million citizens are engaged in performing the myriad tasks necessary for its governance. More than one out of every seven people in the total work force is on the public payroll.

These men and women are the employees of 81,299 entities of government that have been formed to provide public services at the national, state, county, and local levels.

In the past decade, public employment has been the most rapidly growing segment in the American employment, moving ahead of agriculture, manufacturing, and other services. The burgeoning demands placed upon government to meet the social, economic, physical, and security needs of the American people have broadened government's share of the labor market in the number and diversity of skills required. Virtually every occupation and every profession has its representatives in the ranks of government employees. The technological revolution and the complexity of contemporary problems have necessitated government's search for ever larger numbers of Americans with special skills that can be developed only through more and more advanced education. These demands have placed the public employer in increasing competition with private enterprise for graduates of universities and professional schools.

But even with this commanding position in employment, for the average American public service has an indeterminate shape, vaguely defined characteristics, and a distorted image. The term "public employee" may conjure up the picture of the policeman in the prowl car, the teacher in the classroom, the letter carrier on his rounds, the tax collector in his distant office, or the machinist in the shipyard. Or, more likely, the fast-moving agent of the FBI depicted so dramatically on the TV screen. The totality of public service and the problems involved in recruiting, selecting, compensating, motivating, and managing this large and diverse human population are largely overlooked or misunderstood. In fact, many a citizen, far from seeking an understanding of these problems, develops hostility toward those who he feels are largely the beneficiaries of his tax dollars rather than the providers of services for his benefit. The doctrine of the least government being the best has tended to prevail in public opinion, while citizens through their representatives constantly demand more services from their government. While he may exhibit respect toward public servants he knows as individuals, or even adulation for certain government services, the citizen regards public employment in general with less than wholehearted support.

Citizen indifference or hostility is frequently reflected in the popular media. The civil servant, in this world of image-making, is rarely an admired type and is the frequent target of criticism, both serious and humorous. At the time of the initial Soviet success in space there was a popular quip to the effect that the American space vehicle was named Civil Service because "it wouldn't work and you couldn't fire it." At times these dark reflections on public service almost imply a wish for government to drop dead.

The tremendous size and the necessary institutional and organizational patterns of government at all levels have prompted the raising of distress signals in many quarters. These concerns have popularized the term "bureaucrat" with a totally negative implication and "bureaucracy" as the characterization of public employment generally. For many years the magnitude of public employment has been a political issue at campaign times, with the challenging candidate promising impossibly massive reductions and with the incumbent defending the expansion in programs as a response to voter needs while ignoring the attendant swelling of the public payroll.

With the growth in public employment, the public employees, particularly those who have organized and developed their own unions and professional associations, have become potent political forces courted by candidates for office. This political strength of the public employee has led to fewer election-time attacks on the bureaucracy and to promises of higher pay and additional benefits.

Among the categories of public service, the federal establishment has attracted the most national attention through the years. "The vast federal bureaucracy" undergoes periodic congressional scrutiny and executive examination. The portion of the federal budget expended to meet employee payrolls most frequently draws the fire of journalistic criticism. The behavior of the federal career services poses a problem to the incoming President who seeks to guide the bureaucracy in the direction of his policy determinations. Reformation of the federal employment practices attracts the study of individual scholars or the examination of task-force probers. Statistical reporting on federal employment constitutes the measuring rod not only for government growth but also for government efficiency.

The growth in federal employment has been phenomenal, particularly during the last four decades. Since the economic crisis that brought the New Deal to Washington, federal programs have been launched to resolve that crisis, to fight a global war, to achieve postwar reconstruction, to fulfill the commitments of the cold war, to respond to the technological revolution and to overcome the national disabilities of urban decay, social strife, and persisting poverty. Once launched, these programs were funded and staffed for a long voyage and rarely returned to port for either dismantling or mothballing. Executive institutions backed by members of Congress and their constituents have an immortality that even vast technological and social changes cannot overcome.

The infant federal government under the first President started out with nine executive units employing a grand total of 1,000 federal workers. From that beginning, the federal government has proliferated to encompass 2,000 agencies and employ nearly 3 million people. This employment has spread throughout the nation and beyond, with only 10 percent at the seat of government in Washington and the other 90 percent employed in the fifty states and in more than 100 countries overseas. Although the largest concentrations are in the 80 major metropolitan areas, there are federal representatives in each of the more than 3,000 counties and the more than 30,000 cities, towns, and villages that contain a ubiquitous federal landmark, the post office.

The great bulk of federal employment is centered today, as it has been for the past twenty-five years, in three vast federal operations: the civilian personnel of the Department of Defense, the postal clerks and carriers, and the civil servants operating the veterans' services. Nearly half of total federal employment in 1970—just under 1,200,000—was engaged in the civilian support activities of the Army, Navy, and Air Force. This figure reflected a growth necessitated by the widening involvement in Vietnam. This civilian component of the military departments is the most volatile area of federal employment. Its size has risen rapidly in periods of military mobilization and operations—for World War II, Korea, and Vietnam—and has fallen with comparable abruptness during demobilization. But with each receding tide of employment, the level never quite sinks to what it was before the previous war. The military establishment, with its complex logistical systems and with its extensive involvement in technological research and development, has sustained a high but unstable level of employment. This instability has belied the popular conception that public employment constitutes inviolable security. The shifting of missions, the closing of bases, and the changing of weapons systems have forced frequent cutbacks and expansions at a significant number of locations.

The postal clerk and the letter carrier have become well-known symbols of federal employment because their functions bring them into frequent contact with the public. Their numbers have expanded, but not in proportion to the national population or to postal work loads. Even though increases in productivity have fallen so far short of desired goals as to be condemned by a management study of postal operations, greater mechanization and improved processes have held back the growth trend in personnel. If this had not been so, postal employment would have passed the million mark in the early 1960s. At the present level of 730,000, the postal service is one of the largest employers in the land.

National concern for the education, health, and welfare of veterans and their dependents produced a payroll of 169,000 in the Veterans Administration for 1970. The country-wide network of offices and hospitals has generated a rising volume of services as wars continue to produce more veterans and as those who served in previous wars require ever more extensive benefits. This politically sensitive area of federal operations rarely undergoes contraction, and although savings in manpower have been achieved in massive insurance and service activities, the systems analyst can find little relief from the inexorable advance of medical expenditures and staffing.

These three federal agencies—Defense, Post Office, and Veterans Administration—account for nearly 75 percent of the total federal civilian strength. The roster of other departments and agencies, with an employment range of from two for the Delaware River Basin Commission to 116,000 for the Department of Agriculture, totals approximately 750,-000, or roughly equivalent to postal employment levels or a fourth of the total number. It is interesting to note that the Department of Agriculture, identified with the farm and rural population of the country, is an employer of well over 100,000 in a period when only 6 percent of our national work force can produce all the food and fiber required by the total population and a significant portion of the world beyond. This employment total and its relationship to contemporary agriculture has been a frequent point of congressional curiosity. Not entirely in jest, a Congressman introduced a rider to an agricultural appropriation bill requiring that the employment of the department never exceed the total number of farmers in the country.

With the rapid growth of federal social programs, the employment curve in the Department of Health, Education and Welfare showed a constant ascent to the 1968 peak of 117,000. This dropped to 108,000 in 1970; but with the massive infusion of new educational programs, the addition of medical services, an increased awareness of consumer-protection and pollution-control requirements, there is every prospect that the department will continue to expand.

In 1965 and 1966, two new Cabinet departments—Housing and Urban Development and Transportation—were created to give new emphasis and added coordination to federal functions in their respective fields.

Housing and Urban Development came into being with 15,000 employees inherited from predecessor agencies. The first Secretary of Transportation brought together several transportation agencies—the Coast Guard, the Federal Aviation Agency, and the Federal Highway Administration—to form a department of 62,000 employees and to rank in fifth position among the Cabinet departments in the employment box score.

To those who visualize federal employment as restricted to the monumental buildings in Washington, it is always a surprise to learn that a single state, California, provides more federal jobs than the Washington metropolitan area. On the final day of 1967, there were nearly 318,000 federal employees in California and 312,000 at the nation's capital. Other large states—New York, Texas, Pennsylvania, and Illinois—each reported more than 100,000 federal employees on that date. In fact, no state recorded fewer than the 3,300 who were found in Vermont.

In many cities, the federal jobs make Uncle Sam the largest employer. This is particularly true in communities with large Defense installations such as the air bases at San Antonio, Texas, and Oklahoma City, Oklahoma, the naval shipyards at Norfolk, Virginia, and Bremerton, Washington, and the Army posts at Fayetteville, North Carolina, and Columbus, Georgia. Rapid expansions or phased cutbacks have come to have a great economic impact on more and more communities in ever larger areas. The degree of economic dependence in the communities was recognized when Secretary Robert S. McNamara sent special assistance teams into the areas where bases were to be closed.

Nor is federal employment limited in occupation or profession. Depending upon which occupational dictionary is used, the number of identifiable occupational specialties varies in number to a maximum of 15,000. An eager researcher set himself the task of finding an occupation in the dictionary that was not present in the federal government. After an extensive search, he discovered one: stripteaser.

The full range of manual skills in the crafts and trades is sought for maintenance, repair, and manufacturing in the Defense Department. Custodial, food-service, and medical-support personnel abound not only in the facilities of the Defense Department but in the Veterans Administration and the Public Health Service as well. The so-called blue-collar population numbered more than 700,000 in 1970.

The general administrative, clerical, and office occupations number close to half a million. The professions, in turn, find their largest representation in the federal ranks: engineering and architectural (145,000), medical and public health (96,000), the physical sciences (43,000), the biological sciences (41,000), and mathematics and statistics (16,000). And, of course, the legal profession permeates all federal activities, with approximately 8,000 lawyers and 36,000 others in kindred fields.

The diversity in required skills and educational preparation ranges from the lowest to the highest. This vast diversity renders any effort to design a general image for the federal employee an exercise in futility. The diversity in the employing agency, the assigned program, and the work location also injects a multiplicity that forces the manager and the critic to abandon the stereotype and engage in penetrating analysis and creative thought in the search for new and better policies and practices.

But an examination of the dimensions of the federal leviathan fails to take the measure of the other 81,299 governmental entities and their employees. This incredible figure is drawn from a 1967 census of governments that listed the following:

United States government		1
States governments		50
Local governments		81,248
Counties	3,049	
Municipalities	18,048	
Townships	17,105	
School districts	21,782	
Special districts	21,264	
TOTAL		81,299

In 1788, James Madison predicted that "the number of individuals employed under the Constitution of the United States, will be much smaller than the number employed under the particular states." Even with the substantial growth in federal employment in the last forty years, Madison's prediction has been fulfilled. The most extraordinary growth in state and local government employment has occurred since World

War II. In the last twenty-one years, during which the nation's population advanced by 39 percent, federal employment rose roughly in step with it by 38 percent. During this same period, state and local employment increased from 3.3 million to 8 million, an increase of 130 percent. To place these figures in more manageable measures: out of every ten civilians in government work today, three are in public education, five are in other state and local employment, and two are on federal payrolls.

These figures reveal in stark relief the quantitative significance of employment for public education in this country. Expressed another way, the teachers, administrators, and service personnel employed by the nearly 22,000 school districts constitute a larger portion of American public service than the entire federal government. Each district is governed by its own board in accordance with state and local statutes. The employment policies and practices are the product of local judgment, nurtured by local autonomy. Although state and federal agencies provide advice and assistance, the local district pursues its own course of action in hiring, paying, promoting, and managing its personnel. Certain qualification standards are formulated and enforced in the individual states in conjunction with the systems of higher education. With the recent national concern about the quality of American education, teachers have become a more highly valued human commodity and school boards and administrators have taken steps to make teaching a more attractive professional experience. In many jurisdictions this improving trend has not moved rapidly enough for the teachers themselves, and they have increasingly turned to collective action to present their needs to the general public.

The remaining state and local personnel, numbering 5.5 million, cover the broad range of activities that make up the functional responsibilities of the myriad entities of government. At both state and local levels, particular attention is focused these days on the personnel engaged in law enforcement. The police have become an increasingly visible element in our society. The tasks assigned to them have constantly multiplied. The police are required not only to hunt down and apprehend the criminal but also to assure the safety of the streets and highways and the vehicles that travel on them, to search for missing persons, to turn in drunkards and other citizens with antisocial behavior, to cultivate intergroup harmony, and to pursue a broad variety of other tasks. Likewise, the instruments of their trade have become more numerous and complex, requiring higher level skills and more advanced preparation and training. Citizen demands for better police performance need to be matched by citizen willingness to grant this form of public service a more respected and professional status in the community.

State employment has been significantly stimulated in its growth by federal grant-in-aid programs. With federal funds available for complete or partial support of public welfare, employment security, health services, civil defense, highway constructions, and other purposes, the states' hiring needs, while reflecting service to state residents, are influenced by federal program objectives. Certain programs, particularly those specified in the original Social Security Act of 1935, are not merely supported by federal funds; their employment practices are specified by the federal government. On the other hand, the massive federal assistance to highway construction has been relatively free of federal prescription, and it is one of the continuing strongholds of political patronage in public employment.

But it is the municipalities whose public service needs are most evident and urgent. Not only in teaching and law enforcement but in a broad range of occupational and professional categories, mayors and city managers have sought hard-to-find but essential skills. Planners, engineers, public-health officers, public-safety experts, transit managers, recreational specialists, and sanitary inspectors, along with firefighters, city clerks, refuse collectors, assessors, vehicle inspectors, and many others, make up the expanding roster in municipal public service. Increasingly, certain areas of operation move over into the public sphere to expand public payrolls. This has become particularly true through municipal ownership of urban transportation systems.

In its 1962 report, the Municipal Manpower Commission pointed out serious deficiencies in almost every American city's efforts to recruit and retain administrative, professional, and technical personnel to meet the operational demands of a population that was concentrating more and more in the major metropolitan areas. Calling for prompt measures to meet the crisis before municipal government became totally ineffective, the Commission recommended dramatic reforms in public personnel policies and practices. Specifically, it urged higher professional standards, improved compensation, and more extensive training to raise the quality of staffing in every program.

This call for action was greeted with resounding silence. It became the substance of debate in professional associations more concerned about preserving the status quo than ensuring the viability of the cities. Other reports with recommendations for change have gathered dust in governmental archives or have disappeared in the void of inactive legislative bodies.

The multiplicity of public jurisdictions can no longer be tolerated. Their inefficiency and waste are indefensible on many grounds, but they constitute a particularly negative force on the human side of government. The inherent value of citizen participation in government at the local level need not be sacrificed in the reduction of existing jurisdictions. Nor, in and of itself, will this consolidation lower the numbers of public employees, but there are hopes that it can achieve a modest erosion of overhead and the development of broader and more rational personnel policies.

In the final analysis, the American people will receive the public service, in volume and in quality, that they demand. Or, as some critics have stated, the quality of government they deserve. There is need for a greater citizen awareness about that seventh of the work force paid from tax revenues. There is a need for the citizen to exert his opinions. through his representatives for ever more effective performance by public servants. The pervasive desire for a minimum of government cannot be satisfied by demanding a substantial reduction in public employment. In a nation of 205 million people with a highly pluralistic society and with the complexities that have evolved from dynamic growth and technological revolution, a large and diversified body of public servants is an undeniable essential. The basic requirement is to gain an appreciation of this reality and to press for public decisions that will assure that this bureaucracy is positive and responsive rather than a negative and obstructive force in the evolution of American government. The public clamor should be directed toward meaningful changes in attitudes and behavior on the part of public managers and public employees to assure that the necessary skills exist with government to solve the countless problems in the public interest and to provide the highest talent the nation is capable of developing.

The

Anatomy

of Merit

2

In the historical evolution of public service in the United States, the date of greatest significance is January 16, 1883. That day, Chester Alan Arthur, who as Vice President had succeeded James A. Garfield, the President slain by a disappointed office seeker, signed the Civil Service Act to regulate and improve the civil service of the United States. This statement of public policy, which has survived for more than fourscore years as the basic personnel policy for the national government, enunciated merit and fitness as principles for employment. It provided the foundation for the construction of the merit system as a body of standards and practices to govern the selection, advancement, retention, and working conditions for those employed by the federal government. It set in motion the forces that over the years created a meritocracy in government.

In strikingly clear and brief language, the statute called for open competition among all citizens through examinations that would measure the fitness of applicants. It prescribed that examinations should be practical in character and should fairly measure the relative capacity and fitness of the competitors to discharge the duties of the positions they sought. It prescribed that positions covered under civil service be filled by selections among those graded the highest in these competitive examinations. It incorporated as a part of the examining process a period of

13

probation prior to appointment. It laid down prohibitions against obligations to contribute to political funds or to engage in political activity and protected the appointee from removal for political reasons.

Blending idealism and pragmatism, the authors of the legislation left large areas of policy development and procedural formulation to the President and the bipartisan commission created by the act. While circumscribing the appointment freedom of the principal officers of the government, it acknowledged the necessity for executive discretion on the part of the President in determining the method of appointment for what the Constitution referred to as "inferior officers."

Although the act was a response to the evangelical fervor of reformers for the elimination of the spoils system that had plagued the national government since Andrew Jackson became President in 1829, it did not specify the inclusion of any individual employees or groups or classes of employees in the merit system. Instead it placed this responsibility in the hands of the Chief Executive. By spurts and halts in succeeding administrations, the principles of the act were extended to ever larger numbers of employees. Arthur himself started modestly with the coverage of only about 10 percent of the 133,000 positions in the federal civil service of that time, with 90 percent still staffed on the basis of political preferment. Substantial increases in coverage occurred under Grover Cleveland and Theodore Roosevelt. Franklin D. Roosevelt initially lowered the percentage of coverage through the creation of new emergency agencies outside the civil service system, but by the conclusion of his second four-year term he had set in motion machinery that blanketed into civil service a substantial portion of total employment. By the time of the seventy-fifth anniversary of the act in 1958, approximately 90 percent of all federal positions, then numbering in excess of 2 million, were affected by the principles of merit and fitness. But even that percentage figure was not and is not an accurate indicator of the limited dimensions of federal employment available for patronage purposes. The merit conditions of openness and competition were incorporated in new independent personnel systems established for the Foreign Service, the Tennessee Valley Authority, the Federal Bureau of Investigation, the Atomic Energy Commission, and the commissioned corps of the Public Health Service.

The paucity of patronage opportunities has become a source of surprise and disappointment to political leaders associated with each major change of party leadership in the Executive Branch in recent times. In 1953, 1961, and 1969 the victorious party leaders found very limited opportunities for complete appointment discretion, and such opportunities as did exist increasingly called for specialized professional experience in order to serve the needs of the particular office. The objectives set forth in 1937 by the Brownlow Commission for the extension of civil service "upward, downward and outward" have been largely fulfilled.

Some critics argue with some validity that the extent of this coverage is excessive and that an incoming President and his appointees must have a larger number of discretionary positions in order to ensure that the new administration's policies and programs are developed and carried out by officials sympathetic to the new leadership. Others argue that the political parties have been seriously weakened in modern times because of the absence of that earlier political currency—public jobs for the politically faithful. But these arguments largely concern degree, not principle. There is no advocacy for a return to the days of total turnover of federal staffs with a change in party. The growing requirements of professionalism in so much of the government's work call for continuity and stability in employment as well as a high degree of skill. The reality of modern politics necessitates less reliance on job availability in the success of a party. There is no evidence that the limited supply of plums has lessened the vitality of the parties in the national arena.

But the federal example has not been copied, even after all these years, in all the other public jurisdictions. Only slightly more than half of the state governments have their own civil service systems. In certain grant-in-aid programs, the merit standards required by the federal government form a condition for receiving federal funds and have produced the only civil service activity in some states. The counties are even more laggard in their adoption of merit principles for employment. Although a number of cities have long and outstanding civil service records, in many others selection by political leaders is still the rule of the day. The continued prevalence of this spoils system has lessened the regard of both the ordinary citizen and the prospective employee for public service. There is substantial evidence that where civil service standards do not prevail, public programs are more liable to be threatened by corruption or malfeasance. The dependence of the public employee upon continued political backing leads to supervisory problems and frequently to waste and inefficiency. The expansion of federal activities into governmental areas formerly deemed the province of state and local government is at least partially attributable to the inability of the nonfederal jurisdiction to develop an effective body of civil servants.

Even though the federal civil service system has demonstrated its worth and has served the American people well, in recent years it has been the target of mounting criticism based upon the conviction that implementation of its admirable principles has become increasingly rigid and that the system cannot muster sufficient flexibility to respond to the social and technological changes that challenge contemporary government. It is frequently asked whether the merit system, with its origin in nineteenth century American government, can deal with the public problems of the last third of the twentieth century. Only a dynamic merit system capable of adapting itself to changing conditions will survive. There is need today to examine not the principles that underlie the system but the machinery, devices, and procedures that constitute the means for applying the principles.

Over the years since 1883, a vast mythology has grown up around the merit system itself. This mythology is compounded of assorted concepts of what a merit system really is—some vague, some specific, and many contradictory—plus an accumulation of procedural details. In a contemporary evaluation it is necessary to strip away the mythology and uncover the basic principles once again.

Theodore Roosevelt, the patron saint of a vigorous civil service, expressed these principles forcefully in his first presidential message to Congress: "The merit system of making appointments is in its essence as democratic and American as the common school system itself." This is the first basic principle. Democracy, open competition, equal employment opportunity—whatever you call it, the meaning is the same. The second basic principle is job ability. A merit system must select people who are competent and qualified for the jobs to which they are appointed. This was a key point in the basic act. It may seem too obvious to be worth mentioning today, but it was revolutionary in the nineteenth century, when the primary requirement for appointment was to be on the right side with the right people. The third basic principle is that of freedom from political influence or tribute and political neutrality on the part of civil servants. This principle is the basis of the civil service's stability and continuity.

These, then, are the elements a merit system must have. There are others that it ought to have in order to be an *effective* merit system: efficiency, responsiveness to the public, flexibility of administration, adaptability to change. But those are not part of the definition of a merit system embodied in the three essential principles, which in the hands of creative administrators should lend themselves readily to adaptation. The trouble has been that over the years most of the change has been in the form of addition, with comparatively little subtraction. The result is an accretion of nonessentials, which, like barnacles encrusting a ship's bottom, seriously retard its forward movement. Before the decision is made to redesign the ship—or scuttle it—the barnacles should be eliminated.

Part of the accretion consists of practices adopted to implement public policy—practices that have outlived the policy that brought them about. Just as the medium becomes the message, so the practice can become the policy. Some practices go back to the very beginning of the merit system, when the "reformed" civil service had to fight every inch of the way against the entrenched forces of political influence and personal favoritism. Others originated in the days when the government's need for highly trained people in highly specialized fields was very modest and applicants for civil service positions were more than plentiful. Under those conditions, examination and other qualification requirements often served not just to measure relative competence for the jobs in question but also to exclude arbitrarily large numbers of people. Recruiting practices under the merit system must not be allowed to solidify even if they have been highly successful in meeting the needs of government up to recent times. These practices must be constantly and mercilessly re-examined. They are not basic. They can be changed to meet any current need without abandoning what is basic.

It has been popular in some circles to question and frequently to lampoon the tests and measurements used to determine relative ability. One of the questions asked most often about government employment is: Are written tests obsolete? The answer is: Some kinds of written tests, designed primarily to screen out superfluous applicants, are clearly out of date in today's tight labor market in many critical skills. Tests that require abilities far beyond the requirements of the job to be filled never were good tests. This conclusion has been reached only recently, but it has already produced a drastic revision of the federal test program in terms of realistic current objectives. Still, competitive examination should not be abandoned. It is the best method as yet derived to apply the basic principles of competence and equal opportunity, provided that the examinations are truly realistic in terms of job requirements, the labor market, and public policy. Tests may be written or oral, or constitute evaluations of training and experience. If it is necessary to keep changing them in order to keep them realistic, then the changes must be made. This applies to methods of examining as well as to the content of examination. Where the public service faces really fierce competition, as in certain fields of science and in the administrative, professional, and technical areas, any procedure that delays the appointment of an available qualified person is against the public interest. Where the demand for qualified personnel greatly exceeds the supply, "instant appointment" is imperative and possible. Time-consuming procedures, which have become widely identified in the public mind with civil service, are in no way an integral part of the merit system. That is a very popular myth but nevertheless a myth. Regardless of procedure or lack of it, if the public job is filled by the best-qualified person available, the merit principle is fulfilled.

Every civil service expert can name a series of outmoded and vestigial requirements that operate as obstacles to effective personnel management. These features may at one time or another have been justified as public policy but are not relevant to modern labor-market conditions. The public service may be paying dearly today for inflexible and negative restraints calculated to cause hesitation, if not rejection, on the part of the job applicant whose services are most required by the government. Public managers have an obligation to discover these restraints and to present forceful arguments for their removal in the interest of better management.

There is a continuing need to preserve the essential dynamism of the merit system; otherwise today's solutions will become tomorrow's problems. For instance, today's job is made more difficult by the fact that someone in an earlier time cast his thoughts in concrete when they should have been written in wet sand. Only the most significant principles need be graven in stone.

Among the enduring myths about merit is that many things cannot be done without violating or destroying the system. One example is the government's responsiveness as an employer to social objectives, a problem that embraces the whole area of opportunity for the disadvantaged and for minority groups in our population. During the past decade, great emphasis has been placed on special programs to bring federal employment within the reach of these groups. Such emphasis is often criticized on the ground that it necessitates a dilution of quality and consequently makes a mockery of the merit principle. But such criticism overlooks the fact that a basic merit principle is equal opportunity and that all too frequently that principle has received lip service or mechanical adherence and has not achieved genuinely equal results. In pursuing the basic principle of equal opportunity, there has been a need to evolve new and more active practices. Instead of waiting for applicants to come to government with the request to compete, there has been a reaching out into the Negro colleges, minority-group areas, and the poor neighborhoods with government job information and positive recruiting approaches. There has been a rising concern about enforcing the law against all forms of discrimination in all aspects of employment. Through these more assertive practices, it is possible to make equal opportunity a reality and to achieve within the public service an even more genuinely democratic condition than existed before.

One of the traditional features of the merit system that have stimulated an increased volume of complaint has been job tenure. In the original statute, Congress endeavored to protect the jobholder from arbitrary dismissal for political or other causes not related to performance. Over time, this protection has been reinforced either to guard against the repetition of certain cases of abuse or in response to group pressure from employees, until employment guarantees have been assumed by supervisor and employee alike. Virtually every round-table discussion of problems facing public managers will quickly turn to the inability of the manager to discipline nonproductive or insubordinate employees or to dismiss those who have ceased to be productive or constitute chronic supervisory problems. It is the popular impression that once a civil servant secures his position through the machinery of competitive examination, he is all but assured of a lifetime on the public payroll.

There is both truth and error in these understandings. The processes of discipline and dismissal are indeed difficult to traverse. But they are difficult in the interest of employment justice. Managers endowed with both fairness and courage, a rare combination, are able to set standards of performance, to judge subordinates by those standards, and to reward or penalize in accordance with those standards.

The institution of tenure throughout American society may very well produce a condition of excessive employment security and thereby foreclose needed risk-taking and dampen potential creativity. The social researchers could well afford to devote study time to this phenomenon. In public service the extension of tenure to high-salaried managerial and professional posts is particularly inappropriate. The authors of the Civil Service Act had no intention of extending employment protection to the highest level of continuing posts. Without any undermining of the ultimate objective in a public service career, these top posts would gain added skill and capacity if they were placed outside tenure protection. This action would lead to a greater degree of self-selection for advancement because only persons having a dedicated interest in the content and responsibility of a high post plus professional self-confidence would make themselves available. Those to whom tenure was the paramount consideration of employment could logically expect a lower career ceiling.

One fundamental departure from the basic principles of open competition has been the preference extended to the veterans of military service.

Almost from the beginning of the Republic, this form of preference has been public policy. The Act of 1883 permitted a carry-over of this principle, and after World War II the Veterans Preference Act incorporated these preferences in specified details within the body of civil service law. These preferences have gone beyond added points in competitive examinations to extensive advantages relative to reduction in force and in separation from the service. These departures from pure merit have been vigorously defended against occasional but rather weak appeals for modification. The pressure instead has been directed toward additional benefits in public employment for those who served in the military. From time to time, the precedent of veterans' preference has been cited in support of like preferences for others who face disadvantages in labor-market competition. Basically, additional preference of this absolute form should be granted within the context of equal opportunity and fair competition. If the size of the military establishment can be reduced and wartime service curtailed, serious consideration should be given to limiting the forms of veterans' preference to employment opportunity immediately following the completion of military service and to education and training to compensate for inequities and lost opportunities resulting from it.

A controversial accompaniment to the administration of the merit system in the past generation has been the debate among political leaders, public administrators, and personnel experts concerning the functions and the location of the civil service agency. The evolution of the federal agency from its creation in 1883 to its present status has been illustrative of this organizational problem. The original act vested policymaking authority for the civil service in the President but established a Civil Service Commission as his adviser and agent. To assure bipartisan administration, the three-man commission, serving at the pleasure of the President, could have no more than two members from a single party. In the early decades, the commission designed and administered the examining devices for entrance into civil service positions placed under its jurisdiction in the act by the incumbent President. Because of its restraining role on the appointment freedom of department and agency heads, the commission found itself in frequent tension with those officers and occasionally with the President himself. The vigorous and independent Theodore Roosevelt, himself a commissioner from 1889 to 1895, was the reformer's ideal enforcer of the merit system's purity. He bombarded the Postmaster General, the Commissioner of Indian Affairs, and other officials with forceful edicts on the application of merit standards. But other areas of personnel-policy development flowed from the studies of special commissions, from other executive agencies, or from the legislative pressures of employee unions.

With the emergence of big government in the New Deal days and with the concurrent rising concern for improved public administration, the need for a personnel-policy agency was recognized. This recognition reached full flower in the Brownlow report of 1937, which urged the creation of a single personnel administrator with broad policy responsibilities and with clear identification as the President's man on all personnel matters. This organizational concept, along with other administrative reform proposals of that era, was nullified when Congress defeated the reorganization bill in 1938.

But that defeat did not stay the arguments for change. Step by step, in one administration after another, the scope of the Civil Service Commission's responsibilities was broadened to include the administration of personnel programs ranging from retirement and insurance to pay-classification plans and incentive awards. The outlook of the agency became more and more professional as it sought to minimize its formerly predominant role as the policeman enforcing the principles and practices of the merit system. Affirmative and meaningful personnel management became the guidepost of the agency in its relationship with the President and the employing units of the Executive Branch.

In response to a recommendation of the first Hoover Commission in 1949, a chairman was designated from among the three commissioners as the chief executive officer, replacing a commission president who had merely presided over the deliberations of the three commissioners. The rejected Brownlow idea was converted in 1953 as the commission chairman was granted an additional portfolio by President Eisenhower as a presidential adviser on personnel matters. This combination was condemned by the second Hoover Commission, reporting in 1955, and the two posts were filled by two officers in 1957. Concurrently, Congress evidenced concern about the closer proximity of the commission to the Presidency and amended the original act to provide fixed six-year terms for the commissioners, who had served at the President's pleasure for more than seventy years.

During the 1960s the commission chairman, without an extra portfolio, served as the President's principal personnel adviser while directing the multiple activities of the commission. These activities were broadened to include government-wide responsibility for administration of the Equal Employment Opportunity program, for the new policy on labor-management relations, and in 1965 for the providing of federal registrars in carrying out the Voting Rights Act of that year.

The manifold activities performed by the commission produced certain anomalies. The operational and enforcement functions relating to the original statute necessitated a degree of regulation over the activities of agency personnel. While policing the merit system, the commission sought to encourage agency managers to adopt affirmative personnel policy and practices in pay administration, training, and supervision. But this constructive assistance was occasionally complicated by the commission's adjudication of employee appeals in overruling an agency management's decision to discipline or dismiss an employee. Also, the commission as a management agency found itself viewed by employees as its neutral protector of employee rights, or by management as its adviser on the management side of relationships with employee unions. Congress, in turn, classified the commission as an "independent agency" in much the same category as the other multiheaded organizations responsible for economic regulation. Congressional committee chairmen looked to the commission chairman as a spokesman for the President on personnel matters, but there was a continuing concern that this spokesmanship would in some way violate the independence and the neutrality of the commission as an agency.

Regardless of these anomalies, the prospect of the creation of additional executive agencies with personnel responsibility was generally viewed as an undesirable alternative. From time to time, one of the perennial government-reorganization study groups would recommend the separation of personnel-policy functions from the commission and their placement in an office of personnel alongside the Bureau of the Budget in the Executive Office of the President. Labor-management experts have called for the creation of a new labor-management agency that would assume the commission's functions in that area of leadership and interpretation. Civil-liberties and union groups have sought the assignment of the appellate function to a new executive agency or to an administrative court. At some future date, one of these recommendations or others may come to fruition. An argument for such separate units can be justified. But a multiplicity of units in the personnel field would complicate the task of personnel management even though they might make for more rational and less anomalous functional divisions. Concentration of these functions in a single agency with high professional standards, the dynamism and flexibility to meet changing conditions, and close ties to the President can best serve the continuing development of the human side of government.

The federal pattern of organizational relationships has been emulated in many of the state and city jurisdictions where civil service laws have been enacted. In some instances a separate personnel director has also been created, and, at least in New York State and New York City, a separate labor-management agency has been formed. The establishment of these new units has to some degree produced a greater separation of the civil service agency from the chief executive. In all too many instances, this separation has handicapped the civil service agency in planning for and supporting line managers in keeping pace with program-staffing requirements. The independence of the agency has been defended as an essential condition in resisting inherent tendencies to return to the spoils system in the states and cities. Civil service commissioners have been viewed as the opponents of the program directors, and unresponsive to state and city agency needs. The governor or mayor has found the agency unable to develop the creative means for attracting and retaining the scarce skills required in new programs. In its 1962 report, the Municipal Manpower Commission leveled criticism at civil service agencies and urged the formation of personnel staffs more responsive to the chief executive's requirements. This criticism and recommendation drew fire from the personnel professionals that tended to incinerate the helpful findings of the commission.

The insistence upon independence and separation as means for guaranteeing the preservation of the merit system is fallacious. The success of the merit system cannot be the exclusive responsibility of the civil service agency, no matter how intensively it may exercise its enforcement authority. Success will come through acceptance of the basic principles by managers with program responsibility. Only through participation of those accountable officers in the formulation of qualification standards, in the search for candidates to meet those standards, and in the selection, promotion, and training of those judged to be best qualified can these principles survive in the public service. In contemporary government, personnel management must be predominantly an integrated responsibility of the line manager and supervisor, with the personnel professional at all levels providing the staff with advice and the technical tools to assist in fundamental decisions leading to better government through human performance.

Public

Service

by

3 # Contract

The dividing line between public and private employment has become vague and wavering in recent times, especially since World War II. During that war, industry, business, and education were mobilized to serve the total national effort. By means of contracts, the government reached out to secure construction and manufacturing, research and development, and operations and training from institutions in the private sector. Although the ranks of the federal employees rose to an all-time high of 3,600,000 at the peak of the wartime effort, many times that number of men and women were engaged in the government's work while on the payroll of private employers.

The success of this public-private partnership was carried over in pursuing new national goals in the postwar and cold-war periods. As new ventures were undertaken by government action and with government funds, segments of the private sector were linked to federal agencies to take advantage of existing capabilities in nongovernment organizations.

At least two other motivations exerted pressure in the direction of public service by contract. First, counting the number of federal employees had become a favorite political game. The management success of any administration was frequently measured in terms of its ability to keep the count stable or declining. Monthly strength reports were dispatched to Capitol Hill, where each new increase inspired press releases describing the wastefulness of a bloated government. Stability or decline, in turn, prompted self-congratulatory statements from the Executive Branch. Figures were made to appear as large—or as small—as possible; part-time and seasonal workers were added to—or subtracted from—the total to produce an optimum figure. The numbers game could be played by all parties. The Executive Branch leadership produced annual reports with ratios purporting to demonstrate that federal employment had advanced at a slower rate than total population growth or on a more conservative scale than state and local employment.

To exercise even greater control over the agencies' manpower expansion, ceiling figures and clearance processes were added to existing budgetary controls. Considerable management time and money were invested in these multiple controls, with little visible benefit and occasionally serious operational difficulties.

With mounting work loads and staffing limitations, agency administrators turned to the contracting-out device as a means for accomplishing the work. In some cases the contract process could be justified on the grounds of comparative cost, which was frequently claimed as the only reason for such action. Since the counting of contractor personnel was far more difficult, the increased manpower could be applied to the agency's mission without committing the political sin of raising the level of federal employment.

Second, the claim was advanced that government in its growth had moved into functions which were more properly the province of private enterprise and which, in any event, could be more efficiently offered to the government from the competitive market place. Although certain of these views tended to follow ideological fears of "creeping socialism," many viewed the government as an unfair competitor entering an area of operations far removed from the normal governmental functions.

The Eisenhower administration undertook a detailed examination of these claims with the result that certain federal operations were placed in the hands of private enterprise through the contractual route. A federal policy statement declared that government requirements for goods and services would be met in the private sector unless there was a decided cost advantage in government operation or unless reasons of

national security necessitated complete government control. This policy
led to the elimination of a number of defense-support activities performed by government civilians. For example, coffee-roasting plants,
paint-manufacturing facilities, shoe-repair services, and even some food
services were converted to private operation. In most of these cases, the
use of private sources was clearly supported by cost comparison as well
as by policy considerations. The policy was welcomed by many federal
managers because the performance of the particular task by contract
shifted management responsibility to the contractor and relieved the
federal official of staffing and supervising the work within the restrictions
of the federal personnel system. The contractor was held responsible for
delivering the product or the services and for all the attendant operating
problems.

The transfer of the war-born atomic-energy enterprise from the military to the newly formed Atomic Energy Commission in the early postwar years presented the issue of government versus contractor operations
in sharp relief. The Army's Manhattan District had achieved its wartime
objective in producing and delivering a nuclear bomb largely through
wide use of the contract device. With government personnel used only
for contract supervision, security, and financial control, all functions—
research, development, testing, and operations—were performed by a
vast network of industrial, construction, and university contractors.

Upon civilian take-over of this system under the Atomic Energy Act
of 1946, the five civilian commissioners decided to continue the wartime
policy rather than transfer any extensive portion of atomic-energy activities to government personnel. This decision was reached only after study
of the relative merits of each pattern in each function of commission
responsibility. The decision was easily reached with respect to construction because it had long been government practice to contract for architectural and engineering services and for actual construction in the
government public-works programs. It was only slightly less advanta-
geous to continue private operation of large industrial complexes at
places like Hanford and Oak Ridge, and so the commission negotiated
new contracts with General Electric at Hanford and with Union Carbide
at Oak Ridge. But the issue was not so clear in the vital research and

development activities at Los Alamos, Argonne, and Brookhaven; after all, existing governmental laboratories at the Bureau of Standards and in the military service had contributed to nuclear developments. But the national laboratories had been established through contracts with consortiums of universities, or in the case of Los Alamos through a contract with the University of California. Largely on the basis of advice from the laboratory directors and the senior scientists in these institutions, the commission extended the contracts with the universities for the future direction of nuclear research. The scientific staffs themselves preferred university affiliation to government appointment, and they believed that talented scientists would more readily participate in this sensitive research through an ostensibly academic connection. Besides, they pointed out, the compensation and benefits provided through university personnel systems would create a more favorable employment environment than the prevailing federal personnel practices.

Twelve years later, when the American response to Sputnik led to the formation of the National Aeronautics and Space Administration (NASA), these same operational questions faced the first administrator, T. Keith Glennan, who was a former AEC commissioner, and his staff. They inherited the government-run laboratories of the National Advisory Council for Aeronautics at Langley, Virginia, Cleveland, Ohio, and Ames, California, and also certain military space research, particularly at Huntsville, Alabama. Immediate steps were taken to augment the staffing of these laboratories with additional government personnel, but the magnitude of the space venture quickly made it apparent that resources outside government would need to be drawn into the enterprise in substantial numbers.

When in 1961 President Kennedy committed the government to the landing of a man on the moon by the end of the 1960s, the financing of the space program leaped forward, new facilities were planned for construction, the aviation industry became the aerospace industry, and new manpower demands were placed upon limited resources of highly specialized personnel. President Kennedy himself had inquired whether these sources would be sufficient to support the program he was to recommend to Congress. The answer was affirmative, although there is no evidence that the impact of this new demand upon other programs requiring similar personnel was fully measured. But NASA managers moved forward on a broad front to acquire the necessary personnel on its own payrolls, in special industrial plants and in the university laboratories. Because of the diversified operations and the need to integrate various processes at points in the development of the complex vehicles, employees of a number of federal and private organizations were soon working closely together in a common purpose.

The extensive use of nonfederal institutions for the conduct of the government's research and development programs had a debilitating effect on the large federal counterpart establishment. The federal laboratory director, frequently in competition with private laboratories supported by federal dollars for scarce personnel, was at a disadvantage because he was required to operate within the framework of government personnel policies. All too often he found that even the advanced salary levels for scientific personnel in the government were inadequate to match the less inhibited offers of the private contractor. Likewise, the scientists and engineers at the contractor-operated laboratories enjoyed professional benefits not available to the government professional in the form of advanced education, opportunity to publish and to attend professional meetings, and other valued fringe benefits not available to the government scientist and engineer. Even more discouraging than these factors was the general impression that the most urgent and exciting scientific research was not being directed by federal managers into their own laboratories but into those operated under contract.

In the first year of his presidency, John F. Kennedy ordered a searching study of the effectiveness of performing government research and development through the use of contractors. Acknowledging that these practices had accompanied the government's entry into new fields such as atomic energy, missile development, and space exploration, and also conceding the existence of current policies encouraging the contracting out of commercial and industrial activities of the government, he requested a group of top administration officials to formulate recommendations to guide future Executive Branch action in the use of the contract device. He emphasized the importance of exploring "the circumstances and conditions under which contractor operations provide the most effective means for accomplishing the government's objectives." Turning to the problems in federal operations, he requested full consideration of the limitations that made direct federal operations difficult and "to the development of proposals for adjustments and new concepts in direct federal operations which would provide the government with greater flexibility in determining whether the public interest would best be served by the use of contractor or direct government operations."

Reporting in April 1962, the committee advised the President as follows:

1. Federally financed research and development had increased at a phenomenal rate—from $100 million a year in the late 1930s to more than $10 billion a year in 1962, with the bulk of the increase coming after 1950. More than 80 percent of such work was being conducted through nonfederal institutions rather than through direct federal operations. This reliance upon nonfederal organizations had had a striking impact on the nation's universities and industries. While emphasizing the need for improvements in the conduct of research and development work and in the contracting system, the committee concluded that "it is in the national interest of the government to continue to rely heavily on the contracts with nonfederal institutions to accomplish scientific and technical work needed for public purposes. A partnership among public and private agencies is the best way in our society to enlist the nation's resources and achieve the most rapid progress."

2. The direction of these programs necessitated firm control in the hands of full-time government officials responsible to the President and Congress, and a government staff with exceptionally strong and able executives, scientists, and engineers. The most serious obstacle to the recruitment and retention of this talent was the significant disparity between governmental and private compensation for comparable work. This conclusion underscored the urgency of congressional action on the President's previously submitted civilian pay-reform proposal.

3. Stressing the desirability of using a variety of patterns for the conduct of research and development, the committee urged that a standard of relative efficiency and effectiveness, with due regard for the long-term strength of the nation's scientific resources, be employed in choosing the method to be followed.

4. Improvements in the contracting system should be developed to provide more incentive for reducing costs and improving performance, and for strengthening the government's capability to evaluate the quality of research and development work.

5. The erosion of competence in the government's research and development establishment was cited as a consequence of keen competition for scarce talent from government contractors. To reverse this trend, the work environment within the government laboratories should be sharply improved, not only through higher salaries but also through assurance that governmental research and development establishments would be assigned significant and challenging work, along with improvement of laboratory management with greater authority in the hands of laboratory directors to utilize resources and make administrative decisions.

These conclusions became a blueprint not only for the relationship between government and contractor laboratories but likewise for a continuing effort to improve the working environment and employment conditions in government laboratories.

Progress came very slowly. Patterns of organization and management, particularly in the Department of Defense, were changed at a far too deliberate pace. The improvement of the so-called in-house laboratory was a chronic issue on agendas of government meetings. Task forces, management committees, and investigating groups were convened to expedite administrative action. Again and again, the personnel system was cited as the primary obstruction to progress. At one point in 1964, the chairman of the Civil Service Commission sent a personal letter to every government scientist in the upper pay brackets describing the flexibilities and opportunities available to scientific personnel under the civil service system. Three years later, a joint commission-defense team visited most laboratories to assist directly in personnel problem-solving exercises. Although a comprehensive attitude survey of government scientists' views placed less blame on the personnel system than on the assignment of significant missions, a group of senior scientists campaigned for totally separate personnel systems for scientists and engineers.

As will be detailed later, salary reform did come to pass and federal scientific personnel benefited significantly from the frequent upward pay adjustments made possible by that legislation. Still, complaints of superior salary conditions in the contractor organizations continued to be heard. When it was proposed that contractor salary levels be approved by government contract managers, there was instant opposition from both managers and contractors. They considered the proposal an inappropriate invasion of contractor discretion, even though federal funds and federal personnel conditions were involved. Actually, however, a strong argument can be made that if government salaries do indeed reflect the going rate for professional skills in the market place, there is no justification for the federal government to reimburse the contractor for superior salaries he might be paying his personnel. Without interfering with the contractor's management of his own business, the government manager needs to possess more information about the personnel costs and conditions followed by the contractor in performing the government's work. A closer relationship between government and contractor facilities in the same general program can be achieved through improved management without sacrificing the benefits purchased by the government in using the universities and industry in the accomplishment of its work.

Even more serious policy struggles took place on another employment front, in that sector of federal operations described as support activities. This description covers a broad range of services—the programming, operation, and maintenance of computers, the operation of machine shops, the maintenance of facilities, the provision of technical libraries, and even the collection, distribution, and filing of mail. Many of these functions were identical, or at least closely akin, to the functions traditionally identified with federal employment. Here it was most difficult to demonstrate that the services could be more expertly and efficiently accomplished by a contractor than by federal employees themselves. Here, too, in many instances the contractor employees worked side by side with federal employees in the same functional areas. The alarm about these practices was sounded initially by leaders of the federal employee unions. They described the contracting-out arrangement as "a costly, wasteful and inefficient process" and demanded congressional investigation.

These employees were supplied by private contractors, many of whom formed corporations to provide these services or were engaged in activities unrelated to the service performed by contract. Their employees, in contrast to civil servants, took no competitive examination, swore no oath of allegiance, and were not restricted in their political activity, but they frequently drew higher salaries than the civil servants who worked beside them performing the same tasks. These personnel-by-contract operations were running in 1967 at a level of about $8.5 billion a year, primarily in space and defense activities.

The contractors were not without their advocates in this controversy. The president of a large company holding such contracts described the attacks on the arrangement as a power play by federal union leaders eager to swell the ranks of the bureaucracy and of their own organizations. The contractors organized themselves as the National Council of Technical Service Industries and proceeded to defend their multibillion-dollar business.

In response to the controversy, the General Accounting Office and the Civil Service Commission investigated the practices and their relationship to federal personnel requirements. The GAO concluded, after conducting several cost analyses of the system as practiced by NASA, that there was a waste of public funds. It found that NASA could have saved $5.3 million a year if it had done the work it let out in nine contracts totaling $31 million. In rebuttal to these findings, the contractors argued that these analyses did not take into account hidden costs to the government in pension credits and in work-time losses due to allowances for sick leave.

On the matter of policy and legality, Civil Service Commission spokesmen prepared an opinion reaffirming "the principle inherent in our Constitutional form of government that essential functions of government and the employment of individuals required to perform these functions are a responsibility which cannot be delegated to private interests." On the basis of this opinion, general guidelines were laid down for agencies to follow in judging whether or not they were within the appropriate bounds of law and policy in negotiating support service contracts. In this guidance, it was pointed out that "support service contracts are not per se proscribed" and that "no single provision of a contract should be used as the sole basis" for determining whether it would be counter to federal personnel laws. The essence of this position was expressed in this way: "The touchstone of legality under the personnel laws is whether the contract creates what is tantamount to an employer-employee relationship between the government and the employee of the contractor."

These interpretations were generally accepted by the agencies concerned, but continuing reliance in reaching decisions was placed upon the cost comparison between the two methods of operation. In 1967 the House Government Operations Committee, headed by Representative Porter Hardy of Virginia, criticized the absence of precise methods for making a study of comparative costs and concluded that a management decision to contract or go to in-house operation in connection with a support service should not be made without a cost comparison except in special situations. A specific written reason should accompany a decision made without the benefit of a cost comparison and should be reviewed by the agency's top management and the Bureau of the Budget.

But the verdict is still not clear. The government manager has available to him the contract as a means for providing the necessary manpower to perform a particular function. When the contract calls for the delivery of a finished product, the rendering of a complete service, or the pursuit of a defined area of research, the validity of the decision to contract can be more readily demonstrated. The mixing of direct-hire and contract personnel in the same operational setting is fraught with management difficulty in the form of confused supervision even if the Civil Service Commission's standard for employer-employee relationships is met, and with serious morale problems in the inequality of employment conditions, salaries, and benefits. There is no valid brief to support the contention that private employers can attract and retain higher-quality personnel at the same payroll cost as the government. This is particularly true in recent years, when improved federal salaries and more aggressive recruitment have prevailed.

It is essential that persons employed by the government and responsible to constituted authority accept responsibility for the performance of public programs. To assure this accountability, the government must be staffed by strong and able executives advised by highly competent professionals. Extensive contracting out of government programs to private organizations can lower the government's ability to maintain these accountability resources and to plan and evaluate public program execution. Consequently, a decision to contract out should evaluate the impact of that action on the short- and long-term effectiveness of the government agency to manage its programs in the public interest.

The score card on federal employment strength as a measure of management effectiveness should be outlawed as imprecise and invalid. On the other hand, responsible federal officials should be prepared to report to Congress and the public the total manpower invested, whether on government or contractor payrolls, and to defend the necessity of the total number in achieving their mission objectives. Such an accounting would recognize the mutually supporting features of the public-private partnership in meeting national goals. That partnership would be strengthened rather than weakened by a more precise definition of the respective spheres of operation and by full public knowledge of the dimensions of the partnership.

The Meaning

of

Public

Careers

4

A semantic tangle has needlessly complicated public understanding of the public service. The popular use of the word "career" in public agencies has been a major factor in this lack of clarity. This term has been broadly applied to all those who enter public service via the merit system, where job status or tenure becomes the assumed goal. In the minds of many, including the public servants themselves, the concept of a career of employment has become almost synonymous with the concept of merit. Even the term "noncareerist" has entered the governmental jargon to identify those in the meritocracy who serve without tenure for extended periods under a passing parade of political officials.

To a certain degree, these confused definitions are the consequence of a historical accumulation of concepts. As Frederick Mosher describes it in *Democracy and the Public Service,* the United States acquired and "bore a mixed and cumbersome baggage of concepts about the public service and about its role and control in a democratic polity." He properly observes that "each generation had contributed a wave of reform with features and emphases distinctive from any that had preceded and each left lingering contributions and legacies even though some were subsequently modified." These residues of unassimilated reform have piled up to create an opaqueness of view in contemplating and rationalizing the type of public service careers needed today and in the future.

The very diversity of public services perpetuates this confusion of concept. A career as a public-school teacher or as a Foreign Service officer are similar only in the fact that both cover an extended period of employment on a public payroll in support of a public program. Whereas the teacher's career may well be in the same school teaching the same subject for an entire working lifetime, the Foreign Service officer enters a structured career system where he is expected to be a generalist or a many-faceted specialist with extended periods of service abroad in a variety of locations; the presumption is that he will advance upward and onward to greater responsibility and more imposing perquisites. And whereas the teacher faces a career with a relatively flat lifeline where the increase in both salary and emoluments are modest and according to prescribed time and experience requirements, the Foreign Service officer faces a career with a rising line and an expectation of ultimate appointment to a position of high rank.

Police careers more nearly resemble those in a military organization than in other civilian services. The career pattern of the postal clerk or letter carrier has remained fixed to one set of duties and one location, with the less arduous and frequently less responsible duties being made available to senior colleagues; his union aggressively resists a reordering of tasks to secure a more vertical career and advocates higher salaries and benefits with emphasis on seniority as the device to raise the individual's income. Such a pattern is more akin to that prevailing in the blue-collar trades and crafts than to that of clerical and administrative personnel in government.

In the white-collar government occupations, career configurations differ substantially. In the jobs requiring relatively limited educational and experience preparation, those men and women selected through the competitive process tend to be short-timers. As elsewhere in the labor market, low-paid young people who possess a high-school education or less tend to form little commitment or attachment to their employer or to a continuation in the same line of work. In this occupational area, women are employed in large numbers and enter employment with the expectation that they will soon leave the labor market for matrimony or maternity. Both male and female employees in these occupational fields view a job as just a job and have only limited expectations for a government career as such. Recent federal studies indicate that the annual turnover in these categories will run well over 25 percent, and that close to 75 percent of those entering these positions in any given year will have moved on to other employment or activity before the end of the fourth year. Even so, they are euphemistically described as a part—a very large part—of government *career* service.

It is in the growing professional fields, ranging from science and engineering through law and on to administration, where lines of career advancement and development have been constructively sought in the more progressive public service systems. To some degree, this added attention has been a product of competition with other employers. Also to some degree, it has been a reflection of professional expectations on the part of those who graduate in American higher education. Although the benefits extended to these rising professionals differ little from those in the more static employment experiences and amount to a great deal less than in private employment, they will expect more from the public employer in the form of personal development, professional satisfaction, and upward career mobility. The urgent need of virtually every public program for these scarce skills has accelerated the rates of advancement even within the narrow confines of an individual government agency.

It is essential that the existing confusion over career concept be clarified. That clarification should come through the analysis and projection of employment patterns in different occupational and program fields. Any tendency toward uniformity and even consistency in these patterns should be avoided in favor of custom design by responsible managers with ultimate accountability for program results. No categories of employment, even those with high turnover and traditional rigidities, should restrict the opportunity, subject only to the individual performance and aspiration, for growth, development, and improved income. Qualification standards for entry as well as the tests and measurements for relative abilities should be periodically examined, not only in terms of immediate job requirements but also in terms of the individual's future growth. Standards for promotion should be incorporated in these patterns and in close correlation with job experience and training opportunities. Supervisors should be encouraged to view the forming and following of such patterns as an essential part of their administrative responsibility upon which their own performance will be evaluated. In the operation of these plans, tenure and security should be gradually replaced by the concepts of opportunity and growth as the prime motivations. It would be well to lessen dependence upon the expectation of "career" as the principal goal in civil service employment.

A favorite debating topic for civil service reformers is the relative merit of rank-in-man and rank-in-position career systems. The outstanding examples of the former system are the military and Foreign Service with their precise ladder of rising ranks and with heavy emphasis upon required assignments, specified periods in grade, systematic performance evaluation, and "up or out" promotion decisions. These systems are basically closed in the sense that virtually no new entries are permitted into the system above a specified level (second lieutenant or ensign in the military, Class 6 or 7 officer in the Foreign Service) except in periods of rapid emergency expansion. The assignment of these officers is only incidentally related to the duties and responsibilities of the position. In most instances, more complex tasks and broader accountability are associated with each advance in grade. But this is not necessarily so; high-ranking officers sometimes may perform in billets that generally call for a lower grade. Likewise, the exigencies of a particular operating situation or the outstanding performance of the individual officer may propel him into a more difficult set of tasks without any change in rank. The proponents of this system view its flexibility of assignment, systematic management of individual careers, and its precise advancement standards as valuable personnel assets that should be more widely applied in all professional services in the government.

The rank-in-position concept is the prevailing approach for virtually all other career systems, which are based on the initial evaluation of a specific job and the filling of that job with the best-qualified person. Plans of this type have become increasingly accepted not only in government but also in private enterprise during the past fifty years. In the federal government, the framework for this system was initially erected in the Classification Act of 1923. That legislation led to far more rational designs of public positions on the basis of definite duties and responsibilities established by managers and evaluated in accordance with job standards created by a central agency. The original structure has been modified many times, with significant changes in 1949 and 1962. Although there is chronic complaint about and dissatisfaction with the system, which does need modernization, fundamentally it has stood the test of time and has provided a structure of jobs and job relationships in the development of career patterns.

At times the job-classification approach has been viewed as unduly rigid, particularly in its association with the competitive employment process. Under this system, it is possible for any person in the labor market to compete for entry through a matching of skills with other applicants for a particular occupation or profession at any of several specified levels. It is, in short, an *open* system. Incumbents with varying degrees of seniority and at any job-classification level may be faced with competition from a well-qualified outsider. In practice, the great bulk of the professional and administrative personnel enter the system at a job level specified for recent college graduates or for those entering employment with higher degrees. But unlike in the rank-in-man system, advancement is achieved when the individual is prepared, in the eyes of his supervisor and within certain broad limitations laid down in statute and regulation, to perform duties or accept responsibility at the next higher grade level. This can mean that in an expanding or volatile agency, advancement from level to level can be almost as rapid as regulations will allow. It is not unusual to find annual advancement for a particularly able young specialist in such an organization, with the result that high responsibility and complex tasks are assigned to those who have scarcely reached the thirty-year mark.

On the other hand, in a fairly static organization with relatively little turnover and with strictly defined professional requirements, the younger professional may wait for what appear to be interminable periods before advancing to an available set of duties at a higher stage in the hierarchy. To lessen somewhat the depressive nature of such a career outlook, a series of pay steps within a specific grade is provided. In progressive public agencies, a series of rising positions with broad job content has been designed to permit reassignment within a particular grade level and to open up opportunities for reasonably regular advancement on the basis of competitive performance. In such systems, many rank-in-man characteristics have been injected into the personnel structure of the organization without destroying the benefits of assignments based upon position content. In much the same fashion, the rank systems have endeavored to give more precise definition to work assignments and to recognize the necessity of certain professional specialization in their own career lines, even in a system allegedly staffed with generalists.

Studies of career systems for public personnel have revealed career configurations that more nearly resemble the elevator shaft than the pyramid. There has been a tendency for the recent graduate to enter on the ground floor of the career and move to successively higher floors, depending upon the expansion and dynamism of his organization. The passengers on the elevator have a relatively limited view of other professional experience that may exist outside their own organization in related professional or program fields. Whatever career motion exists tends to be controlled by the organization of their employ, whether it be the Kalamazoo school system, the New York City police force, the California university system, the U.S. Department of the Interior, or the Social Security Administration. This is particularly true once the individual has passed the initial five-to-ten-year stage of his career.

Mobility between governmental organizations and levels of government or between government and the private sector is limited, occurring only on a casual and unplanned basis. This static situation works to the disadvantage of both the individual and the government organization. It fails to take advantage of professional similarities and the self-renewal made possible through constructive changes in employment environment. In law enforcement, for example, benefits would accrue from steady movement through experiences at the local, state, and federal levels punctuated with periods of general or specialized training. With so many governmental functions now a part of federal-state or federal-local grant-in-aid partnerships, experience at different levels of government can be complementary aspects in the same field, whether it be public welfare, job training, urban renewal, or some other critical area of governmental activity. A strong argument can be made in favor of staffing federal positions in such programs *only* with those who have been directly involved in the operation of the program at the state or municipal level.

In contemporary government, more and more programs involve close interrelationships between government and industry, government and the universities, and government and nonprofit organizations. The public official who has a period of direct experience in industry, education, or nonprofit organizations will be better equipped to make balanced judgments in exercising his governmental responsibility.

On a more limited scale, such mobility should be encouraged within the several sectors of government. An economist can enhance his public value by serving in a number of different social agencies as well as in the Bureau of the Budget, the Council of Economic Advisers, or the Federal Reserve Board. A physicist can broaden his public contribution through research and development involvement in the Bureau of Standards, the Atomic Energy Commission, NASA, or the Defense Department. A lawyer can find supplementary experience in virtually every other government agency beyond the boundaries of his own. In the management staff specialties—financial management, personnel, procurement, systems analysis, and an ever growing array of other services to the program manager—there are common denominators throughout the government. There is perhaps more mobility among these specialists in public administration than in any other field, but most of the mobility is self-generated. Even in the federal government, where administrative machinery is perhaps the most highly developed, there has been an inability to develop lines of lateral as well as upward progression in these common fields. And the most important of the public cast of characters, the manager, would benefit himself and public management generally if his career afforded practice for his skills in a variety of program situations. In some instances the degree of technical knowledge necessary to manage the program will prohibit his selection from another field, but frequently these specialized demands are overstressed and a competent manager proves to be a quick student in entering a new field where he can bring to bear his talents for leadership in the public interest.

The meaning of public careers cannot be expressed in a few simple phrases. The meaning is as myriad as the occupations and professions that make up the employment mosaic of public service throughout the United States. But the term "career" should not equate exactly with civil service or with the merit concept. Large portions of public employment must be short-term and must be oriented to the individual job. Wherever possible, an objective of individual growth and advancement should be designed in a form reflective of the character and substance of public programs. There should be a minimum of uniform statutory or regulatory requirements and a maximum of discretion for the responsible manager, who can achieve his program purpose only through the efforts of the people who work under him. The adoption of a closed or open system, the acceptance of rank in the man or rank in the job, will provide the solution. There must be open opportunity for all Americans to compete for positions at all levels, and there should also be a justified expectation that persons who enter public service and gain experience over time will always have a qualifications advantage over those from the outside. While regular advancement through evaluation and competition is essential to every career system, such advancement without reference to the job content and responsibility of a position will be wasteful and will produce career distortions. In the acceptance of a principle of equal treatment, there should not be the mistaken expectation that every person entering the public service will sooner or later advance to the top post. The numbers at successively higher levels will be smaller as the number of higher-ranking tasks diminishes and as the workings of relative competition reduce the number qualified for advancement. The term "career" can be truly misleading if those entering it assume that they are on the first step of a smoothly rising escalator.

Individual career designs should not be constructed or operated in isolation within an agency. The vista of career opportunity should be broadened to include related experiences on a wider plain of public services. No assured route with required stops in other organizations should be mapped across that plain, but signals should be erected for clearly identifying the growth potentials in other programs and jurisdictions. With the expanded capacity of information systems it should be possible, without any violation of privacy, for intergovernmental groups, professional societies, or other broad-based organizations to collect information about qualified persons with an interest in filling, on either a short-term or a long-term basis, assignments in other organizations where their own professional or administrative field is represented.

Because the human element is fundamental in the successful accomplishment of the public mission, policymakers and citizens alike should demand dynamism in public careers. Obstructions to such dynamism in the form of arbitrary or restrictive personnel policies, outdated governmental organization, or the perpetuation of antiquated programs should be eliminated. When the Peace Corps was formed as an innovative and imaginative government agency, its leaders consciously restricted the time span of service to five years on the reasoning that a longer career would produce unfavorable human conditions that would seriously hamper the agency's performance. They designed what they called "the five-year flush," whereby a change in personnel would be guaranteed after that period. Although this original intent proved unduly restrictive and prompted many exceptions for individuals with five years of service, the approach is worthy of emulation on a more flexible basis. If high levels of human skill can be developed through more frequent changes in organizational structure, operational practices, program direction, or top leadership, such changes should be encouraged. Both the individual and the government will benefit from assurance that a career of thirty-two years of experience will not be just one year's experience repeated thirty-two times.

No matter what structures or specifications are applied to these career systems, the individual and his personal goals should remain foremost in the minds of the system designers. No organization should be allowed to become so fixed and no set of policies so prescribed that the individual cannot exercise free choice in pursuing his own development in public service. The demand for fairness and equity should not submerge manifestations of individual motivation that justify special recognition. The creative person, the nonconformist, the exceptionally able should not be forced to develop in a standard career mold cast for the nonexistent average man. In any event, flexibility of definition, policy, and practice should be maintained to permit the shaping of new patterns to meet the ever changing demands of public service.

Government

Seeks

the College

5 # Talent

"The presence of the federal government as a recruiter of college talent is proof of growing government dominance and the advanced state of socialism in this country." So commented a large metropolitan daily in 1966 at the time when the federal government stepped up its recruiting effort to secure a larger share of the college-graduate market to staff critical public programs. But this was a lonely dissenting voice that has become more and more muted in the intervening years.

It is now recognized that government must seek and select a significant number from the top talent pool in the country. In doing so, government will be unsuccessful unless it becomes an effective competitor with the best of the private employers. This is a fair and healthy competition, a free labor market at work where the young man and young woman are offered employment choices among an array of bidding employers.

Government has not always entered the labor market place as an effective competitor. In many jurisdictions, the lingering aura of political spoils has created the impression that those interested in government must first secure a political passport. Where the merit system has become the established entry route, there has been a traditional assumption that able people will come forward, file their applications, undergo the examination, and await the results of the rating process. Only in relatively recent times or during previous periods of dire emergency has the government employer waged the type of selling campaign that can attract hard-to-find professionals and specialists. Even when public managers were infused with the competitive spirit, they found themselves obstructed by legal or regulatory barriers that frustrated the use of recruiting techniques acceptable in the private sector. As late as 1967, congressional committee members were critical of federal efforts to secure authorization to pay applicants' travel to a federal agency for interviewing.

If the public employer is to prevail in securing the skills required, recruitment processes must be better planned, more aggressively pursued, and more critically evaluated. These processes do not commence when the federal official visits the college campus or when the recruiting brochure is delivered to the university career counselor. They begin when program objectives, organizational patterns, and financial authorizations are converted into numbers and types of jobs. The difficult task of determining staffing requirements is an essential first step. Far too many public agencies fail to take this step and merely launch a recruiting campaign based on the premise that they need as many of the trained physicists or engineers or economists as they can attract to their organization. These requirements must be cast in the light of a reasonable approximation of the talent available at the time required. Although handicapped by uncertain program projections and the vagaries of annual appropriations, the manpower planner must recognize the time factors in the attraction, selection, and training of even the most skilled manpower for the task to be performed. Manpower waste and program failure may very well accompany an assumption by management that the time cycle in acquiring personnel can be continually shortened. It is true that in the development of manpower requirements and forecasts there will always be a number of unknowns. But the speculation can be partially reduced through a penetrating analysis of employment experience in the program and the occupational fields involved. Managers can review employment experience from similar current and previous operations. What has been the performance experience with those recruited previously? What has been the pattern of professional growth? Which recruitment sources have been productive of the highest quality? At what

career points does the most significant turnover take place? Which training programs have proven most successful in terms of program results?
These and many other questions should be raised before quantitative or
qualitative requirements become recruiting objectives.

The actual skill requirements of the positions to be filled need to be
critically analyzed to ascertain the appropriate levels desired. When
college graduates are plentifully available or when a zealous program
manager insists on high educational standards, a qualification standard
in excess of the true performance requirement of the position is liable to
be imposed. A classic example of this type of planning error occurred in
the initial staffing of the security-guard force of the Los Alamos project
of the Atomic Energy Commission. Impressed with the high sensitivity
of nuclear research and the national importance of the laboratory, the
new managers of this enterprise in 1947 determined that all security
guards should be college graduates who received the highest rating on
a competitive examination designed for such graduates. Several hundred
young men were selected in accordance with these standards, only to find
that standing guard in remote areas of the laboratory or directing traffic
in the company town was not the career expression of their collegiate
preparation. Both morale and performance suffered, the cost of physical
security was excessively high, and a complicated redesign of standards
and restaffing of the operation, which took nearly ten years to achieve,
became the only means of correcting the original error.

With skills scarce and the market competitive, job engineering designed to reduce the number of positions to be filled from higher educational sources is absolutely necessary. In public service, many tasks can
be regrouped in such a fashion as to be within the capacity of the
high-school graduate who has received the appropriate in-service training. With current emphasis placed on identifying the employment opportunities for the educationally disadvantaged and potentially underemployed, this form of job engineering in advance of recruitment can
serve broad social purposes as well as specific objectives.

Many young professionals who enter public service motivated by personal ideals and thirsting for significant action are crushed by finding
that their initial assignments are not only uninspiring and far removed

from the critical issues with which they hope to deal but also are capable of being performed at levels of skill or intellect substantially lower than their own. This experience has been a cause of discontent and frequent losses of talent during the early months of employment—another by-product of the failure to apply research and judgment in advance of recruitment.

Too few public agencies study the characteristics of the professional labor market. In specifying advanced degrees as prerequisites, they fail to recognize the inelasticity in the output of the nation's graduate schools. The increase in the number of those schools and their graduates has in no way kept pace with the nation's demand for professional talents. The requirements have often been set at such a high number that individual government programs have established demands in excess of a fair portion of the professional talent flowing from the graduate schools.

When the national space program was accelerated in 1961 to assure the landing of a man on the moon by the end of the decade, the statement of manpower requirements for this crash effort was a minor item in the plan presented to President Kennedy. He was assured that there would be no problem in securing essential personnel. But through the attraction of exciting work and higher salaries, scarce skills were drawn away from other areas of research and engineering. In one of the early forecasts, the requirement of the space program for Ph.D. mathematicians was estimated at a number in excess of the total national supply for the year in question. Nor has this type of planning been the exclusive province of crash research and development programs. At one point the state university system in California formulated an expansion plan that would have called for employment of the total output of Ph.D.s from all American higher education.

Whatever the difficulties inherent in the forecasting of manpower requirements, it is an absolute necessity. Obtaining an adequate public service is first of all a matter of recruitment, for which the assessment of current needs is little more than a statistical exercise. Recruitment programs must be directed toward the needs of next year and the year following and five years hence. Very few jurisdictions have undertaken any kind of comprehensive manpower forecasting. According to the 1962 Municipal Manpower Commission report, only three out of sixty governmental units reviewed were even attempting advance planning of their staffing needs. One of the commission's priority recommendations was that "local government should first undertake long-range manpower planning—three to five years ahead."

During the 1960s, moves were made to begin a series of analytical projections of staffing needs for federal agencies as an aid in more effective long-term and short-term program planning. For the first time on a government-wide basis, the Civil Service Commission undertook projections that incorporated turnover rates, hiring rates, and other statistical information on a wide variety of occupations representing the full range of employment in the federal service. Projections of expected manpower supplies and labor-market conditions were provided and an over-all assessment was made of the supply-demand outlook in each field. As background in developing this program, extensive information was collected on recent agency employment experience in the then critically short fields of engineering, physical science, and mathematics. This survey indicated, among other things, that more of the total staffing needs were caused by turnover than by incremental growth, that more were filled at higher levels than by entry-level recruitment, and that success in competitive hiring was largely determined by the number of applicants available in the general labor market, in graduating classes of professional schools, and by current economic conditions. Although changing program conditions within the government and economic conditions in the labor market nullified certain of these projections, they provided the first guidance for the federal recruiting effort and gave the labor market some indication of the magnitude of impact to be expected from federal demands.

On the assumption that recruiting goals have been formulated from the planning and forecasting process, recruiting strategy and tactics must be developed as a major management activity in every public agency. This function is too crucial to delegate to even the most successful recruitment practitioner. Particularly when the search is for professional talent, the public official in the profession must play a large part in covering the potential sources of supply through his personal involvement. The potential candidates will want professional information about the nature of the program, about its professional goals and environment, and about their prospective colleagues. In many cases, the professional reputation of the laboratory director, the agency general counsel, or the chief economist will be the primary attraction for the young person making his first professional career decision. In recruiting, the governmental representative must seek out the candidates through personal visits to the campuses. These visits must be more than an annual episode. Whenever possible, the governmental representative should establish professional colleague relationships with faculty members as well as recruiting relationships with the career counseling office. He needs to possess information concerning recruiting experience at given institutions. He needs to have identified the career-influencing forces in the institution. He needs to utilize attractive and persuasive written material concerning the employment possibilities he describes. He must be enthusiastic in his own commitment to the program for which he is recruiting but must stop short of overselling its benefits. He must be able and willing to communicate with a degree of empathy in student discussion sessions. He must be sufficiently adaptable to deal with controversial issues and to handle excessive rhetoric without emotional or irrational response.

There is an unsettled argument as to whether a relatively young recruiter or a better-known senior representative is more effective in this duty. It all depends upon the individual, upon his sensitivity and rapport as well as his personality.

Public recruiting differs in one significant way from private efforts with the same objective. Because it is public, it is essential that all institutions, prestigious or obscure, highly rated or barely accredited, must be covered in the campaign so as to fulfill the equal-opportunity precept of government. But even if this precept were not a factor, it is in the public interest to make known the needs of public agencies at all institutions. The validity of this policy was confirmed in research recently conducted by both the federal government and the telephone system. It revealed that the level of academic performance on the part of an individual was a stronger indicator of subsequent professional success than the relative reputation of the institution he attended. Although an Ivy League educa-tion has been generally assumed to be the most promising doorway to success, a high-ranking student in a lesser-known institution can be a strong competitor in career advancement within large organizations. This widespread search pattern means that public recruiting efforts must be planned and supported with sufficient resources to make a significant impact.

In studying student reaction to public employment, there has always been a reflection of confusion and lack of understanding with respect to the different employment routes offered by the broad and diversified array of public service recruiters. In a move to lessen this confusion, the federal government consolidated a number of different civil service ex-aminations designed for college graduates. In 1955, the Federal Service Entrance Examination was announced by the Civil Service Commission as the principal entry route for careers in the federal service, supplanting separate examinations for different fields of study. That one examination, designed primarily to measure relative ability and relative promise for future success, attracted tens of thousands of competitors each year and was used by federal appointing officials to fill from 6,000 to 12,000 positions annually. The principal federal recruiting effort at the bachelor-degree level has been concentrated on this particular examination. Printed materials and recruiting visits have been designed to urge the student to file an application for this examination, which has been con-ducted at more than a thousand locations, many of them university campuses, seven or eight times each year. Some state and municipal governments have shown an interest in considering eligibles from the examination for their own staff requirements. This might be a beneficial practice in many instances, but a single public service examination for college graduates to cover all public jurisdictions would probably be impractical. Certainly it would destroy the recruiting advantage that comes from a direct relationship between the potential recruit and the representative of a program or organization in which he might be inter-ested.

Within the framework of the Federal Service Entrance Examination, the federal government has continued the competitive selection of a smaller group of outstanding college graduates for appointment as management interns in many elements of the federal government, primarily in Washington. The competitors for this jet-assisted start on a career in public service have taken additional written exams and have exposed themselves to an oral interview by a federal examining panel. About 10 percent of the competitors are judged eligible, and out of that group from 300 to 700 are employed each year. Those who are employed undergo special training and are given agency assignments to prepare them for early managerial or professional assignments. The group has occasionally been criticized as "fair-haired" or "crown prince," but it has provided the introduction and first step for a large number of the rising junior managers in important federal programs. The turnover is high, but no higher than is experienced by other employers who select from the very top of the graduating classes.

The necessity of an examination in recruiting college graduates has frequently been a source of contention in public employment. Critics of examinations have frequently alleged that they are culturally biased, that they overemphasize verbal ability, that they do not constitute an accurate measure of relative ability, and that they are a deterrent in attracting the superior talent unwilling to undergo yet another examination to qualify for employment.

Such criticism has risen to the action point. A group of black federal employees have filed suit in United States District Court charging that the Federal Service Entrance Examination was culturally and racially discriminatory. In charging the Civil Service Commissioners and HUD Secretary Romney as defendants, these eight employees contend that the examination "has served systematically to exclude qualified blacks and members of other minority groups from obtaining managerial and professional level positions in the Federal Service and has by other means denied plaintiffs and their class equal employment opportunities." They claim that "the ability to score well on such written tests is obviously related to the cultural background of the individual taking the examination."

The content of such examinations must be periodically evaluated to

determine whether they are truly responsive to the performance requirement of the positions to be filled and whether they are free of questions
that may exclude segments of the population which come from different
cultural backgrounds. Little evidence has been offered to support the
claim that the examination requirement deflects promising candidates.
Many private employers also utilize examinations at some point in the
recruiting process. In several prominent companies, the recruit is questioned about the rating he received on the Federal Service Entrance
Examination. For some time, most graduate schools have required an
examination as a part of their admissions process. In any event, the
selection of qualified candidates through the competitive process necessitates the use of a device for measuring relative ability if there are more
candidates than available positions. Recruiting efforts should be aimed
at building up the supply of applicants with the expectation that increased competition will produce a larger share of well-qualified eligibles.

Where the supply of qualified candidates falls far short of the number
of positions to be filled, the examination can be waived in favor of
evidence of the appropriate degree or professional attainment, as has
been done for most scientists and engineers for more than a decade. This
has meant that recruiters were able to offer appointments at the time of
initial interview if the candidate could present the necessary credentials.
In some jurisdictions this waiver has not been authorized, with the result
that the recruiter was at a competitive disadvantage. Yet even with these
more flexible conditions, the public recruiter has the obligation to assure
the public that his search has covered all possible candidates in all
qualifying institutions.

Many a recruiter has explained that money isn't everything in achieving success, but he has been unable to determine what is in second place.
Public recruiters must be reasonably competitive in the salaries they offer
to the prospective recruit. For many years, public service recruiters were
at a serious disadvantage in not being able to offer competitive salaries.
This condition still prevails for many state and municipal agencies,
which are virtually forced out of the market because their salaries are so
unresponsive to the prevailing market conditions. The federal government has long been aware of the salary competition. Back in 1958, it

improved its competitive position by ruling that graduates in the top third of their class could receive pay equivalent to two grades higher at the time of entry. In the Salary Reform Act of 1962, the basic principle of salary comparability with the private sector was established to improve the competitive situation with almost annual frequency. In addition, that statute permitted the Civil Service Commission to advance the salary range to any point within 30 percent above the base level where evidence could be adduced to prove a shortage in the required occupation and a generally higher salary level prevailing for it in the market. This flexibility has been helpful and has strengthened the federal recruiter when promoting his case for federal careers with the hard-to-find professional prospect.

The sales pitch offered to students in support of a career decision in public service has been based on a number of different arguments. Most recruiters emphasize the principle of service to the people and the social significance of the work. They stress the satisfaction in directing one's profession toward broad public goals in a career where initial selection and subsequent advancement are based upon relative merit. It has been demonstrated again and again that these arguments carry far greater weight than those stressing economic security, generous fringe benefits, and similar characteristics of public service. The more able candidates are fully aware of the fact that their educational level and inherent abilities constitute a reasonable guarantee of continued employment. This is particularly true since none of the recent college generations has more than a historical familiarity with widespread economic insecurity for college graduates. Unfortunately, some recruiters tend to reflect their own insecurity and press these points in their effort to communicate with college students. All too frequently, the recruiter's personal interest in a liberal retirement system will lead to undue emphasis on that aspect of public service in seeking a new generation of public servants. Although some in the student generation ask questions about the relative retirement benefits of competing employers, they tend to be the least attractive candidates. Most students today assume that any employer they select will support a retirement plan with a reasonably adequate annuity, and anyway the last element in their future for which they have particular concern at that point in their lives is the period of retirement.

Some recruiters may advance more subtle arguments for public service. With the current emphasis on "power" in various segments of the society, a number of recruiters have been highlighting the inherent powers that can be exercised by those employed by government—the power to regulate, the power to enforce, the power to collect taxes, the power to issue rules, and other alleged power performances in the bureaucracy. Generally, however, this line has been neither attractive nor widely utilized. More important in recent years, campus involvement in public issues has turned students to public service rather than to the profit-making market place. This turn of interest was particularly evident in the early 1960s, by a large volume of student applications for public service and by an outpouring of interest in voluntary service in the Peace Corps and VISTA. Students tended to focus their attention on specific programs of public service, particularly those related to social problems, and to local government in contrast to the national and state levels. The interest was also whetted by a desire to pursue a social goal as an individual outside large structured organizations, and recruiters had to answer perceptive questions about the nature and environment of the work to be performed in the public agency. This social idealism also led to initial periods of disappointment and disillusionment as the determined young professional shattered his lance against the established mores of the bureaucracy. Accusations have been made that the language in recruiting brochures and the rhetoric of the recruiters constituted a misrepresentation of the work situation to be faced by the newly hired civil servant.

The opportunity for summer employment became a major attraction in government service during the 1960s. Six to ten weeks of summertime service in Washington became almost a prestige hallmark in many universities. Federal organizations, alumni associations, professional societies, and other groups were barraged with requests from students for lively vacation employment in the nation's capital. Only a limited number of such assignments were available, and that number was diminished substantially as a result of the increasing concern for the employment of the disadvantaged during the summer. Nevertheless, several thousand college students moved into Washington each summer to work in the Capitol or in the marble palaces along the avenues and to live and play in Georgetown or some other student mecca within the city.

In many organizations, the numbers became so great that the opportunity for a meaningful experience was eroded. Agency employers were urged to provide training experience in connection with the summer job, but such experiences varied broadly in quality and impact. Until the numbers outgrew the capacity of any convention hall, programs were offered to the total body of students in which they could come into direct contact with leading legislative and executive figures and could aim their penetrating queries at the visiting dignitaries. The climax of the summer experience was a visit to the south lawn of the White House for an address by President Kennedy or President Johnson. Both Presidents found these occasions stimulating, and they served in their own ways as the highest-level instructor and recruiter for the public service. Words uttered on those occasions found their way into the recruiting brochure of the following year. In fact, a presidential message concerning public service became a leading declaration in the quest for quality on the college campuses.

Because of the popularity of the summer experience, questions were raised about the manner in which candidates would be selected for appointment. In view of the expense and complications of a competitive examination, the Civil Service Commission was reluctant to design and operate this traditional process for selection. But when political preferment and congressional recommendations began to enter the application file, so that the offspring of federal officials and residents of the greater capital area formed a predominant portion of the summer employees, it became necessary to put into effect an examining process that besides determining relative ability would permit equitable competition for applicants from more distant locations. The examination proved a highly popular one, with 40,000 to 50,000 candidates taking the examination for less than 10 percent of that number in available jobs.

The number of the summer employees who return to government following graduation has been disappointingly small. In the summer of 1964 several hundred student lawyers who worked in the various federal departments were canvassed on their interest in future full-time service. Only about 20 percent evinced even a moderate interest and an even smaller number were actually available for selection after graduation. For them, summer work in the government was just that and not a preparation for a government career.

From the recruiter's point of view, the most successful programs were those in which the student who passed and received an eligibility rating on a regular civil service examination could be given a regular appointment for the summer, a leave of absence to complete his education, and a career appointment following graduation. For such a student, the summer experience became part of the preparation for a career job. Astute agency administrators continued communication with the former summer employee while he was completing his academic work and was exposed to the blandishments of other prospective employers. In the technical and scientific fields, programs of this type were particularly rewarding. The student was assigned to a laboratory or some other technical operation during the summer, and his experience with professional colleagues, the importance of the work assigned, and the high quality of the facilities available worked in the government's interest when the ultimate career decision was made.

In other public jurisdictions, similar recruiting programs and more extensive efforts can be used to secure quality candidates. California has pioneered in such approaches on a nation-wide basis, and Michigan and New York State have made great strides in recent years. Among the local jurisdictions, Los Angeles, Detroit, Denver, and New Orleans have made noteworthy progress.

But what is the true attitude of students toward public employment? All too little research has been directed at seeking an answer. Undoubtedly the most significant work conducted to date is that of Franklin P. Kilpatrick, Milton C. Cummings, Jr., and M. Kent Jennings in 1959–60 under the auspices of the Brookings Institution. In that study, the student population was requested to compare the chief advantages and disadvantages of government versus private employment. A number of viewpoints emerged from the data. In general, high-school students had the most favorable attitude toward federal employment and graduate students the least favorable, while college seniors held views close to those of the graduate students. Interestingly, security and fringe benefits were the most commonly mentioned advantages of government employment among all three student groups. The pay and self-development opportunities in government looked best to the high-school students. Their attraction was decidedly less for college seniors and graduate students, but those two groups saw opportunities for interesting and enjoyable work in government more often than the high-schoolers; the equipment and facilities offered by the government had a particular appeal to graduate students. They and the college seniors considered the biggest drawback in government employment to be restrictions on the individual's autonomy or an absence of self-determination with respect to his work. This criticism was frequently expressed in complaints about excessive bureaucracy and red tape. The student impression conjured up an employment environment fraught with restrictions on one's freedom of action in the job, cumbersome procedures, and inadequate opportunities and rewards for the truly able person who wished to get ahead.

The findings as a whole pointed to a fairly substantial attractiveness at the high-school level that was dissipated as the individual student moved upward through college and graduate work. In assessing both positive and negative features of federal employment, women were clearly more favorably inclined than men. Whereas college students with lower averages tended to put more emphasis on government security and fringe benefits, college seniors with the highest grades placed relatively greater emphasis on lack of self-determination, the existence of poor personal relations, and excessive bureaucracy. These findings may have been substantially altered during the last decade: student attitudes toward government may be both more substantially positive and more substantially negative because of an increased campus activism and a much stronger passion among students with respect to public issues. But in any event, continuing research of this type is important for future government recruiting efforts and in gauging government's capability to attract and retain the high skills that future programs will require.

With all of the attention college recruiting has received from the public service in the past decade, an assessment of campus response to these efforts is always being sought from faculty spokesmen, particularly those in the disciplines most closely related to government service. In 1966, when many of these programs were approaching what their advocates considered to be full flowering, a summary assessment was sought from faculty representatives in some twenty institutions in various parts of the country and with varying ratings in the academic pecking order. This summary uncovered the same points of criticism on government recruiting at each institution. Unhappily for the government advocates, the criticisms were generally similar to those expressed over a long period. They were:

1. Too much emphasis on the part of government representatives with respect to employment security in the federal government and too many general banalities offered about pay and benefits.
2. Minimal discussion concerning substantive program opportunities except in the most general terms, and an unwillingness on the part of the recruiter to say anything about the possibility of opportunities in governmental organizations other than those represented by the recruiter.
3. Inability or unwillingness to make firm position offers with definite reporting dates even when the required examinations had been taken and individual ratings made available.
4. Little expressed interest by the recruiter in the student's desire to match his own university experience and personal aspirations to specific governmental jobs.
5. Little subsequent follow-up on the agency's initiative with the persons interviewed, with the result that the student was often left to make the necessary follow-up with some distant and vaguely identified personnel office.
6. Multiple arrivals of recruiters who were generally not of high quality and who were seldom accompanied by officials concerned with policy issues.

Even when these observations are discounted for limited knowledge of recent developments and for local misunderstandings, they reinforce the need for a more determined effort by public agencies in planning and conducting recruiting activities in the important arena of the universities. Whether or not any single criticism strikes an individual target, it is essential that each critique be countered in the future performance of public recruiters.

Making

Equal Opportunity

a Reality

6

Assailed by accusations that Uncle Sam is a bigot and that he is practicing discrimination in reverse, the government employer has been at stage center in the drama of equal employment opportunity.

No issue has received more thoughtful deliberation or more vituperative condemnation in the past ten years than fair employment practice for American minority members in the public service. It was the issue that projected public employment into the civil-rights revolution of the 1960s. As demands for equality in voting, housing, education, and private employment reached new intensity, public administrators were forced to look beyond time-worn policy statements at the reality of employment opportunity for Negroes in government service. As civil-rights statutes outlawed discrimination and segregation, the performance of the public employer was assessed against ever more realistic standards and was frequently found wanting. When other employers endeavored to improve their own practices, through their own volition or under mounting public pressure, they turned, frequently in vain, to the federal government in search of appropriate models.

Where civil service concepts prevailed, public agencies were committed to equal opportunity as personnel policy. Competitive selection of citizens on the basis of their ability and fitness could function equitably only if the broad competition was open to everyone. But many govern-

mental bodies were not guided by a civil service policy and had selected
their employees on an admitted basis of discrimination—political preference. Such preferential employment not only led to a high degree of
political party homogeneity but also to a remarkable degree of sameness
in color, creed, and ethnic background. As late as the winter of 1970, a
newly appointed executive of a local public agency inquired about the
number of Blacks in his agency, only to be informed that there were no
Blacks and that agency employment was not even open to Italians.

In most government organizations, however, the administrative task
in pursuit of equal opportunity was the conversion of well-intended
policy statements into the reality of equal opportunity for all Americans
and in all employment judgments—initial selection, promotion, discipline and reward, training opportunities, and adjudication of complaints.
Whereas the rhetoric of the policy statements usually sounded noble and
clear, the application of those words in government offices, plants, and
installations was frequently slow and confused. The policy itself was
generally accepted as sound and equitable. In fact, most public managers
and supervisors were convinced that they had been following it. They
disputed any charge of discrimination or prejudice in their personnel
decision, and they always claimed an absence of personal bias. Inevitably
they could cite a few individual instances in which they had been instrumental in giving a Negro or a Mexican American what they considered
to be an employment break. Frequently they attributed the absence of
minority workers to the functioning of the personnel system: no Negro
eligibles had passed the competitive examination, or the examination
standards established excessively high hurdles for minority employment,
or Negroes' preparation for certain occupations was always inadequate.

When President Kennedy signed his Executive Order in March 1961
creating the Presidential Committee on Equal Employment Opportunity
and calling for an affirmative program within the federal government and
among the private employers under contract to the government, he was
not taking an innovative step. Presidents Franklin Roosevelt, Truman,
and Eisenhower had, each in his own way, emphasized the need to
overcome discrimination against American minorities in public and
related employment. The formula "employment without regard to race,

color, creed or national origin" had carried the presidential imprint in other times. But as with the equal-opportunity provisions in the Civil Service Act, there had been a serious lapse in applying the presidential principle. Also there was a widespread conviction, particularly among the growing group of civil-rights advocates, that government had failed to set the pace for equality in employment.

There had been previous breakthroughs in Negro employment in the federal service. Washington during World War II witnessed a massive entry of Negroes into clerical positions when previously they had been confined to jobs as messengers, laborers, or the lowest-level clerks. By 1942 and 1943, black faces could be observed in more and more jobs and previously all-white cafeterias were displaying a diversity of color. By 1960, certain public institutions, particularly the Post Office Department, had become a significant arena of opportunity to upwardly mobile Americans of all backgrounds. In many large northern cities, work as a postal clerk had afforded an improved income and status for large numbers of Blacks—so many that the post offices in cities like Chicago, Philadelphia, and Detroit had some predominantly black work shifts.

The merit system had opened employment doors for first- and second-generation immigrants. Foreign-sounding names, European and Oriental, appeared on governmental employment rosters long before their presence in any large number could be found in equivalent private employment. The basic purpose of civil service in establishing a representativeness of the total population had admirably overcome the elitism that was the hallmark of government service in the early days of the Republic.

But such progress was not enough. The limited available employment statistics revealed a concentration of minority groups in the less skilled and lower-paying positions, and very low proportionate minority employment in certain sections of the country. The very absence of adequate data led to inconclusive judgments concerning the effectiveness of equal-employment efforts. During the Eisenhower years, preliminary surveys of minority employment had been conducted in selected cities, but by and large there was a prevailing reluctance to secure information of this type on the ground that the act of collecting the data would in and of itself be discriminating. The equal-rights efforts of the 1930s and 1940s had outlawed the recording of race or creed or color on employment records. A subsequent move forced the removal of photographs from application forms. Records such as these were judged to be an open invitation to discriminatory action, and they often were. But the absence of identifying information deprived the administrator intent on designing a positive program of the essential analytical tools he required. The lack of information had become an excuse for inaction in many quarters. "We don't discriminate; we don't even keep any records of minority employees; we just select and promote the best qualified." Such an answer, clothed in official piety, frequently covered employment practices that did not encourage the competition of Blacks for public employment.

President Kennedy designated Vice President Johnson as chairman of the newly created committee of federal officials and distinguished private citizens. At its first meeting, the Vice President called for a pledge from all federal department and agency heads to adhere to equal-employment standards, to review existing practices within their organizations, and to join the Civil Service Commission in initiating steps to improve the total personnel system as it related to minority Americans. An immediate census was undertaken to secure reliable data on minority employment and to form a statistical basis for measuring future changes. The college recruiting campaigns of the federal government were redirected to assure that predominantly Negro colleges in the South and large northern universities with significant Negro enrollment were thoroughly canvassed and not neglected because they had offered few candidates in the past, and Negro students were counseled and encouraged to compete in available examinations.

President Kennedy underscored his commitment to the effort at a Cabinet meeting during the first sixty days of his administration. The new President had observed that the passing cadet corps of the Coast Guard Academy in the inaugural parade had not a single black face. This observation prompted renewed attention to the recruiting of Blacks for enrollment in the service academies.

Within the government, new training programs were instituted to give managers and supervisors a clear understanding of the President's intentions and to promote an understanding of the government's role as a model employer in equal employment opportunity. Sessions of this type were not limited to the seat of government. In major centers throughout the country, federal officials, civil-rights leaders, educators, and business-men were drawn together for meetings, frequently addressed by the Vice President himself, aimed at developing special efforts within the local community. These sessions frequently pointed up the need to improve more than existing employment practices. A chain of environmental deficiencies led to inadequate preparation on the part of many Negroes and Mexican Americans for available employment openings. Deficient education at all levels, the absence of vocational-training programs, the poor condition of housing and community facilities, inadequacy of diet, and unremedied medical defects made up a constellation of disadvantage.

When the statistics for the first full year of the program became available late in 1962, there was evidence of a marked increase in minority employment on a national basis. There was an absolute increase in the number of Negroes and also an increase, though a relatively small one in comparison to the whites, in Negroes at higher pay and supervisory levels. There was increased minority visibility in high positions, particularly in those where the President or a top appointing officer had total discretion outside civil service. Blacks began to appear in professions where their presence had been undetected previously. President Kennedy sought Cabinet status for the Housing and Home Finance Agency, with the declared intent of making Robert C. Weaver the first Black Cabinet officer. This intent was finally consummated by President Johnson when in 1965 Congress authorized the creation of the Department of Housing and Urban Development. Negroes were among the Kennedy appointees to federal courts, U.S. attorney posts, and ambassadorial assignments where only whites had served before.

If there was any satisfaction in these early gains, it soon vanished as civil-rights militancy in the South revealed prevailing deficiencies in federal government practices.

In May 1963, Birmingham, Alabama, had drawn national attention as marching Negroes under the leadership of Martin Luther King, Jr., were forcibly restrained by city police. In an effort to mediate the increasingly violent dispute, Burke Marshall, the Assistant Attorney General for Civil Rights, went to Birmingham and talked with representatives of the marchers and the city leadership. He learned that the Negroes sought admission to the white-collar trades, especially in retail establishments, where they had been traditionally excluded. When Marshall conveyed this reasonable demand to the leaders of the business community, he was faced with the retort: "Why should we employ Negroes in white-collar jobs when the federal government in Birmingham doesn't hire any?" A quick check demonstrated that except for postal and Veterans Administration hospital jobs, there was evidence of only the most limited Negro employment among the federal agencies. Several federal offices had no Negroes at all. Some offices had hired Blacks but had placed them in positions concealed from public view. Virtually all Negro employment was at the most menial level.

A task force of personnel specialists was dispatched from Washington to Birmingham to examine these conditions and to organize a drive to change the existing employment pattern. What was discovered was a blow to federal managers who had claimed substantial progress in the two previous years. Almost no recruiting had been conducted in predominantly Negro schools or training centers. Local representatives of federal agencies had established little communication with the Negro leaders in the community. Many civil service examinations had been closed to public applications for long periods. There was little awareness of the equal-opportunity policies so vigorously pressed by the administration in this area.

Fortunately a new Social Security office was being staffed in Birmingham. With the cooperation of all parties concerned, new examinations were announced, incumbent federal employees of both races were canvassed for possible transfer and advancement to the new organization, previously neglected sources of black candidates were cultivated, and community leaders from all segments of city life were made aware of federal employment opportunities. As a result, nearly forty Negroes were appointed to white-collar jobs in accordance with civil service practices during the ensuing sixty days. But the impact of this Birmingham experience extended far beyond those jobs. It had proved that policy statements

from on high in Washington, broad national recruiting efforts, and special management training were not enough to change practices and
ensure justice in employment.

City-by-city reviews of existing employment conditions as they related
to equal employment were conducted immediately and were continued
in subsequent years on a regular basis. They were not limited to the
South, although there was an initial concentration on other cities in the
Southeast in order to detect other cases of the Birmingham syndrome.
These community-action reviews resulted in a highly publicized initial
meeting of each center's federal managers, civil-rights leaders, principal
employers, officials, and news media. Attention was directed to the most
recent federal employment census for the metropolitan area concerned.
The data were analyzed, agency by agency and occupation by occupation. From the data, agency managers were queried with respect to any
seeming imbalance in employment. They were asked to forecast employment plans and to describe their proposed actions to assure genuinely
equal opportunity. The current condition of civil service examinations
was assessed. Past recruiting and employment-publicity procedures were
criticized and improved. Where outside community factors, such as
education and housing, were instrumental in frustrating equal employment opportunity, they were called to the attention of responsible local
officials. In many cases, federal programs would be enlisted to help
finance the identified corrective action under existing but neglected programs. From the discussion, combined efforts were organized among the
federal managers to solve particularly difficult problems.

These sessions were conducted in more than eighty centers across the
country. No community, no matter where located and whether large or
small, was immune from criticism in its accomplishment of the federal
objectives. Although the problems were frequently different in the
North, they were no less severe than in the South. Many but not all
problems were solved. In some localities employment turnover was low
and there were no new offices to staff. In other cities, even the most
intensive efforts failed to attract Negroes qualified for available positions.
And everywhere, the minority complaints continued to rise along with
an increased awareness of individual rights. Many of the complaints

came from within federal agencies where black workers stressed the absence of advancement opportunities more than an unavailability of initial employment. Without an overt intent to discriminate, supervisors frequently gave the impression that they were purposely selecting whites over Blacks. Where supervisory discretion led to the selection of Blacks over whites, there were occasional complaints of discrimination in reverse. This allegation gained wide currency late in 1963 when two Negroes were promoted to supervisory positions in the Dallas post office. There was an outcry for a congressional investigation from the politically powerful postal unions, which while supporting the equal-opportunity objectives showed little taste for Negro advancement in their own ranks. The facts of the actual promotions and the administrative regulations involved were so complex that no convincing argument either for or against the promotions could be presented. However, the clamor unquestionably intimidated supervisors and curbed any tendency toward compensatory promotion action.

The word "compensatory" was used by some critics of federal progress toward employment equality. Some civil-rights advocates believed that the normal workings of the system, with its applications, examinations, ratings, and other competitive devices, would never permit the Negro, who had suffered generations of disadvantage, to compete on equal terms. Instead of urging Negro applicants to take tests that they could not pass or to compete for promotions that could convincingly be denied them, they argued for an open and drastic change in approach. They urged an overt preference for Blacks in filling certain jobs or a certain portion of all jobs as compensatory employment, at least until a greater equality existed between Blacks and whites in the competitive labor market. But without statutory sanction, such preference could not be extended to Negroes or to any other group even if such action was judged to be sound public policy. At no time was there enough serious executive or congressional support for such a position to produce extensive public debate on the issue.

The heads of major federal agencies devoted considerable time in communicating their expectation for changed conditions throughout their organizations. Secretary McNamara at the Defense Department insisted that all military and civilian managers give the program high priority. He instructed each unit to review the employment circumstances of every employee to assure against underutilization of skills. This process revealed Negro employees with college degrees who worked in mail rooms or at other jobs with skill requirements well below their educational level. These utilization surveys gave support to claims of limited opportunity for the upgrading of black employees in low-level jobs and led to more forceful action in providing training and improving promotion systems.

The Administrator of Veterans Affairs, John Gleason, called the managers of VA establishments with poor records of Negro employment to headquarters and exhorted them to exercise ingenuity in attracting and selecting Negroes. "Use the same skill now to employ Negroes that you applied in the past to exclude them," he admonished them. He pointed to the irony of widespread Negro employment in patient-care positions in the hospitals while relatively few Negroes had been appointed to office positions with far less intimate interpersonal relationships. Secretary Orville L. Freeman, in the Department of Agriculture, called for special efforts to bring immediate improvement in the agricultural agencies in southern rural areas where the social and economic conditions of the Negroes were most depressed.

Such high-level emphasis was absolutely essential to sustain progress down the line. Frequently the local managers, thwarted in their efforts to comply, would plead for a definite percentage or a specific quota to serve as a target in minority employment. Such requests were resisted because quotas would have undermined the basic objective of equal opportunity, causing separation rather than unity among the diverse elements in the work force. No absolute number, no specific pattern, could constitute successful implementation of the program. Instead there needed to be a general atmosphere of opportunity, confirmed by a reasonable and regular recruitment of minority workers and by their advancement through the organization on the basis of their ability and training.

During this period the charge was frequently leveled that existing tests were biased or else measured skills irrelevant to the job to be performed.

Consequently, they were considered a part of the discriminatory machinery. These charges were partially true. Many tests were inherited from an era whose general assumption was that in filling any position the person with the highest skills or the greatest educational ability would be the best performer. Under the pressure of the new goals of equality and of matching skill to task, there was a turn away from written tests and a greater reliance upon the job-element approach, in which the individual's experience record and general aptitude were measured in direct relationship to the job functions he would perform in the desired employment.

With the accelerated tempo of college-level recruiting for Blacks, the Federal Service Entrance Examination came under close scrutiny. The Civil Service Commission had known for a number of years that applicants' scores on that nation-wide examination were always lowest in the Southeast, but there were no data with respect to the performance of Negro applicants. When such data became known through testing at Negro colleges, they revealed once again the serious deficiency in the education provided for Negroes. Where the percentage of competitors passing the nation-wide test was 45, it was a rare Negro institution whose graduates could reach a 4 to 6 percent passing rate. These results were initially assumed to reflect a lack of interest or confidence in federal employment on the part of the better-prepared Negro candidates. This proved true to some extent. There was some improvement in succeeding years as more Blacks applied, passed, and were appointed, but never to the degree expected. To facilitate the participation of Negro students in these examinations, arrangements were made to conduct them on the campus, a practice extended to more and more campuses to ease the student's part in the recruitment process. There had been reports in certain southern communities that Negro competitors considered federal buildings where the tests were ordinarily conducted to be the white man's preserves. On one campus where testing was undertaken college officials alleged that the tests were rated in a discriminatory fashion because none of the candidates passed. Although this allegation could not be proved, the test was administered once again under close monitoring. Again, every competitor failed.

These examining experiences led to ever more critical reviews of both the substance of the test and the relative performance on the job of competitors with varying scores. Although test and job performance showed a relatively close correlation, the test was largely a measurement of white college graduates with reasonably similar educational and cultural backgrounds. The specter of possible cultural bias could not be completely laid. The financial and manpower resources available for extensive research were minimal, as they were for any form of comprehensive personal research in the area of tests and measurement. Only through the active interest of the Educational Testing Service and the generosity of the Ford Foundation was it possible to initiate extensive evaluation of tests in later years. The findings from this research are still incomplete and inconclusive, but the necessity for assessment of this type has been substantiated as an essential feature in designing devices for the equitable measurement of relative abilities.

With the passage of the historic Civil Rights Act of 1964 came an equal employment opportunity statute applicable to all employers. As a result, the record of the federal government in that area of civil rights became a prime model in achieving these goals in all employment situations. Early the following year, the Equal Employment Opportunity Commission became the applicable enforcement agency. The Community Relations Service, created by the same act, moved forward to strengthen the capacity of each community to resolve its own race-relations problems. With this reorientation of civil-rights responsibilities in the federal government and with this added emphasis on equal employment opportunity, President Johnson, through a new Executive Order, assigned responsibility for administration and enforcement of the equal-opportunity goals in federal employment to the Civil Service Commission, the central agency for personnel management in the federal government. In so doing, he assigned the mandate to federal managers that he had expressed in his Howard University speech on civil rights: "It is not enough just to open the gates of opportunity. All of our citizens must have the ability to walk through those gates. This is the next and most profound stage of the battle for civil rights—not just equality as a right and a theory, but equality as a fact and as a result."

While commending the progress of the four previous years, President Johnson pointed out that the progress told a story of uneven results, agency by agency and in the states and metropolitan areas across the country. He set as a goal the establishment of the federal government, the nation's largest employer, as a showcase of achievement in equal employment opportunity and as a model for other employers.

To achieve this objective, a program based on four objectives was inaugurated by the Civil Service Commission late in 1965:

1. A renewed attack on prejudice itself, with the goal of eradicating every vestige from the federal service.
2. A painstaking reappraisal of job structure and employment practices—with the goal of providing entrance and advancement opportunities that could fulfill the fair expectations of more of the economically and educationally disadvantaged, whether Negro or white, Puerto Rican, Mexican American, Oriental American, or Indian.
3. A new emphasis upon training and upgrading employees already on the rolls—with the goal of removing from the system any feature that discriminates against full participation by minority employees in all occupations, in all organizational units, in all levels of responsibility, and in all geographic areas.
4. An extended campaign for community involvement—in participation with other employers, with the schools and universities, and with other public and private groups in cooperative action to improve employment opportunities for minority groups and other disadvantaged citizens.

These goals were intended to reinvigorate the program, with clear policy directives, with specific and practical plans of action, and with thorough follow-through and enforcement. But no set of policies and goals could create instant change. Supervisory attitudes, employment patterns, and community environmental factors that had evolved over generations could not be modified without a continuing effort and occasional tensions. As Blacks' demands became more militant, some whites were less inclined to apply the extra effort. Where some personnel actions had the appearance of discrimination, others were contested capriciously by complainers. Certain communities became chronic sources of friction and complaint, necessitating special reviews and evaluations. Those responsible for the programs never ceased to be surprised at the emergence of one problem area after another in the face of unflagging special effort. Investigative teams of increasing skill and sophistication were dispatched to diagnose and treat employment situations that failed to live up to the standard expected of a model employer.

Civil-rights leaders directed their fire at the procedures by which discrimination complaints were resolved. There was dissatisfaction with the delay in adjudication, with the equity of the process pursued, and with the ultimate decision, which in the vast majority of cases proclaimed the absence of discrimination. The complaint most often raised about the handling of such cases was that the same agency officials who might have committed or condoned the offense served as investigators, prosecutors, judges, and jury. It became evident that an affirmative program alone would not correct the conditions that provoked complaints and that the complaint settlement must follow due process to a greater degree in order to gain the confidence of those using it.

To improve and simplify the collection of employment data concerning minority employment, an alternative reporting device was developed in 1966. The earlier census-taking had been accomplished through a visual count by individual supervisors of the employees under their direction without self-identification on the part of the individuals involved. This method had unquestionably led to inaccuracies and lack of completeness. It also failed to provide information in sufficient detail to identify true patterns of discrimination or to trace progressive trends in minority employment. No matter what system was used, it was essential that no record identifying minority classifications be associated with an individual personnel file or be used in making employment judgments. Through use of computer processing, the new system would make possible the storage and retrieval of self-identification information without relating the minority classification to given individuals. The data thus made available could be readily used in analyzing and evaluating the employee population.

After a successful trial run in the Department of Agriculture, this new method was offered to all departments as an alternate record-keeping process. It was greeted with an unexpected negative reaction, particularly on the part of whites. A substantial number of protests against self-identification were forwarded to members of Congress, particularly to Senator Sam Ervin of North Carolina who was undertaking an evaluation of employee allegations of invasion of privacy. The protest reaction was also reflected in intentionally inaccurate returns. For example, a large number of employees in the New York City post office recorded themselves as American Indians. Large numbers of employees failed to return the identification form. In view of this negative reaction, the census the following year reverted to the more familiar means of the visual count by the supervisor. This experience illustrated once again the difficulty faced by managers who seek, without imposing on employees, the requisite information to administer an employment program designed to assure equality.

Throughout these years, the concentrated concern on the employment rights of the Negro frequently threw the Spanish-speaking American into the background. Puerto Ricans in New York and Mexican Americans in the Southwest pressed for broader opportunity in federal employment. By way of response a Cabinet Committee on Mexican-American Affairs was formed and staffed to assist agency heads in meeting the special problems of this particular American group, which was also given special attention in community-action reviews in metropolitan areas with sizable Mexican-American populations. Kelly Air Force Base in San Antonio became the prime focus of their discontent. That maintenance and supply establishment employed more than 20,000 civilians. Civil Service Commission and Air Force inspectors probed again and again the practices at the base to ferret out the causes of the militant Mexican Americans' dissatisfaction. The U.S. Civil Rights Commission held hearings in San Antonio that turned the spotlight on the federal government's performance. As in the case of the Negro dissenters, the main disaffection was not over the number of Mexican Americans employed; they constituted a large segment of the total work force. Rather it was their seeming inability to achieve advancement and the failure of management to place Mexican Americans in supervisory or other senior positions. To an appreciable extent, the negative interpersonal relationships on the base tended to be a reflection of community attitude, and consequently the locally oriented "Anglo" supervisors found it difficult to foster new job opportunities for Mexican Americans. The language problem itself aggravated the cultural adjustment. The Mexican American was forced to learn English, but the Anglo never learned Spanish. The development of bilingual and bicultural objectives had not been accepted by the leadership in the broader community and consequently was resisted in the work situation at the base.

The problems of the Mexican American were raised to a pinnacle of executive concern in hearings conducted by the Cabinet committee in El Paso late in 1967. Five Cabinet officers, the director of the Office of Economic Opportunity, and the chairman of the Civil Service Commission listened to carefully prepared presentations by Mexican-American leaders on an array of social and economic problems, and were subjected to probing questions concerning federal action to correct deficiencies in programs for which they were responsible. They all carried back to Washington long lists of required actions relating to the grievances of this group. Substantial gains were subsequently made in employment opportunities for Mexican Americans. Certain jobs were identified as bilingual, and special training was offered to improve proficiency in English and to impart other skills that would permit more equitable competition for advancement. Most important of all, impressive gains were recorded in the number of Spanish names on the federal payroll.

A survey of minority employment in November 1967 showed that members of minority groups held nearly one in five jobs in the federal service—496,000 of the 2.6 million full-time positions surveyed. The employment of Negroes reached a new high of 391,000, or approximately 14.9 percent of the work force. In the five southwestern states, Spanish-surnamed employees numbered nearly 55,000, or 10 percent of the area's total employment. In addition, there was an increase of 38 percent in Negro employment in the middle grades and 65 percent in the top grades over a two-year period. Although there were continuing increases near the top, the Negro portion of the top three grades (unfortunately labeled "supergrades" in federal parlance) totaled only 66 among the 5,492 officials in these grades. Largely on the basis of these statistics, Julius Hobson, a black militant leader and a federal employee himself, elaborated his charge that Uncle Sam is a bigot in a *Saturday Evening Post* article in April 1968. It was difficult to accept such an indictment at the time when Blacks were participating in the deliberations of the Cabinet, the Supreme Court, the Federal Reserve Board, the Atomic Energy Commission, the Export-Import Bank, and many other federal activities. But it illustrated the necessity for a continuing and never slackening drive for practices and conditions supporting the achievement of equality as a fact and as a result.

In public jurisdictions outside the federal government, progress toward this objective has been even more difficult. In many jurisdictions only limited effort has been evident. Large cities, however, have tried to increase the black proportion of their police forces so as to match more nearly the color composition of their population. Public-school systems and public universities have been prodded to increase the number of teachers from minority groups. The addition of black teachers and their integration into the white teaching staffs in many schools is still a source of community tension. The same effort to open opportunity has been seen in social work, legal assistance, urban renewal, and other state and municipal operations.

In the South, previously segregated public activities have been abolished under the pressure of civil-rights statutes and the persuasion of federal funds. In the early 1960s it was discovered that the merit standards required for certain federal grant-in-aid programs had not included equal employment opportunity, so that federal administrators had approved merit-system plans for many states without prohibiting practices that made employment for Negroes an extremely limited prospect. Corrective steps toward new standards were taken, with beneficial results.

When public officials and legislators critically examine their personnel policies and systems to assure equality of opportunity for all Americans, they must recognize their obligations to press for an elimination of conditions that exclude a significant segment of the population from reaching the gate of opportunity. With more and more government organizations calling for higher skills, education and training assume an even more direct relationship to ultimate employment opportunity. The initial employment of minority workers was only the first step in practicing equal opportunity. Within public service there must be an employment climate in which equality is a factor in promotion, transfer, discipline, recognition, and training. In the effort to put opportunity within the reach of all, another problem should be frankly faced. There must be an avoidance of what might be called the tyranny of color. If an incompetent is allowed to hold onto his job only because of his race, equal opportunity will be sacrificed. It is a delicate balance to achieve but it must be achieved. The personnel decision-maker must achieve a balance of equality in the public interest in this time of revolution without obscuring the fundamental purpose of government itself: efficient and effective service to all the people.

"Every Day
Is
Ladies' Day"

7

Sex discrimination in public employment is another matter. Militant feminists representing such organizations as the National Organization for Women (NOW) have protested against the operation of government by "gentlemen's agreement" without equal opportunity for the fairer sex. For some peculiarly masculine reason, the objective of equal employment opportunity for women has been a subject to be lampooned or caricatured. The truth is that existing conditions, even after the changes in the past decades, are no jesting matter but a tragic waste of talents in a society that can ill afford to overlook the power of women.

A new awareness of equal opportunity failure with respect to women was underscored by the findings of the President's Commission on the Status of Women, formed by President Kennedy late in 1961. That commission was the final act of public service by Eleanor Roosevelt, who served as chairman and provided inspiration in behalf of equal rights for women in American society. The commission discovered in its inquiry into federal personnel practices that a long-standing policy permitted federal appointing officers to limit consideration for appointment or promotion to men only or women only, without regard to the duties to be performed. Although civil service examinations had always been open to men and women without discrimination, agencies requesting eligibles from those examinations asked for men only for the vast majority of

83

professional and executive positions and for many lower-grade jobs as well. At the request of the commission, the President had the legal sanction for that policy examined by the Attorney General, who in declaring it invalid opened the way to more job opportunities for women. The right of agencies to specify the sex of employees was immediately limited to a few specific positions that had to be approved by the Civil Service Commission, after obvious discrimination had been allowed to function for nearly thirty years without serious challenge.

While these steps were being taken, the Civil Service Commission began to require agencies that requested men only to give reasons for this limitation. This requirement had a prompt effect. Virtually every subsequent request was submitted without a sex preference expressed. It was apparent that an outmoded practice had been continued automatically and that those following it were unable to justify it.

The commission's extensive canvass of federal civilian employment revealed no significant differences in the treatment of either sex in terms and conditions of employment such as pay, premium pay, leave, insurance, retirement, and appellate rights and procedures. Federal employment conditions in these regards were and remain clearly superior to those prevailing in the private business. Not until legislation was passed over heavy opposition did women there gain equal pay for equal work.

The distribution of employment, however, followed the pattern in private enterprise: a heavy concentration of women in the lower-grade office positions and a heavy concentration of men in the professions (other than nursing) and in middle and upper administrative managerial posts. Less than 2 percent of high-level positions were found to be filled by women.

At the request of the commission, comprehensive studies of employment profiles and advancement patterns were conducted with respect to separation rates and their causes, grade levels reached, and attitudes affecting promotion, with data given by sex. Women's voluntary resignations were found to be nearly three times those of men, a figure attributed to the fact that women predominated in the younger age groups and low-paid occupations where turnover is higher for both men and women. When comparisons were made by age groups, salary levels, and occupations, it appeared that women's rates, while still higher, were much closer to men's: the loss of employees by turnover decreased significantly with advancing grade levels. Women of middle age were a more stable group than either men or women under twenty-five; women who entered the labor market in their forties showed very low turnover rates compared with other women.

Almost half of the women who left federal agencies gave reasons related to family responsibilities. The reasons of single women for leaving were similar to those of men. Nearly one woman in four left for the same reasons given by almost half of the men—to receive broader experience or better pay elsewhere, or because of dissatisfaction with the working situation. The third-ranking cause among women was ill-health or voluntary retirement.

While the advancement rate of men and women differed considerably according to occupation, the over-all difference in median grades in federal white-collar occupations was about five grades. Some three-quarters of the men were in grades reached by only one-quarter of the women. Differences were less sharp in such highly professional groups as attorneys, but in most cases women with comparable education and years of service were at lower grades than men. The women in higher grades were somewhat older than the men; more of them had college degrees. Typically they were not married; those who were married had smaller families than the men in the same grade. The advancement of single women was noticeably but not strikingly greater than that of married women. Women in the upper grades were quite as involved in their careers as men; they engaged more frequently than men in professional activities related to their jobs.

A very large proportion of men at all grade levels believed that men were better supervisors than women. A somewhat smaller number believed that men did better in nonsupervisory posts as well, though actual experience in working with women as supervisors or colleagues modified the strength of such views. A majority of women thought there was no difference in performance of men and women. The prevalence of negative attitudes among men concerning the ability of women emphasized the need for research on the sources of such views and attitudes, and the adoption of positive policies to diminish prejudice where it existed and to improve women's performance where grievances were found to be justified.

One of the commission's primary concerns related to the government's inability to take advantage of the availability of women for part-time employment, the only type possible for many able women, including highly trained professionals. Existing employment and fiscal policies tended to frustrate the arrangement of part-time assignments to utilize these skills. The commission urged the design of innovative work situations to open employment for women on a schedule more flexible than that usually followed.

These findings and recommendations were incorporated in a shiny report with findings and recommendations on other areas of national concern relating to the status of women. When the document itself was presented to President Kennedy, a little more than a month prior to his assassination, Eleanor Roosevelt was no longer present to add her personal eloquence to the proposals. She had died the previous November.

After the assassination, President Johnson moved promptly to place in motion the recommended implementing machinery. In the course of the following year, similar commissions were appointed by the governors in all but two states. The leaders of those commissions came to Washington annually to exchange views and to stimulate further national action to eliminate job discrimination against women. In all these deliberations, public employment policy received priority attention. This was one area that was reasonably understandable and in which corrective action was assumed to be reasonably achievable.

To demonstrate an instant response to the call for greater participation by women in government, President Johnson launched a special and personal campaign to attract women into high posts in his administration. He urged all of his department and agency heads to do likewise in filling the key position in their organizations. Between January 1964 and October 1965, President Johnson's talent search resulted in the appointment of 120 women to key positions. During the same period, federal agencies appointed or promoted over 3,500 women to positions at salaries of $10,600 and above. Many of those appointments represented breakthroughs into occupations formerly held exclusively or almost exclusively by men. The search for qualified and available women became so intensive that the President's recruiting team claimed that their theme song had become that old popular tune, "Every Day Is Ladies' Day with Me."

The President's pressure for feminine recognition was not limited to new appointments or promotions. When he received the winners of the Public Service Career Awards in the Rose Garden at the White House in the spring of 1965, he quickly noted that all of the winners were male and then proceeded to honor them with a forceful criticism of the selection committee for failing to include at least one woman. In subsequent years, that panel never failed to honor at least one woman in each such group.

But even with the prestige of the presidential commission and the continuing pressure of the President, the position of women in government was not substantially improved. There was a growing concern that many doors in administration and the professions were still closed to them, even while it became more apparent every day that women were an increasingly indispensable element in the American work force. The obstacle repeatedly encountered was that too few women had sufficient preparation for professional careers. As in the case of minority groups in our society, discrimination had been practiced against women so long that many lacked the incentive to gain the education and make the effort needed to develop their full potential. From inquiries in high schools, colleges, and universities, the same lack of incentive appeared to exist among many talented girls.

The sign saying "No Women Need Apply" had been removed from all the doors of opportunity, but they remained closed to those who lacked the necessary training. It was necessary to work at both ends of this problem at the same time. It was not enough to remove barriers to employment; barriers to preparation for employment must also be removed. This has proved to be much more difficult because incentive is a personal, individual matter.

To provide motivation is a task that transcends any government responsibility. It requires intensive efforts from many other sources, among them educators, private employers, counselors, and parents. There is need for a new recognition of the value of women as a critical and vital resource in the economic life of the nation. There must be a realization that equal employment opportunity for women is not a favor but an economic necessity. Women are more than one-third of the labor force of the United States. The fact is that the high levels of economic activity we continue to enjoy cannot be maintained without the extensive employment of women, both in government and in industry. The economy is in great need of women's service. In the next decade alone the country will need 900,000 additional school teachers and college instructors, 1 million additional specialists in the health services, 800,000 additional science and engineering technicians, 700,000 additional scientists and engineers, and 4.5 million state and local government employees, exclusive of teachers. The requirements in these fields alone will be 110,000 additional trained specialists every month for the next ten years. That requirement cannot be met by men alone. More and more of these professions must be open to women, and the means of training them for these professions must be established immediately.

It is sad that while opportunities for women are increasing in both private and public employment and traditional barriers are being lowered, few women are found in many professions and occupations. Nor is the prospect bright, since relatively few are being educated for such professions and occupations. Of the 29 million women who work for a living, three-fourths are clerks, sales personnel, or factory workers; one-fifth of all working women with B.A. degrees are secretaries.

This is a highly complex problem, made up of individual and group attitudes, educational and social patterns, and other interrelated factors.

First of all, there is a dropout problem that has received far too little attention: the dropout of girls after high school. Relatively more girls than boys finish high school, and with relatively more than their share of honors. But what happens to them after that? About 51 percent of the 1964 high-school graduating classes were girls, but only 45 percent of the group that went on to college were girls. Proportionately only three-fifths as many women as men twenty-five years of age and over are college graduates, and the farther up the educational ladder, the farther behind the girls fall. The most alarming aspect of this situation is that it is getting worse: women obtained 40 percent of all master's and second-level degrees in 1930, but only 31 percent in 1963. Similarly, while in 1930 women received 15 percent of all doctorates and equivalent degrees, by 1963 their share had fallen to less than 11 percent.

This educational fallout is due largely to lack of motivation, but a negative attitude on the part of parents toward college for their daughters is another influential factor. I think that fathers are especially responsible for this. Fathers, in particular, need to abandon the assumption that their daughters really cannot learn mathematics, or that it is not quite feminine to major in physics or chemistry, or that the engineering degree is strictly for males.

For many years now, the socialization and education of girls has been preparing most of them for a world that has vanished in the United States and many other countries. Many of the adults who significantly influence girls and boys—parents, teachers, counselors, and others—are inadvertently encouraging girls, and the boys they will marry, to ignore the facts of women's lives in the world of today and tomorrow.

Many adolescent girls continue to make plans on the assumption that marriage will permanently end their participation in the labor force. For some this will still be true, but for a great many it will not. Here are the facts on working women in the United States today: More than 36 percent of our total work force are women—more than 29 million. More than a third of all married women work. Five million women are heads of households. It is estimated that nine out of ten girls in school today will be employed, most for a substantial period, during their lives. Twenty-six years have been added to the American woman's average life expectancy since the turn of the century, from forty-eight years to seventy-four. Along with marriage and child raising, the modern American woman literally has a half-life of added years for constructive work either from economic necessity or to contribute a skill to society. What is she doing—and what will she do in the future—with these added years?

If the predominant influence on the girl during her educational years is toward a view that any education or training she may acquire is for "a contingency," a kind of life insurance against some vague day of possible need, with the hope and expectation that if she succeeds in marriage her husband will provide adequately thereafter and she will have no need to work, then she is bound to have low career interests, motivation, or aspiration.

Another general attitude destructive of employment progress for women is the masculine-feminine occupational concept. This is based upon erroneous assumptions of wide sex differences in intelligence, special abilities, aptitudes, or interests. One of the more interesting manifestations of this concept is how it has tended to separate the sexes even in the same broad occupational fields, always with the women in the lesser positions. Here are a few instances:

Nurses are women; doctors are men.

Bookkeepers are women; accountants are men.

Clerks, stenographers, and secretaries are women; administrators and managers are men.

This concept was described effectively by Dr. Rebecca Sparling of General Dynamics: "There is nothing inherently *feminine* about mixing a given batch of materials, exposing it to a definite temperature for a definite time, and producing a cake. There is nothing inherently *masculine* in mixing a batch of materials, exposing it to a definite temperature for a given time, and producing iron castings. I have done both and find them satisfying occupations."

The third of these general interrelated attitudes that stand as barriers to equal employment opportunity for women is an outmoded image of many professions. Occupational images far removed from current reality are still projected and act as deterrents to career selections by girls. This is true of a number of fields, particularly of those which are in very short supply and will continue to be for the foreseeable future.

First, there are the engineers. It is not uncommon to see the stereotype of the engineer as a rugged young man, fully equipped with field boots, hard hat, and a fistful of blueprints, sleeves rolled up to reveal a tattoo, in sole command of activities at the outdoor site of a major construction project. Yet probably a high percentage of today's engineering jobs are performed at a desk or in a laboratory, probably with substantial assistance from a computer. They can be performed equally well by either trained men or trained women. But the truth is that less than 1 percent of the engineers in the United States today are women. The latest figures on engineers now graduating from college give little indication that that number will be substantially increased in the near future.

Second, there are the medical doctors. The stereotype of the medical doctor is frequently projected (for the TV viewer to the point of overexposure) as an extremely overworked man with no regular hours, subject to the beck and call of his patients twenty-four hours a day, seven days a week, with little or no time for any personal or social life. And yet many fields of medicine conform to normal working hours similar to those in other occupations and professions. And although doctors need not be men, women comprise only 5 percent of American medical-school graduates. The situation is far different in many other countries. For instance, in India 35 percent of the medical students are women; in England 25 percent; in Thailand 28 percent. In Yugoslavia it is estimated that more than a third of the doctors are women, and in Russia more than 70 percent. In some of the developing nations of Africa, notably Nigeria and Uganda, a much higher percentage of women are entering the medical profession than in the United States.

There is an imperative need for employers and educational institutions to recognize and adjust to the changing pattern of women's lives. One wise person has observed that the basic problem may not be discrimination as such but rather the fact that women do not fit easily into situations designed by men for men. One essential fact that must be accepted is that women do leave the labor force for the responsibilities of maternity. In the future as in the past, a great majority of them will probably not want to go on working while their children are young. But increasing numbers of them will want to return to work at a later time—and they will be increasingly needed.

Educational institutions must make suitable provisions for these women to keep their skills up to date. Both public and private employers must make necessary adaptations of present working structures to permit the use of their skills when they are available. This is where the flexibility obtained through the use of part-time services is particularly important. There are many professional and technical positions where adherence to a rigid eight-hour day, five days a week, is totally unnecessary.

These issues penetrate to the very core of our social mores. Fundamental attitudes toward the education of women for work and toward their capability to perform that work must be altered throughout our society. When discrimination on the basis of sex was inserted in Title VI of the Civil Rights Act of 1964, it was pointedly placed there by members of Congress who opposed the other prohibitions against discrimination in employment. The intent was to ridicule a national policy of no discrimination by introducing an area of discrimination that was largely the subject of bad jokes and chronic misunderstanding. A year later, when the Equal Employment Opportunity Commission held a conference to discuss its responsibilities in eliminating discrimination against women, even the good gray New York *Times* reported the event as though it were the opening night of the latest Neil Simon comedy. Serious representatives of business downgraded the event by asking questions about the necessity for male stewardesses on airliners or male bunnies in Playboy Clubs. Rare were the observations about basic equity or about national manpower needs.

With this kind of recent record, it is not surprising that employment progress for women in the public service, even in the federal government, has been very limited. Statistical evidence in 1968 showed imperceptible gains in the number of women in senior positions at the federal level. Of all women employed, only 0.02 percent held the top professional jobs in grades GS-16 and above. In the larger group of GS-13 and above, women held only 3.7 percent of the positions. The vast majority of women continue to be employed in the traditionally feminine occupations, most of them requiring limited preparation and enjoying limited compensation. Aside from a few highly publicized presidential or gubernatorial appointments, there are probably fewer women in high governmental posts today than there were in the 1930s. There has been virtually no advance in the feminine population in elective office. It is doubtful whether there are more women federal judges than twenty-five years ago —and no President has yet seen fit to appoint a woman to the Supreme Court.

To conclude this discussion on a slight upbeat, there have been a number of significant professional breakthroughs during these years of increased emphasis but only moderate results. The space program has attracted able women in physics, astronomy, and space engineering. Letter carriers are no longer all men. Women have entered the accounting field in increasing numbers. The Department of Defense reports a growing roster of women in its research and development activities. Since the "male only" label has been removed, women are employed in increasing numbers in positions that require traveling, a development that Eleanor Roosevelt would have viewed with particular understanding and appreciation. And federal recruiting in the colleges is paying off. More and more women college graduates are applying for the Federal Service Entrance Examination, are passing it, and are being selected for junior professional and administrative posts. Since 1961 the percentage of women in these appointments has advanced from 17 to 38. This augurs well for an increased number of women in the higher professional grades if the old inhibitions on advancing women to higher responsibility can be overcome.

Emphasizing Ability, Not Disability

8

The opening of public employment to all citizens has revealed a broad range of excluded groups. Under the pressure of manpower shortages during World War II and the Korean War, the employment search spread into areas previously overlooked. While the initial motivation for the search may have been totally pragmatic, the ensuing selection, training, and adaptation of those previously disadvantaged by physical or mental defects were sustained through humanitarian interest. The process was accelerated through medical and therapeutic developments for the rehabilitation of those suffering from disabilities. Compassionate concern for disabled veterans opened the way to new recovery possibilities for those who had suffered disability through accident or inheritance.

The World War II experience in the federal government proved in terms of productivity that it was good business practice to employ the physically handicapped. It proved that previous requirements for a perfect physical specimen for every federal job were indefensible. It demonstrated that existing standards of physical performance were unrelated to the performance of certain required tasks and that the utilization of job engineering to group tasks so as to meet the capability of an employee with physical limitations could significantly increase the number of qualifying workers. Although the count was not entirely accurate, the records show that more than 165,000 physically handicapped persons

95

were employed by the federal government during that war period. These handicapped workers rarely missed muster when the whistle called their shift to work. Their turnover was less than for nonhandicapped workers and the hard work had a therapeutic effect far beyond expectations. Evidently a handicapped employee, properly placed, was not handicapped at all. The rallying cry became "emphasize ability, not disability."

Immediately following the war, all federal positions were reviewed by medical and personnel specialists to specify those occupations which could be performed by persons with certain impairments. In the course of the succeeding years more than 15,000 positions were surveyed and adapted for placement of the handicapped.

The doctors conducting the survey, in the beginning and even at present, often found resistance on the part of supervisors to changes in operating practices to accommodate persons with certain physical limitations. When a supervisor told them that a man had to stand at a certain workbench, he was questioned as to why the workbench could not be lowered to wheelchair level. Very often it could be and was.

Congress decreed in 1944 that any disabled veteran otherwise qualified for federal employment was entitled to have ten points added to his civil service test score and thus to be given decided preference in federal employment. This statutory mandate, along with the alert pressure by veterans' organizations, accelerated the process of matching the disabled man with a job he could perform. But the serious obstacle in the path of this employment program was made up of inherent prejudices and chronic apathy in making the extra effort to achieve the matching. The educational, soft-sell approach was largely followed in the program, which was permissive rather than mandatory. Special tests were designed to be administered to blind or deaf applicants. In the case of blind applicants, many tests were prepared in braille or with recorded material. In an effort to facilitate the job placement of the unsighted, legislation was sought and passed in 1963 to permit the employment of readers to assist on work assignments.

Advisory bulletins were issued to give supervisors the facts about diseases, illnesses, and handicaps. Well-reasoned arguments pointed up the logic of employing persons who suffered from these afflictions. The availability of rehabilitation services was made known to encourage the development of more advanced capabilities. But, as in the case of the equal-opportunity programs for minorities and for women, the pace of change was disappointingly slow and the professional efforts had little effect.

To add momentum to the program and to create a policy conscience within each operating organization, the President's Committee for the Placement of the Physically Handicapped and the Civil Service Commission conceived the idea of a coordinator program. The coordinator would be an official, designated by top management, who would serve as the middleman between the handicapped citizen looking for the work and the job that was open. Ideally the coordinator should be high enough in the organization to make his presence known but not so high that he was unfamiliar with job content or too busy to devote time to this mission. He was supposed to be armed with facts on which of the jobs at his establishment could be filled by a handicapped person and with facts that he could use to dispel prejudice wherever he found it. Whenever the opportunity presented itself, he talked up the merits of hiring the handicapped person to any supervisor who would listen. In seeking a placement commitment from the supervisor, the coordinator used logic, not compassion; he invoked the element of progress, not pity. He endeavored to convince the hiring officer that the handicapped applicant was entitled to receive full consideration lest the organization pass up a good employment opportunity. In this process the regular civil service procedures were adhered to and the handicapped candidate would have to qualify through the required test and have his name certified for selection. Should the supervisor decide that the handicapped person on the list was clearly not the best candidate for the job, he was free to hire the person who was best qualified. In cases of this type the coordinator was not expected to twist the supervisor's arm, because the objective was not to produce a situation in which discrimination in favor of the handicapped became the established pattern. Many a coordinator who came to know the handicapped person who had met civil service standards would pursue placement possibilities in a nearby job in another federal installation, in an industrial job, in local government, or wherever there might be an opening. In many communities the coordinator developed a network of his counterparts among employers so that job opportunities could be offered on a much broader basis.

This local placement approach gave vitality to a national policy at the point where jobs were actually being filled. It placed in a single staff officer a continuing responsibility for results. A statistical analysis of the program over its first six years demonstrates its degree of acceptance. In 1957, the first year of the program, only 6 of every 1,000 persons hired by the federal government were handicapped. By 1961, when more than 2,500 coordinators were operating, the proportion of handicapped persons hired rose to 15 per 1,000. The following year, when 1,000 more coordinators were functioning, the handicapped accounted for more than 19 of every 1,000 appointed. Thus, in five years, the percentage of handicapped persons hired tripled. Although this rate of increase has not been sustained in each of the subsequent years, a marked annual increase has generally been recorded.

An anomaly has developed in relation to this program. More and more public personnel systems provide disability retirement for career workers no longer able to perform the duties to which they are assigned. Under the federal system these retirement provisions are particularly liberal and permit an employee to retire if he is disabled for the job he happens to hold rather than for all jobs in the federal service. Consequently, at the direction of President Kennedy in 1961 all federal managers were requested to interview each employee who came up for disability retirement and to offer him another position that could be performed within the limits of his disability and thus retain his service in the government. No defense could be offered for the retirement on disability payments of workers who could readily perform tasks that newly hired individuals with similar handicaps were expected to perform. Far too little imagination was applied in seeking another position within the employee's existing capabilities for the longtime worker whose disability may have been at least partially attributable to the work he performed in the service. It may well be that as a matter of public policy the existing standard for disability retirement should be tightened to prohibit retirement unless the disabled person cannot perform any work reasonably related to his previous skills or whose disability creates an unsafe condition for himself or his fellow workers. Disability retirement is never a humane solution for the disabled person or his family. The compensation level, even in the most liberal plans, is insufficient to sustain the individual, and departure from the work environment often aggravates rather than ameliorates the disability.

If the placement of the physically handicapped has proved difficult in public employment, the placement of those with mental disabilities has been far more so. In 1961, for the first time, the federal government tackled in earnest the matter of employing the skilled person who had been restored to health after suffering mental illness. Managers and coordinators were told, at every official and unofficial opportunity, that mental illness like physical illness can be treated and often cured. To facilitate this understanding, written guidance was provided for applicants who had suffered mental illness. Questions on the application that implied ineligibility for former mental patients were modified or eliminated. Special procedures were developed whereby employing organizations could work with psychiatrists in mental hospitals in designing rehabilitative steps that would lead the former patient back to society through a gradual return to utilization of his skills.

Accompanying this effort was a more thoughtful and constructive approach toward the employee who suffered mental or nervous problems while employed. Managers were urged to give particular attention to such persons, to grant them generous sick leave while undergoing treatment, and to carefully design the work situation at the time of return.

But the mentally ill were more difficult for supervisors and fellow employees to understand than the paraplegic or the sightless. The causes were far more elusive. The behavior was frequently aberrational and disruptive of work routine. The burden upon the supervisor was frequently heavy and called for a knowledge and patience not generally considered an inherent part of the supervisor's responsibility. Consequently, relatively few successful placements can be cited. Those few occurred in government activities with medical rehabilitative missions. In the Department of Health, Education and Welfare and the Veterans

Administration, the placement process was closely associated with their mental-hospital programs, where it was possible to arrange in-hospital work assignments as the first phase in the new employment experience. During the initial adjustment in these work assignments, in close proximity to therapeutic treatment, the former patient was able to move on to new tasks at new and progressively more distant work locations. As recovery progressed, the work responsibility could be greater and the employee given more personal responsibility and granted fewer returns for hospital treatment or observation. Although experience data are limited, personnel officers with extensive participation in this program have estimated that under such favorable circumstances only about 50 percent of these successful transitions from patient to worker were accomplished the first time.

Similar programs have been undertaken in city and state mental hospitals with generally similar results. If this form of rehabilitation is to be advanced significantly, more concentrated attention must be applied through research and evaluation. With nearly half the hospital beds in the country occupied by mental patients, with a serious shortage in psychiatric and associated personnel, and with the demonstrated therapeutic benefit in returning to work, this area of disability deserves the focus of official attention at least in equivalent proportion to that directed to the placement of the mentally retarded in the federal government during the period starting in 1963.

President Kennedy had an intimate interest in mental retardation, having observed this disability within the circle of his closely knit family. The charitable work of the Joseph P. Kennedy, Jr., Foundation has been largely devoted to research and rehabilitation work with the mentally retarded. Early in his presidency he directed his personal attention toward the federal government's programs in this field, and pressed for legislation that would increase the federal resources devoted to this serious health problem within American society. He convened under White House auspices a conference of experts to formulate new programs of action. He designated a presidential special assistant to oversee these programs and to make sure that operating plans were in fact activated within the labyrinths of the federal government, and he directed department and agency heads to emphasize employment of the mentally retarded in federal activities across the country. He requested that reports on the progress of this program be sent directly to him from the Civil Service Commission. He appeared in the Rose Garden November 8, 1963, with General Melvin Maas, chairman of his Committee on the Employment of the Handicapped, and talked to assembled representatives of the state committees on employment and rehabilitation of the handicapped about the challenge of this new program to open up therapeutic employment opportunity for those who had been previously doomed to virtual exclusion from meaningful work.

Before President Kennedy was able to receive evidence of the unusual progress made toward the goals he set, he was struck down in Dallas. But President Johnson sustained the effort with a frank and straightforward statement: "I must confess that until I became President I was rather oblivious of what was happening to our mentally retarded people in this country, I didn't know much about it, it did not consume a lot of my time or my interest. However, there is not a committee in existence that I have more interest in or more concern for than the President's Committee on Mental Retardation. I hope that each of you will be a walking messenger to go forth to every State in the Union to try to make other people as aware of our problem—and what good we can do—as you have made me aware."

That awareness of the problem and what could be done about it was the first step toward a commitment with two major goals: to enable suitably trained retarded persons to achieve self-support and self-respect in needed work and to prove to other employers that it could be done.

It was not an easy job to open employment opportunities to the mentally retarded. It was especially difficult in the face of the traditional civil service practice of appointing persons who ranked highest in competitive examinations weighted according to mental ability. Initially, many managers questioned the existence of legitimate and necessary jobs in government that mental retardates could fill capably. Some professed concern about "welfare operations run at the expense of federal agency programs" if special arrangements were designed for this group. And a few did not want to be bothered with anything they had never tried before. But during the next three years these classes of doubters were converted through solid evidence accumulated in the operation of the program.

First, it was established that most agencies did have some work that retarded persons could do well. More than that, it was shown that in some jobs a suitably trained retardate can be a better worker than others not thus handicapped—that for such jobs a retardate is in fact a quality appointee.

Second, the retarded employees proved that they not only earned their pay but were indirectly saving money for the agency through a lessening of the high turnover common in the types of jobs that the retarded could perform.

Third, the employment process was operated outside the traditional competitive process, with the placement of the retarded person determined on the basis of performance tested during training and certified to by vocational-rehabilitation authorities. It was a collaborative process involving the vocational-rehabilitation agency on the one hand and the manager and the personnel official of the agency on the other.

Placements resulted in sixty-four different occupations. Retardates were hired as laborers, clerks, mail handlers, messengers, janitors, laundry workers, mess attendants, office-machine operators, building-maintenance workers, warehousemen, elevator operators, and bindery workers. But they were also employed as engineering and physical-science aides and as library assistants and medical technicians, all jobs with skill requirements. In less than four years, 3,562 persons were gainfully placed in necessary and productive work. This was not "made work." No jobs were created for the mentally retarded. The federal employer identified the simple and routine but still necessary tasks that the retarded could do well, and then considered for those tasks any retarded persons who had been trained to do them.

Each job placement was made with particular care. The basic philosophy underlying and influencing all aspects of the program was that the agency was seeking quality rather than quantity in the employment of the mentally retarded. From the outset there was heavy stress upon the necessity for the careful matching of individual persons with individual jobs. Each successful placement was regarded as a major achievement that helped to break down barriers of prejudice against hiring any but "normal" workers and thus helped to improve employment opportunities for retarded persons everywhere. Each unsuccessful placement was regarded as a serious setback: in addition to dashing the hopes of one individual and perhaps undermining his confidence and his courage to try again, it would support the prejudice and reinforce the barrier against hiring other retarded persons. Hence there was resistance to the frequent suggestion that numerical goals or quotas be established. Instead, the emphasis was upon making placements that would be long-range successes. In support of this objective, the placement procedure started with a written agreement between the Civil Service Commission and forty-one individual employing agencies. These agreements were designed to protect the interests of both the retarded worker and the employer. They included, among other things, a commitment by the employer to use the state vocational-rehabilitation agency services in any postemployment counseling the employee might need and in advising his supervisor about his on-the-job training and supervision. The only requirement for terminating the employment of a retardate was that the agency first consult his counselor. This provision was of particular importance because it not only reassured the employer that he would not be forced to retain an incompetent employee but also reassured the retardate that immediate steps could be taken to provide him with continued rehabilitation service or other help if that proved necessary.

The agreements called for involving the coordinators for the handicapped in all agencies, for internal training sessions with supervisors, and for furnishing appropriate materials to guide execution of the program. It was suggested that prospective supervisors visit nearby rehabilitation centers to see for themselves the remarkable training given to retardates and the remarkable work that trained retardates could actually perform. On the basis of such visits they could more readily examine the jobs under their direction with an open-minded and imaginative approach. They were advised to enlist the expert help of local vocational-rehabilitation people in matching workers and jobs.

The record of success was clear—93 percent of the placements were so judged by responsible supervisors. A survey showed that the separation rate for retardates for all causes (including termination of seasonal employment, the family's moving away, and other causes not related to work performance) was actually lower than the over-all rate for the government. Only 7 percent of all retardates appointed had to be released because of failure to meet performance standards or to make necessary social adjustments. In a number of cases, the retardate's performance on the job was considerably better than satisfactory. Fifty-four of the 3,562 received Outstanding or Excellent efficiency ratings, forty-two had been promoted, and a few received special awards for above-average productivity.

Perhaps the most deeply meaningful observation to be derived from this program is that successful employment can actually develop increased ability in the mentally retarded. With the growth of confidence and self-reliance came a growth of interest and courage to reach out toward a wider horizon of learning and accomplishment. As impressive confirmation, some retarded employees had been promoted to higher grades and a number had participated successfully in regular competitive examinations leading to career civil service status. A girl who was appointed as an office-machine operator in March 1964, one of the very first appointees under the program, was given an Outstanding performance rating and a cash award of $200 for sustained superior performance under the Incentive Awards Program. Making copies on a Xerox machine, she averaged about 850 copies a day, freeing several higher-grade secretaries from that part-time chore. She also distributed mail within the office, provided messenger service, and answered the telephone when alone in the file room. She worked tirelessly and conscientiously, had a pleasant and cooperative disposition, never missed a day of work, and was always on time. In another success story, a mentally retarded mail handler in the Muncie, Indiana, post office received a regional award "for performance above and beyond the requirements of the position he occupied."

The program was conducted as an unsheltered workshop. There was no secrecy about the activity. Those responsible for it were most gratified to be contributing to the breakdown of the old defeatist attitude, the once-prevalent assumption that the blind can't see, the lame can't walk, the mentally retarded can't learn, so we just quietly put them aside somewhere and take care of them and don't talk about it.

In the early days of the program, there were jokes to the effect that the federal government was largely staffed with those who were already mentally retarded, so why multiply the liability? But many managers came to be enthusiastic backers of the program and obviously gained added individual satisfaction through participation in a campaign that paid such significant human dividends.

The ripples spread. Programs were developed under the Manpower Development and Training Act in some private industries following the same certification and referral procedure negotiated in the federal agreements. Several state merit systems adopted programs along these same lines. The National Jaycees established a special action program to promote employment of both the retarded and the emotionally restored throughout their organization. Individual success stories in the program stimulated these advances. The following examples paint a more individualized picture of the program and its impact.

In the first case, the employee, from a family of six children, spent four years in special education classes in high school. He was never able to find employment until the Veterans Administration hired him through the program for the mentally retarded. When sudden and severe illness struck his stepfather, the boy's salary helped the family to weather the storm and made it possible for his older brother to continue working his way through college. The employee performed exceptionally well on the job, an achievement that was all the more remarkable since, in addition to being retarded, he suffered a degree of spastic paralysis.

In the second case, the man, aged twenty-nine, had spent twelve years in a state school for retardates. In addition to his retardation, he had a congenital heart defect that required major surgery. He left the school in 1958 and, except for eight months in 1961, was never employed. An orphan, he was on public assistance and receiving $1,871 a year. Through the joint efforts of the state vocational-rehabilitation department, the Civil Service Commission, and the General Services Administration, he was hired as a custodial laborer, becoming a taxpayer rather than a tax recipient. He was assigned to cleaning an area that was formerly the responsibility of two employees, and the only difference the agency found was that while the two men were able to mop the floor every other day, this man now mops it every day. A supervisor reports, "I wish I had a dozen like him."

In the third case, the man managed to eke out a bare living as a busboy in a dairy company's employee cafeteria before being hired by the Post Office Department. His pay stretched only far enough to cover room and board; there was nothing left for other necessities. His only relative in the city would have nothing to do with him. After he received his first check as a government employee, the young man went out and bought himself new work clothes. He was so proud of himself and so pleased with these new clothes, bought with his own earnings, that he went to the postmaster to show them off.

Experiences such as these make each successful placement particularly rewarding. Countless others provide the human dimension to this program and make it among the most successful undertaken in the extension of opportunity. The growing appreciation of the worth of the mentally retarded as employees and their special value in jobs that are difficult to fill and keep filled because of their narrow and repetitive nature is a cause for continuing optimism in contemplating future developments. Manpower shortages are causing employers to consider previously underutilized sources and to search for ways of re-engineering jobs so that these less broadly skilled employees can do them. Trained retardates have demonstrated after a relatively brief period of public employment that they are an excellent source of manpower and need not be a continuing burden to themselves, to their families, or to their government.

Accompanying the increased attention to the placement of the handicapped has been a mounting awareness in public service of the broad field of occupational health. There has been a growing recognition that a good employee is most valuable when he is healthy and that management should do what it can to keep him so. There has also been an increased investment of resources in providing employees with on-the-job services that promise to reduce absence due to illness and injury, to lower the incidence of early retirement due to disability, and to contribute to

maintaining skilled human resources at peak efficiency. This new concern for the physical and mental well-being of employees has been justified not only from the obvious humanitarian standpoint but from the
pragmatic dollar-and-cents view as well.

After more than ten years of interagency study and interorganizational disputes concerning jurisdiction, President Johnson took decisive
action in this area and ordered in mid-1965 that health-service programs
for federal employees be expanded. He directed the Civil Service Commission, with professional assistance from the Public Health Service, to
enlarge and improve existing occupational health programs. Since that
order was issued, provision has been made for greatly increased access
for employees to traditional health-room services. In addition, there has
been search and experimentation with new means to provide preventive
health service. New significance has been given to safety and environmental health at all work locations.

In a most daring and controversial step forward, practical policies and
methods were openly discussed with respect to employees with drinking
problems. It was apparent that too little official concern about help for
these employees had been demonstrated in existing health programs.
Clearly, alcoholism was a chronic national health problem, and, once it
had adversely affected an employee's job performance, it had become an
employer's problem. No matter how successful the employee-selection
process might be in excluding applicants who were already problem
drinkers, it was only self-deception for management to assume that no
problems existed and that no employees had developed drinking habits
subsequent to public employment. It would be totally delusory to continue to cover up the substantial time and productivity loss from the high
incidence of alcoholic cases.

In this area, the federal approach was in step with a general philosophy
of conserving human resources and achieving economies through preventive health maintenance. To initiate the program, department and
agency heads were requested to designate a representative to attend a
planning conference in Washington. This conference was designed to
educate public officials and to formulate recommended guidelines from
which practical programs to deal with alcoholism could be formulated.

The conference, which had been viewed with some uncertainty and dismay by the more timid public officials, proved to be a success. Besides providing necessary knowledge, it created a wave of favorable comment within the government, from the press, and from other interested organizations. Its published report became a best-seller, and in less than a year there had been some measurable progress. Many agencies started promising alcoholism programs. The National Institute of Mental Health's Center for Prevention and Control of Alcoholism provided valuable technical assistance to agency managers, and the following basic program principles were spelled out as guidance for a government-wide effort:

First, there is open acknowledgment that alcoholism is a treatable health condition.

Second, the public employer has a responsibility to conduct an educational program to keep his employees from acquiring this condition and to make rehabilitative assistance available to employees who do contract it. This effort should be sustained as a part of a larger occupational health program in conjunction with the personnel-management effort of the federal government.

Third, every safeguard should be adopted to avoid the appearance or the fact of a witch hunt for alcoholic employees. Management should stay away from any invasion of an employee's privacy. The person who comes under the scope of the program should be one who has already a drinking problem and, if not in the program, would be facing disciplinary action based on his unsatisfactory work performance.

Fourth, the procedure for dealing with problem employees should not be altered. Before the program was instituted, the federal supervisor was restricted to reprimanding, suspending, or taking steps to remove employees whose problems were caused by drinking. But the typical supervisor, in a misguided attempt to be "a nice fellow," resorted to indefensible tactics to cover up for the alcoholic employee as long as possible. Such covering up was a decided disservice to both the supervisor and the employee. Under the new program, supervisors were provided with the alternative course of referring the problem employee to an approved source of rehabilitative assistance. If the employee refused to admit his problem, if he refused to cooperate, or if in the course of rehabilitation he failed to achieve professionally acceptable results, the supervisor was obligated to resort to the usual disciplinary procedures.

Fifth, management would not concern itself with an employee's drinking as long as it did not affect his work performance adversely.

Last, the program was built to rely mainly on federal cooperation with existing health resources for rehabilitative assistance.

But policies, principles, procedures, and organizational arrangements do not add up to immediate results. In this area, as in many others promoting change, success will come slowly if at all. Evidence of progress will be more difficult to measure than in the case of the mentally retarded. Meanwhile, management's concern has been pragmatically demonstrated and the veil of taboo has been lifted. Throughout the entire occupational health field, an acceptance of management responsibility has been recognized. No longer does the federal government limit its concern about an employee's health to his initial physical and mental capability to perform the job and to his fitness or unfitness for continued employment in the event of disability or retirement eligibility.

Still other areas of exclusion through personal handicaps will be revealed in days ahead. Public agencies must be alert to the necessity for thought and action to overcome these disabilities through meaningful work experience and to permit all citizens to offer their services in the public interest.

Public Employment as an Instrument of Social Change

9

Concern for the disadvantaged forced the public employer to examine the degree to which the socially and economically disadvantaged shared the benefits of employment on the public payroll. The national goal of bringing unemployment to an irreducible minimum underscored the necessity for government to pursue that goal in its own practices while seeking to convince private employers of their social obligations. With a national effort directed at the upgrading of skills through manpower training, the government's own practices came under closer scrutiny. A campaign against poverty could be successful only in terms of more and better jobs for people disadvantaged through limited income and inadequate educational preparation. It was not enough to cite the government's policy of equal opportunity and nondiscriminatory competition for public employment. Could the public employer fulfill the operating needs in support of government programs and use public employment as an instrument of social change? With government generating an ever higher demand for an ever larger share of the labor market, the impact of its decisions in this area assumed increasing importance.

To many observers determined to eliminate poverty through the creation of jobs, the ultimate answer was the use of government as "the employer of last resort." In other words, if the private economy could not produce a sufficient number of jobs or was unable to provide an upgrading of skills, government employment would become the final means for assuring employment for all. Government would become the employer that offered the job route out of poverty and, through work tasks and training programs, overcame disadvantage. Such an objective served rhetorical rather than political purposes. Its fulfillment was never seriously advanced for legislative consideration, but it did put pressure on the private sector to expand its corporate efforts in behalf of the poor. The National Alliance of Businessmen, established by President Johnson early in 1968 under the leadership of Henry Ford II and subsequently of Donald M. Kendall and Lynn Townsend, became the joint venture between industry and government in engineering new job opportunities following the riots of 1967.

Government as the employer of last resort was a concept that jarred the complacency of government managers and led to intensive thought on the impact of government employment policies in the major metropolitan areas. This examination forced a new recognition of the pressing problems of the real world. When post-riot employment conditions for ghetto dwellers were evaluated, government employers were revealed as unresponsive to existing needs. Traditional merit machinery—competitive examinations, standard jobs, inflexible qualifications—had to be re-evaluated in the light of government's responsibility to serve as an instrument of social change. There emerged a belief that government could become the employer of *first* resort for those on the outskirts of hope and in the center of hard-core unemployment. There was a renewed belief that the fundamental objectives of the merit system could meet the challenge presented by the disadvantaged. With the greater concentration on this goal in private business, government organizations learned that what might have been interpreted as welfare practices were really good business. One business leader after another called for programs of industrial leadership in helping ghetto residents acquire the skills they needed to obtain jobs. There was an acceptance of the belief that the only real long-term solution to the plague of poverty was productive employment that would enable those currently unskilled, unschooled, and unemployed to achieve a sense of dignity as well as a source of income through work. There was a realization that employers could not stand back and wait for the unemployables to appear at the personnel office or the employment window. It was necessary to search out, train, and hire these men and women. There was widespread shock over the discovery that these victims of disadvantage did not possess even the most elementary understanding of the culture of work. They were unprepared culturally as well as educationally to survive in the work environment.

Evidently positions needed to be re-engineered, with the most elementary skills grouped together in new jobs which could serve as entry points for the relatively unskilled. This did not mean lowering standards for more complicated jobs. It meant creating simpler jobs with more limited requirements. There was less emphasis upon previously required credentials for employment, a search for persons able to learn and perform a job rather than for diplomas or licenses. There was the ever-present need to relate training to specific jobs. In many instances, false starts were made in which training programs were organized and conducted without relation to the jobs that would be available. In certain training programs, increased disillusion was the product when those who had left idleness for training were forced to return to that idleness when the training was completed.

To move along a parallel path with business, government fashioned new policies and techniques within the traditional framework. The Civil Service Commission issued a number of special examinations geared specifically to persons with limited education and skills, covering such jobs as the worker trainee and office aide. Most of these examinations were conducted without written tests, the competitors being rated on their relative capacity to perform the constituent job tasks. These new examinations would result in new hiring among the unemployed only when agency managers agreed to strip away the simple tasks from complex jobs and create positions in which the uneducated and unskilled could be employed.

One such program, called Operation MUST, an acronym for Maximum Utilization for Skills and Training, involved job engineering to separate from professional or technical jobs the lower-grade duties often found in them. The primary purpose of MUST was the redesigning of jobs so that lower-grade duties were eliminated from higher-grade positions to create new and useful entry jobs for persons with appropriate skills. Managers were urged to review continually the job mix in their installations and apply the job-redesign concepts of MUST to reap a dual benefit: they could serve the national interest by creating additional jobs for the needy and contribute to better personnel management within their own agencies by freeing highly skilled professional and technical workers from routine and unproductive tasks.

A major feature in the MUST program was a new worker-trainee examining plan based on motivational research. Starting from the proven premise that labor turnover in low-grade jobs had been highest among employees with the highest scores on written tests, a plan was developed whereby maintenance and service workers were able to get jobs without the usual written test. No experience was necessary, and they were selected on the basis of their likelihood of succeeding in the particular job, not on the possibility that at some future date they might advance to a supervisory position. The job requirements were confined to simple and basic needs: the prospective employee must be reliable and be able to follow directions and handle whatever loads and weights the job entailed. In the past, in filling positions of this type there had been complaints from disadvantaged applicants of low skills and little education that they had been passed over in favor of someone whose capacities could have been put to a better use in a higher-level job. The new selection technique reduced the number of such complaints. While benefiting the hard-core unemployed, it also cut the cost of recruitment and training and resulted in a better use of employee skills.

Such a policy did not weaken the merit system but strengthened it. It did not mean a change in standards as much as a change in attitudes. It did not mean reducing competition but extending opportunity. It directed the search on a broadened and extended basis that included the poor, the uneducated, and the unskilled.

There was an implicit understanding that the unemployed or disadvantaged would not remain forever in menial tasks. Once the jobless and inexperienced person gained some successful experience on routine duties, he would be given a chance to move up. The public employer, like his counterpart in private business, had the obligation to find methods, through training and supervision, to develop the best among these workers into prospects for more responsible assignments. This called for a strong new emphasis on training programs within the service and upon individual guidance and counseling for the employee.

Sometimes the federal government became host rather than employer of the disadvantaged. In such programs as the Neighborhood Youth Corps, College Work Study, Vocational Work Study, Adult Work Experience, and to a lesser extent the Job Corps, federal agencies provided work stations for trainees and in some instances paid a small part of their salaries. When the training was completed, the enrollee could be given a permanent federal appointment by establishing his eligibility on a competitive examination. Two of these programs had a direct impact on the problems of disadvantaged youth, the age and social group among which unemployment continued highest. These were the Summer Youth Opportunity campaign and the Stay-in-School campaign. Both were devised and initiated in 1965 to provide full-time employment in summer and part-time employment during the school year for people between sixteen and twenty-two. These became major management efforts with special financing and distinct employment goals. For example, in the summer of 1967 approximately 44,000, or half of the total number of young people employed by the federal agencies, came from disadvantaged backgrounds. The following year the target was to raise the number to 70,000. Although there were cases of poor performance and maladjustment, the vast majority of these young people, who in most instances were gaining their first involvement in work, were judged to be productive. Many a supervisor spoke with pride about a ghetto youngster who under his guidance became a well-adjusted and productive member of his organization. Support of the Stay-in-School campaign faced greater difficulty, although at its peak during the academic year 1966–67 it had more than 38,000 needy students employed on a part-time basis with federal agencies.

Studies of the disadvantaged in urban poverty areas disclosed that isolation had become one of their most persistent problems. They were isolated by lack of transportation, by the "closed society" aspects of the ghettos, and sometimes by language differences. These factors necessitated special and innovative techniques in recruitment. Special transportation arrangements were required. Jobmobiles that would accept applications in the ghetto areas toured the inner city. Recruiting messages in Spanish were broadcast over radio to penetrate the language barrier.

Despite all these well-intentioned changes in practice and technique, the rate of progress was slow, the cost of job engineering and training was high, and the processes of individual and group adjustment were difficult. High supervisory skill and additional supervisory time were required to achieve the adjustment to work and the acceptance of production standards. The government manager was under multiple pressures not only to play the role of social innovator but also to increase productivity, respond to public inquiry, and meet increased work loads with lower unit costs. The growth of the program was severely inhibited by financial pressures, and the specter of massive employment of the disadvantaged faded when the total costs of such a venture were computed. Many necessary work projects were deferred because of lack of funds or space. Even a higher standard of maintenance and service in public operations could have created many new and useful jobs, but the public decision-maker suffered from an automatic inhibition when challenged to hire the disadvantaged when he viewed his limited budget for sustaining essential services. It would have been better to appropriate additional funds for employment and training programs for the disadvantaged in the Post Office and Defense Departments, the General Services Administration, and other large federal agencies. Instead, virtually every program had to be absorbed within current operating budgets.

The momentum for public-sector response to hard-core employment has continued to stimulate hiring reforms at all levels of government. States and cities have joined in reviewing their personnel systems to open up opportunities for hundreds of thousands of the urban poor who are willing and able to enter or train for genuine jobs that are not being filled. Following many of the steps initiated by the federal government, there has been a drive both to pull together and expand limited and scattered efforts that have proved successful in various jurisdictions. There has been a revision of rigid regulations, selection standards, and tests that did not necessarily reflect the job's requirements or the applicant's ability to meet them. There has been a strengthening of recruitment, orientation, placement, and probation procedures, along with an improvement in the climate of acceptance of the disadvantaged on the job. There has been a redesign of jobs to provide new entry-level positions and opportunities for promotion combined with training and the development of special skills for the disadvantaged, such as ability to deal with other ghetto residents or to use the language of most effective communication. There has been increased cooperation with private organizations working toward the same goals.

Under the leadership of the National Civil Service League, there has been a new emphasis upon this program through research and publication, conferences with state and local officials, and technical assistance to interested governmental organizations.

California has led the way in reforms. Early in 1968 businessmen under pressure to hire the disadvantaged complained to the governor that the state's own employment practices were not in keeping with what they were being asked to do. A new program was undertaken to match public service manpower needs with people who were unemployed or were already working for the state government at lower skill levels than their abilities warranted. The program was concentrated in such fields as hospital work, aid to parolees, and social service, resulting in the new career ladders with higher prospects.

Washington State has been successful in overhauling its civil service system in the Departments of Probation and Parole, Employment Service, and Public Assistance, with the major breakthrough in cracking the credentials requirements.

Seattle has pursued a program with exclusively city funding and with concentration on male trainees for office jobs. One group of recent trainees included 27 percent with arrest records, 60 percent with previous employment income under $4,000 a year, and 65 percent unemployed at the time of application.

New Jersey has inaugurated a career-development program in a number of fields with some success in recruiting through civil rights groups, poverty organizations, and ghetto schools.

To varying degrees, programs of this type are in process of development at the state or local levels or both in Pennsylvania, Connecticut, Florida, Texas, Ohio, Michigan, and Illinois. The experimental and demonstration experience will revolutionize public employment and give a new definition to employment and promotion of low-income people in civil service jobs under merit principles.

Precise estimates of the numbers of people who could enter local and state government by this route are difficult to prepare. On the basis of several studies at least 140,000 public service jobs in governments of the largest cities appear to be available for ghetto residents now. With state governments increasing employment by nearly 70 percent, or 1 million employees, and local governments by 55 percent, or 2.4 million employees, in the past decade, increased opportunity in public service for the disadvantaged cannot be withheld.

With unemployment rising in 1970 and 1971, Congress turned to public employment at the local level to open new jobs in essential but unfinanced areas of public service. The 1970 bill, passed by overwhelming majority, was vetoed by President Nixon on the grounds that this was an inappropriate approach to reduction in unemployment. But the 92nd Congress returned to this proposal with early hearings in 1971.

If public employment is to serve as the instrument of social change, more definitive public policies to that end must be established by executive and legislative action in terms that accommodate the conflicting objectives of more jobs for the disadvantaged and greater economy in government. The first steps have been taken, but even that limited advance will be lost unless a more solid policy base is laid and public management is more insistent upon visible, measurable results. Those results can only be obtained if the extra costs of job engineering, manpower training, and extended supervision are fully recognized and underwritten.

Labor-Management

Relations

in the

10 # Public Service

Public-employee labor relations, for all too long a topic for academic and theoretical debate, have risen rapidly on the agenda of critical concerns in recent years. No other aspect of public service now attracts the same degree of citizen discussion.

Today, the voice of the public employee in all sections of the country has risen to a sustained and insistent pitch. He is demanding a fuller and more effective participation in decisions that relate to his working conditions, his compensation and benefits, and his relationship with public management. The accumulation of these demands has brought about a rapidly expanding union movement whose significance and impact have found many public managers and legislators unprepared. Where these demands have been thwarted or ignored disputes have erupted, threats of strikes have been proclaimed and work stoppages, frequently of dramatic proportions and in sensitive locations, have finally occurred.

Strikes by transit workers, schoolteachers, sanitation workers, policemen, and firemen in the City of New York in 1966, 1967, 1968, and 1971 have made public labor relations a persistent and critical factor in the life of the nation's largest city. The demands of sanitation workers for recognition by the mayor of Memphis produced the dispute that brought Martin Luther King, Jr., to that city and to his assassination in April 1968. Hospital workers in Savannah, Charleston, and San Francisco,

119

have injected their disputes with public managers into the consciousness of the public where the ill and injured receive care. Although Calvin Coolidge made his political reputation in overcoming the police walkout in Boston back in 1919, he did not leave behind any rational pattern for the resolution of disputes which have boiled up in police departments across the country. In another area of public safety, the discontent of firefighters has led to emergency discussions to prevent work stoppages. The disruption of these essential public services that so closely relate to the daily life of the citizen has sounded an emergency alarm with mounting frequency.

The rise in the number of public service strikes is confirmed by Bureau of Labor Statistics reports of experience during the ten-year period 1958–68. The total number of strikes a year jumped from 15 to 254 in that period and the number of workers taking part rose from 1,700 to more than 200,000. Most of this rising ferment has taken place at state and local levels of government and not at the federal level, where since 1962 labor relations have been governed by policies set forth in presidential Executive Orders and by a statutory ban on strikes that until recently has been occasionally threatened but generally observed.

Tension and militancy have been magnified especially in the urban centers, where union demand for higher wages, more costly benefits, and extensive operational changes coincide with widespread dissatisfaction over the inadequacy in government services, rising taxes, and a general deterioration of the quality of life. There has been a contagion from city to city and from one municipal occupational group to another as public employees find themselves falling behind others in the laboring community and suffering at the same time from public criticism and disrespect. Public officials are in the middle, with pressure from both sides: the citizens' pressure for more and better services and less onerous tax burdens and the employees and their unions pressing for greater outlays, improved employment security, and higher status in the community. These responsible officials rarely possess sufficient authority to respond to even the most reasonable demands from the unions. They may sympathize with the need for better working conditions and may have advanced strong arguments for improvement, only to suffer defeat in the budget or appropriation process. They have little discretion within their limited budgets and find employee benefits a low priority with legislative bodies. A high official, exposed to a different set of political pressures, frequently must become a party to the negotiations in which his hands may be tied by civil service laws and regulations that run counter to the basic tenets of labor-management relations. Concepts designed and applied to government long before the growth of unions are necessarily incompatible with union recognition and serve to restrict natural areas of negotiation. The unions tend to be ambivalent while they oppose the reduced scope of bargaining.

No unit of government is today immune from the prospect of labor disputes. Many units are functioning under closely specified labor-relations procedures embodied in statute and with a basic prohibition on strikes by public workers. The prime examples of this type are New York City and State, the locus of the most serious labor-relations problems. At the other end of the range of experience are units with virtually no experience and often with a negative attitude toward the formulation of policies to deal with potential strikes. They all too often reflect the view that "it can't happen here" and that the mere act of formulation of policies and processes will invite the growth of unions and attendant disputes. When a dispute does arise in these jurisdictions, the unprepared public official either yields all too readily to the demands or adopts a negative attitude that heightens the community tension.

One paramount necessity in the public sector in the 1970s is the establishment of affirmative policies with respect to the relationships between public managements and unions in their organizations. Orderly processes for participation by employees in matters affecting their working conditions must be jointly arrived at to avoid the confusion of improvisation. The creation of systems to settle disputes must be defined so to avert the intolerable situation of public employees' withholding their services from the public they are employed to serve.

Although the arrival of public labor-management issues at stage center is relatively recent, the presence of unions in the public service has existed for more than over a century. Prior to the Civil War, craft unions were formed in the naval shipyards. By the 1880s, unions of postal employees were organized to campaign for the so-called eight-hour law for government workers. This action heralded the evolving role of federal employee unions as a political force to impress employees' views and needs upon decisions of Congress. These activities were sufficiently compelling in 1912 to lead to the passage of the Lloyd-LaFollette Act, which formally legalized the right of federal employees to organize and prohibited federal executives from interfering with the right of employees to petition Congress. Thus protected, union organizations developed the additional power that flowed from both increased membership and persuasive capability with members of Congress and ultimately developed the art of lobbying to a most effective level.

Unionization became a predominant pattern in the Post Office Department, where over the ensuing fifty years seventeen different organizations were established and more than 80 percent of the employees became members of one or more organizations. The early union activity in the shipyards led to the representation of workers in the crafts by the appropriate international unions under the coordination of the Metal Trades Council of the American Federation of Labor. For white-collar workers elsewhere in government, the National Federation of Federal Employees was created during World War I. When part of its membership seceded in 1931 to form the American Federation of Government Employees, affiliated with the AFL, NFFE continued as an independent union with broad white-collar and blue-collar membership. The AFGE grew separately and became the prototype of the government industrial union, with a membership of 350,000, the largest in the federal service, by 1970.

During the New Deal period, although labor-management relations became a central theme of government action and when the Wagner Act of 1935 created the National Labor Relations Board and machinery for granting union recognition and representation, no executive or legislative action was taken by President Roosevelt with respect to policies relating to the government's own relationships with unions. To the contrary, the only statement flowing from the White House during those years was a restrictive presidential statement in 1937 to the president of the National Federation of Federal Employees—a decided departure from the President's position on the role of the unions outside of government. The historic Roosevelt position read this way: "Since their own services have to do with the functioning of government, a strike of public employees manifests nothing less than an intent on their part to prevent or obstruct the operations of government until their demands are satisfied. Such action, looking toward the paralysis of government by those sworn to support it, is unthinkable and intolerable." This same negative tone was incorporated in 1955 in legislative action prohibiting strikes or work stoppages on the part of federal employees and requiring that an oath subscribing to this prohibition be administered to every new employee. Making it a felony for any federal worker to strike, this law provided a maximum penalty of a year and a day in jail plus a $1,000 fine and rendered mandatory, after hearings, the removal of any worker who asserted the right to strike against the government or belonged to an organization asserting that right.

Against the backdrop of these historical trends and attitudes, President Kennedy took the initiative in June 1961. "The participation of federal employees in the formulation and implementation of employee policies and procedures affecting them contributes to the effective conduct of public business," the President declared when he appointed a task force on employee-management relations in the public service. This charge to the task force acknowledged the affirmative role of unions in government and directed the task force to design a labor-management system based upon cooperative participation by the unions. For this policy exploration, the President chose a unique task force constituted entirely of federal officials appointed by the President, and endowed with ultimate responsibility to assure that the system to be designed would be effectively administered. The official who chaired the task force, Labor Secretary Arthur J. Goldberg, had been a leading labor lawyer with access to the best experience and thinking in the labor-relations field. The President set a deadline for the task-force report and the necessary implementing executive documents. This date was met. The task-force recommendations were accepted by the President, and on January 17, 1962, he signed an Executive Order that for the first time promulgated presidential guidance for federal managers and unions alike.

The order in no way modified existing statutory requirements, including prohibition of the right to strike, nor did it curb the traditional right of the unions to lobby with Congress for benefits beyond those the Executive could provide. It recognized that many issues of primary importance in industrial labor relations were excluded from negotiation because the Congress retained the power to set most federal salaries, to authorize all fringe benefits, and to set certain general working conditions. Nevertheless, it acknowledged the importance of cooperative and constructive relations between recognized unions in all levels of federal management. It created a structure of recognition at three levels: informal for small organizations (the right to be heard), formal for organizations having as much as 10 percent of the membership of an employee unit (the right to be consulted), and exclusive for organizations representing a majority of a unit's employees (the right to negotiate agreements). It specified conditions under which agreements could be negotiated between agency and installation managers and units eligible for exclusive representation of employees. While emphasizing that the public interest was paramount in such agreements, it fostered a new system of communication with respect to employment conditions not controlled by statute or civil service regulations. In view of the presumed absence of the ultimate union weapon, the strike, there was an earnest endeavor to create conditions that would resolve grievances as promptly as possible and foster more open discussion of common problems at the actual work location.

The 1961 task force faced up to the basic issue of the relationship of the merit system to collective bargaining. It determined that there could be an acceptable compatibility and that the negotiation of agreements with unions gaining exclusive recognition could be developed without violating the basic merit principles. This meant that federal employees would continue to be selected on a competitive and open basis and that the union shop and the closed shop were inappropriate patterns of labor relations for the federal government. On the other hand, the task force was sympathetic toward the need for some device that would assist in the maintenance of union membership and recommended further consideration of the feasibility and propriety of the withholding of dues for members of union units recognized as having exclusive representation.

The following year the Civil Service Commission responded favorably to this proposal and issued regulations under statutory authority for employee payroll allocations permitting the withholding of union dues for members of unions with formal as well as exclusive recognition. This particular step was accomplished without expense to the taxpayers through reimbursement of collection costs by the unions, which it did much to strengthen. Before that, every union had faced serious problems in the collection of dues to support its activities.

The installation of the new policy created an immediate need for widespread understanding, not only of the provisions of the order but also of the management attitude and practices that would flow from it. Since the local managers would have primary responsibility for the determination of units, the level of recognition, and the negotiation of agreements, there was a need throughout the country to train management officials. Management relations with unions had existed in certain agencies prior to the order, but they had none of the bilateralism which now became a requirement. Many officials had found the less formal and less demanding atmosphere of the earlier period more to their liking than the new program, which required them to accept an obligation for cooperation with a recognized union. Many others, however, welcomed the precision of guidance and collaborated with recognized unions in devising the processes for early compliance. The Labor Department had been designated in the order as the federal organization to adjudicate disagreements over unit determination and recognition, while the Civil Service Commission had been assigned the responsibility to interpret policy and practice, to train management officials for the program, and to evaluate agency compliance with the program. The major burden of implementation fell upon the largest employers, the Post Office, Defense Departments and the Veterans Administration, in each of which extensive training programs were conducted in the following weeks with the active participation of the Civil Service Commission.

From the outset, management representatives viewed this program as a "moderate" approach to labor relations in the federal community. The label was applied to the task-force recommendations by Secretary Goldberg when they were presented to President Kennedy and again by the

President himself when he ceremoniously signed the order. It was hailed in union circles and in the press as the beginning of a new era. One union leader dubbed it the Magna Carta of federal employee relations. It had endorsed the activities of federal employee unions and had delineated for the first time the respective rights and obligations of both agency management and the unions. Many of the program's provisions stopped far short of those advocated by union representatives. Other provisions recognized the pragmatic necessity to minimize adverse impact upon existing organizations and upon traditional management practices during the transition to a more advanced and sophisticated labor-relations program. Standards of conduct for employee organizations and a code of fair labor practices, issued in May 1963 as sequential documents to the Executive Order in defining the conditions of federal labor relations, were also moderate in their language and intent.

With the need for extensive training in both management and union ranks, the program advanced slowly during the first few years. This period was devoted to the establishment of representation rights and the subsequent consultations and negotiations. There was frequent impatience over the span of time necessary to move from the initial application for recognition through the entire process to a complete agreement. In some instances, exclusive recognition was granted and neither party moved toward the consultation table for the formulation of an agreement. In a few cases, the negotiation moved into an impasse stage. Since final decision rested with the agency head, his unwillingness to compromise management positions virtually terminated discussion, to the irritation of the recognized union leaders. Delay was also produced by reluctance on the part of agency headquarters or national union leadership to allow delegated action by their local representatives. This reluctance was understandable because early agreements might establish precedents with far-reaching implications for future local negotiations. In fact, some agreements were consummated in such haste that management was criticized by other agency negotiators dealing with the same unions for having "given away the store" in their novice enthusiasm to cooperate.

The pace of the program, and of federal labor relations generally, quickened in 1965 as unions gained in membership strength, financial resources, and program understanding. With increased interest by national labor circles in the organization of government employees, professional assistance was provided for organizing drives. Competition between unions affiliated with the AFL-CIO and the independent unions was heightened to heated rivalry. And there were jurisdictional conflicts between affiliated unions with craft and industrial objectives.

The drumbeat of militancy on the part of public employee unions in the states and the cities, notably New York, and in Canada and in other countries was heard and re-echoed in the federal ranks. Union dissatisfaction with certain features in the federal program, expressed repeatedly but moderately during the initial year, became so insistent that most of the large postal and other federal unions were mandated by their national conventions in 1966 and in 1968 to apply added pressure for statutory union recognition and rights in Congress. The 1966 AFL convention adopted a resolution to "support enactment of legislation prescribing true collective bargaining for unions of federal and postal employees, with appropriate disciplinary measures for management violations of this principle." A second resolution committed the AFL to seeking "legislation which will allow, where prohibited, public employees to negotiate union security provisions." Convention rhetoric heated up to the point where more moderate leaders were placed under heavy fire and resolutions to eliminate no-strike pledges from union constitutions and to test the no-strike law were introduced by activist members.

Although there was no clear consensus among the patchwork of federal unions on specific changes to be sought in the executive program, these were the most generally expressed proposals offered by union spokesmen:

1. Establishment of an independent federal labor-relations board to oversee the program and make definitive interpretations and rulings of the law.
2. Impartial third-party decisions on disputed matters, either by the board or by arbitration, including arbitration of negotiation impasses.

3. The right to negotiate all terms and conditions of employment other than those set by law.
4. Penalties for management officials who do not accord unions status and consideration in accordance with their rights.
5. Various union security provisions.

But dissatisfaction was not limited to the union side. Agency representatives were unhappy over the system of multiple forms of recognition. Union drives to organize and negotiate for supervisory as well as rank-and-file employees produced problems of conflict of interest and diffusion of management responsibilities. Open criticism by union leaders and frequent misrepresentation of facts concerning agency management action were seen as prejudicial to public confidence and damaging to operational improvements through cost reductions. The lack of provision for skilled mediators, fact-finders, and arbitrators familiar with the special conditions of federal employment made agency managers balk at involving third-party assistance to resolve disputed situations.

It is easy to overemphasize these dissatisfactions because they were delivered at a higher decibel level than the reports on the benefits wrought by the program. Agencies did report marked improvement in their communication with employees and significant improvements in such areas as tours of duty, health and working conditions, safety practices, control of sick-leave abuse, and the handling of grievances. It was readily evident that employee unions had gained substantial status, had secured far larger and more stable membership, and were exerting significant influence on the development of agency personnel practices and working conditions through the formal consultation and negotiation rights. The membership statistics alone underscored the growth of labor-relations activities during the first five years of the new program. Union membership rose from an estimated 760,000 in 1961 to more than 1 million in 1966. In the initial days of the program, 26 exclusive units were recognized. Five years later the record showed 1,170 such units. At the outset of the program, 19,000 employees were covered by the exclusive units. In 1966 the rosters totaled 1,054,000. Finally, the number of negotiated agreements had risen from 26 to 598. These figures do not include the thousands of local exclusive units and agreements within the 34,000 post offices across the country. Of the 1,054,000 employees in exclusive units, 620,000 were in the Post Office Department, up from 472,000 in 1964 and 515,000 in 1965.

Faced with pressures for change, the federal officials responsible for the program recommended to President Johnson in 1967 that a new task force be designated, with the same members as the 1961 group, to evaluate the program and to consider possible changes urged by both labor and management leaders. Such changes would be studied in the pattern of recognition and the rights conferred with each form of recognition, the means for facilitating negotiations and resolving impasses, the definition of management rights and improved agency administration, the structure of the grievance processes, standards of conduct for federal unions to conform more closely to the regulatory provisions in the Landrum-Griffin Act of 1959, the enforcement of the code of fair labor practices, and the respective roles of the Department of Labor and the Civil Service Commission. The desirability of establishing a central authority for program decisions and of changing the program by further executive action or by act of Congress were to be given renewed attention. The President recognized the need for further review and designated a new task force. It held hearings in the fall of 1967 in which management and union representatives, labor-relations experts and interested citizens offered testimony with respect to the need for program changes. For the most part, the hearings reflected the moderation of the original program; for example, there was no campaign for the right to strike. Although certain unions sought greater union security while management opposed moves in that direction, most of the proposals followed the general assessment of the officials who had been most closely identified with the program. By the spring of 1968, most of the parties had agreed upon provisions of change, but in the waning days of the Johnson administration it was not possible to secure total agreement. The President concluded that his successor should have the opportunity to consider the advice of his own advisers and to form his own decision in this sensitive public policy area.

As a consequence, these issues were brought to President Nixon's attention early in his administration. He appointed a study group, consisting of the Secretaries of Defense and Labor, the director of the Bureau of the Budget, and the chairman of the Civil Service Commission. In its report, submitted in September 1969, this group conceded that the 1962 order had "produced some excellent results, beneficial to employees and management alike," and that it had been "sound in concept and . . . effective in practice." The great growth in union representation was also noted. By that time more than 1.5 million employees—more than half the entire federal work force—were represented by labor organizations. The number of labor-management agreements had risen to 1,200, with a much larger number of supplemental agreements in effect. In the words of the report, "the tempo of organizing activity and the negotiation and administration of agreements is at a very high level." In the face of such conditions, the report acknowledged growing difficulties in operating programs under the original policy and a general dissatisfaction on the part of union officials and agency management because of past failure to adjust the program to these changing conditions. It recommended changes to update policies and to provide new arrangements to improve future labor-management relations. These improvements were:

1. Designation of a federal labor-relations council, composed of federal officials to oversee the entire labor-relations program, to provide definitive interpretation and decide major issues and to entertain appeals from decisions on disputed matters.
2. Change in the pattern of recognition, with elimination of informal and formal recognition and with changed standards for exclusive recognition and the creation of new standards for that recognition.
3. New definition of supervisors, with the understanding that those holding supervisory positions should not engage in the management or representation of labor organizations representing other employees.
4. Machinery for the resolution of disputes on unit, representation, unfair labor practices, and standard-of-conduct matters through an Assistant Secretary of Labor.
5. Improvements in the negotiation and administration of agreements

through clarification of arrangements and through specification of national and local responsibility.

6. Procedures for resolution of impasses in negotiation through the services of the Federal Mediation and Conciliation Service and through the creation of a federal service impasses panel to assist the parties if they were unable to reach agreement through other available means.

7. Improvement of grievance procedures through the availability of arbitration for the resolution of disputes over the interpretation and application of a labor-relations agreement.

8. Broadening of the standards of conduct for labor organizations through the promulgation of rules by the Assistant Secretary of Labor for financial and other reporting-and-disclosure requirements.

9. Extension of the code of fair labor practices to provide equal obligations on the part of management and labor for consultation and negotiation as required by the order, and through an amendment to the provision on strikes and picketing to clarify the language relating to prohibited picketing and reflect the responsibility of the labor organization to take affirmative action to prevent or stop any strike or prohibited picketing by its locals, affiliates, or members.

10. Continuation of the voluntary dues-withholding program.

11. Extension of the program to cover federal employees paid from nonappropriated funds.

In a significant and prophetic conclusion, these officials of the Nixon administration stated that they recognized that "any effective system of labor-management relationships must be fashioned to fit the particular circumstances and that problems of the federal government are different from those in other sectors of public employment. It is our belief that a federal labor-management relations program as adjusted by these proposals may contribute ideas useful to the constructive resolution of state and local problems. In our deliberations we have been mindful of the fact that in all the operations of government the public interest is paramount. This has been our guiding consideration in developing these recommendations. We believe that the principles enunciated will improve labor-management relations in the federal service and thereby contribute significantly to the effective conduct of the public business."

On the basis of these recommendations, President Nixon signed his Executive Order on October 29, 1969, as the modernized and improved charter for federal labor relations. The improvements received mixed reactions. Federal management was generally satisfied. The affiliated union leaders viewed it as progress, particularly in the machinery to resolve disputes and impasses, although they deplored the absence of increased union security. AFL-CIO President George Meany gave the order his enthusiastic support. The independent unions, which had been the principal beneficiaries of informal and formal recognition as differentiated from exclusive recognition, released press statements in opposition to the new order. There were some renewed demands for legislative action that would override executive policy declarations and would prohibit future presidential discretion to change the program. As in previous years, there was little enthusiasm among the members of the appropriate congressional committees for definitive legislative action. Instead, Congress accepted the President's new version with limited response, as it had in 1962, and reflected concern only about federal labor relations in view of potential crises inspired by the behavior of the Professional Association of Air Traffic Controllers (PATCO) and certain postal unions, which had escalated their militancy to the point of advocating massive use of sick leave or outright strike action.

The Federal Aviation Administration, the employer of the air-traffic controllers, took a strong disciplinary stand against the mass-sickness technique and sought outside advice in the resolution of the complaints about employment policies and conditions among the controllers. The sensitive task of the controllers in connection with the safety of thousands of airline passengers served to dramatize the significance of the employees' complaints. The employees had demonstrated the vulnerability of the management position when amid crowded air-traffic conditions they insisted on following to the letter the aircraft spacing requirements set by the FAA for safety purposes. This literal compliance with regulations produced extensive delays in the landing and take-off of scheduled airliners, with resulting confusion and dissatisfaction on the part of passengers. Then, too, the more militant representatives of the controllers raised the apprehension of airline travelers by emphasizing the understaffing and inadequate equipment in the air-traffic control system. This form of criticism raised new problems for the management with the public as well as in its relationship with the employees.

With an epidemic of strikes spreading among state and municipal employees and the pressure for higher pay and additional fringe benefits, it was not surprising that the threat of strikes, so long a taboo on the federal scene, became at least a part of the rhetoric of federal labor relations. Though the loudest such rumblings came from the most muscular centers of federal unionism, the postal employee organizations, they were not the only source. During the 1967 hearings before the Johnson task force, an officer of the National Association of Government Employees (NAGE) warned management to be on the outlook for a rash of wildcat strikes. Within six months of this warning, an NAGE local in New York City was deprived of its exclusive recognition and its dues-withholding privileges after member employees picketed the Weather Bureau's New York office in protest over working conditions and personnel policies then under negotiation. Management's action was the first instance in which sanctions were exercised against the union under the antipicketing provision in the labor-management program. These sanctions were clearly authorized in the code of fair labor practices, which prohibited picketing in connection with federal labor disputes.

During the period from 1962 to 1968 there had been fifteen incidents of potential strike, work stoppage, slowdown, or picketing in violation of the law. All but three of these potential violations had been averted. The only strike was at the Tennessee Valley Authority in August 1962, and the eighty-one employees involved were discharged. Aside from the picketing at the Weather Bureau, the only other case was a walkout in 1967 of some postal employees in New Jersey.

The threats finally became action. The no-strike law was violated. For the first time in nearly two hundred years, the postal system suffered a work stoppage. It happened in New York City on March 18, 1970, when locals of the letter carriers' union failed to report to their duty stations. The dire prediction was fulfilled, and it involved postal employees in the New York area, where public employees at the state and local levels had lived in almost perpetual dispute with public management.

The strike spread to every region except the South, ending after eight days through the use of military forces as postal workers and assurances of higher pay. This action by the postal unions had far-reaching consequences, some immediate and others still conjectural. Respect for the statutory prohibition was destroyed, and its impact on future federal labor relations is seriously depreciated. The capability of national union leaders to guide their locals was undermined. The policies and procedures formulated after eight years of labor-relations progress proved unavailing. The paramountcy of public service was disregarded.

It can be claimed that a complexity of factors and forces had peculiar implications in the 1970 crisis. This is true. As in so many labor relations conflicts, the points at issue were blurred. The striking workers proclaimed demands for higher starting pay and quicker advancement to the top of the pay range, for greater government contribution to pension and health-benefit programs, and for improved working conditions. All these issues were beyond the capacity of the Postmaster General or the President to resolve. They were clearly within the province of Congress. And the unions preferred it that way. The history of at least the past twenty-five years had demonstrated the political power of the postal unions with members of Congress. Time and time again, administration leaders from both parties were forced to compromise on salary increases well above the level they had proposed because of the combined pressure of the postal unions and their friends in Congress. The reform proposal first advanced by President Johnson and strongly supported by President Nixon for the creation of a nonprofit corporation to operate the postal establishment instead of the Post Office Department was bitterly opposed by the postal unions even though the plan would permit collective bargaining between the new postal authority and its unions. The union leaders had studied the record. They had more generous friends in Congress than they would ever have on the management side of a corporate table even if negotiation impasses were subject to binding arbitration. In the legislative maneuvering for the new corporation, 1969 and 1970 pay increases for postal and other federal employees had become bargaining factors. The combination of delay and misunderstanding had exacerbated relationships and fueled the militancy of local leaders, who became tired of the legislative maneuvers in which their leaders were engaged on Capitol Hill.

Running through this train of circumstances was the employees' deep-seated resentment concerning general working conditions prevailing in the postal service. While postal salaries had been increased, the department and Congress had failed to keep pace with physical improvements in the post-office plant. The volume of mail had far outstripped the capacity of existing buildings to accommodate the flow of letters, publications, and packages and the people who were required to handle it. Major metropolitan construction had been practically nonexistent in the years since the New Deal's public-works program constructed facilities to meet the demands of that depressed time. The investment in research and development had been niggardly in proportion to need for use of new technology in processing mail, with the result that mechanical and electronic benefits utilized by other employers with mass operations were not widely applied in the Post Office. Even the procurement of vehicles had been behind the times or without sufficient regard for employees' safety.

The employment system itself, designed and preserved by the alliance of unions and Congress, frustrated individual achievement. The great bulk of the jobs were either labeled "clerk" or "carrier" and all of them were paid at the same basic rate. There was a failure to recognize different levels of skill requirements with different levels of pay. There was a tenacious adherence to a single rate that applied not only to many different operations but also to post offices in all parts of the country. This practice produced pay rates that might in fact be inadequate in New York City or San Francisco but in excess of the local banker's salary in Enid, Oklahoma, or Orono, Maine. These deficiencies had been identified in hearings before congressional committees, but they were decried by spokesmen for the postal unions who invariably cited the inequality in compensation for postal workers by comparing their pay with that of unionized occupations in the highest-paid markets.

The Post Office Department was also plagued with the conflict between and among the unions themselves. The large and strong craft unions, the letter carriers and clerks, were opposed by a growing industrial union, the National Postal Union. As a vestige of the days of segregation, a union with predominantly Negro members, the National Postal Alliance, sought recognition in certain post offices. Still another belligerent on the battlefield was a union of more than 30,000 supervisors who, though exercising supervisory responsibilities within the post offices, behaved like trade unionists. But that was not all. The postmasters themselves were organized, not in just one but in two organizations, which experienced difficulty in encouraging their members to stand firm on the management side in labor-relations disputes. And permeating the entire patchwork complex was a perceptible strain of politics. Postmasters were certified through competitive civil service examinations, but there was undercover clearance for the eligible person among the top three who was most satisfactory to the political representative of the President's party. With Congress setting salaries and postal rates, these processes of determination were less rational and more political. The political importance of the rural mail carrier perpetuated outmoded practices and excessive compensation. Where the closing of post offices would have resulted in efficiency and improved use of personnel, local political interests stood in the way and forced the continuation of post offices where the revenue collected did not even pay for the postmaster's salary.

Against such a backdrop it is difficult to assess blame or to propose new solutions. There is hope that the new corporate authority to manage the post office, free from political interference and operated on the basis of business standards, can correct many of these deficiencies. If Congress will delegate to its management the establishment of salaries and fringe benefits without political interference, a pattern may emerge that more nearly resembles industrial labor relations. If this is to be the development, the relationships of the postal corporation to its unions should be placed in a context similar to that of other public service industries— transportation, utilities, and health and welfare services. Not that existing procedures for the resolution of disputes are satisfactory or responsive to the public needs, but with the blurred line between public service performed by private corporations and that performed by governmental agencies, there needs to be a more nearly common approach with more effective deterrents and more solid guarantees against work stoppages.

While recognizing these similarities between public service and private employment, one must also emphasize the decided differences. As long as employees are paid by tax revenues collected from the citizenry and are assigned duties to carry out publicly authorized functions, certain distinct conditions must exist. One of the greatest obstacles in the search for effective solutions in public service labor relations is disagreement on the question of whether government service is essentially different from private employment. In any governmental jurisdiction, unless the parties can agree on an affirmative answer to this question of difference, the road of labor-management relations will be too rocky for the public to travel. The government involved and the public that supports it will be too suspicious of unionism to permit it to flourish. Conversely, if the government and the public it serves believe that the union recognizes and accepts the essential difference, then all the problems of equality of status and methods of operation in particular aspects of the relationship will have a good chance of resolution.

The essential differences between public service and private employment are threefold when it comes to labor relations.

First, in private enterprise authority is located clearly at the top. The subordinate organization and delegations of authority usually are clearly drawn. In democratic governments, on the other hand, as in unions, ultimate authority is at the base rather than at the top of the structure. The general membership or the citizens themselves decide the organizational framework, elect their representatives, define their authority within constitutional limits, and provide internal checks and balances or oversight arrangements to ensure that the will of the majority prevails in decision making.

This difference in the location of basic authority, and the way in which operating authority is limited and diffused among governmental leadership, is at the heart of much of the difficulty in public service labor relations. Unions constantly complain about their inability to deal, as in private enterprise, directly with the source of final authority to say "yes" or "no." This attitude, which denies a reality that cannot be changed, must itself be changed if progress is to be made. After all, it is a cardinal principle in unionism that management should not inject itself into the union's internal affairs, particularly into its internal authority and disciplinary arrangements. This principle cuts both ways.

The second difference that affects relationships lies in the way that management authority actually is exercised in democratic governments. While government leaders do have defined authority to act as management, the nature of their action is strongly affected by the need to weigh and balance divergent interests of major groups among the citizens they represent.

The 1968 teachers' dispute in New York City, in which public schools were closed for many weeks, provides a dramatic illustration. In this dispute, 52,000 teachers denied their services to the schools and the lives of more than a million children and their parents were deeply affected. To the union, the issue was not pay but job security, protection of the working rights of its members. But to the city government and the school board the issue was by no means that simple. The parties in confrontation were not just labor and management; they included many other groups representing educational, civic, political, racial, and religious interests. So the real issue was one of public policy—in this case, public educational policy. And it was surrounded by a mixture of pressures, politics, and prejudice so complex as to block any solution through dealings with the union alone.

This leads to the third main point of difference. Many of the working conditions of public employees that are regarded as uniquely different and perhaps less beneficial than those in private business are the product of public policy. If it is a policy of any significance, the amount of pressure for change brought to bear by an employee union seldom has much to do with finding a solution. Indeed, it is probably unfair that labor relations should get a black eye for what happened in the New York teachers' dispute. The task of resolving questions of public policy is the task of government; it is a burden which should not have to be borne by a labor-management relationship.

These essential differences between public service and private employment need to be accepted by union leaders and reflected in their attitude and approach to labor relations in the public service. This does not mean that the role of labor unions in public service should be more limited than in private employment. Instead it means that the test of labor's success should not be scored in terms of the forms and techniques of collective bargaining in the private sector but in terms of similar results for the worker through whatever form of representation is best suited to the public jurisdiction involved. Form and technique should fit the authority and organizational pattern of the parties in the work setting. Labor-relations arrangements properly differ not only between private industry and government but from one government to another. Good experience that can be transferred in whole or in part from one setting to another may prove beneficial, but the main effort should be to develop forms of representation that are best suited to the actual circumstances in each public domain. There are significant opportunities to develop creative new patterns to meet the needs of public organizations in public programs independent of prototypes that may exist in industry or other forms of government.

Regardless of the particular form of representation that evolves in the public sector, there is need to keep searching for new patterns of direct employee participation in the arrangements that relate to their working experience. In our rapidly changing society, one constant has become obvious: the reach of the individual for involvement, the rising demand for more meaningful participation by the individual. The symptoms of this growing demand for personal involvement in decisions that affect the individual's status and well-being are evidenced in universities, churches, political parties, and labor unions as well as in the government services. Where that demand is not satisfied by involvement and added influence, an increasingly militant and organized reaction has developed against the institution of the established order. We have seen this in recent times in the government unions themselves: changes in leadership, refusal to ratify settlements, a lack of interest in or opposition to labor's long-standing policies and goals. It has been observed in the ranks of government employees themselves: youth, women, racial and nationality groups, older workers, veterans, professionals, supervisors, and even managers all have a new interest in the policies that affect them. All want serious and meaningful consideration of their views.

The force of this new interest will continue to put a premium on administrative initiative, on the development of ways in which individuals and groups can participate more effectively at all levels where decisions are made. The term "participative democracy" has gained a certain popularity and attracted a certain skeptical criticism, but it must become more of a reality than it has been to date in all institutions. Those who lead will sustain their leadership if they can demonstrate organizational and attitudinal progress in this direction.

The alternative is a breaking down of any established order and a frustration of the purposes for which unions and governments and all traditional institutions exist. The forces of innovation in government must develop human and individual arrangements within the context of bigness, for much of the unrest reflected in group and individual actions is basically a discontent with being only one relatively ineffectual element; it is an assertion of identity as an individual in an ever expanding and increasingly complex institutional setting. Employment arrangements must seek to involve all groups, for the recognition of the needs of some tends to develop negativism and discontent in the others and, in turn, makes for divisiveness rather than unity in the organization.

Concentration on federal labor relations is neglectful of the predominant arena of labor dispute in government. It is in local government that the former advantages of public service have been most seriously diluted in recent times. The pressure of the citizen for extended and improved services, the decay of the inner city with the related social problems, the superior economic gains for those employed at similar skill levels in the private sector, rising living costs, and the instability of the political environment have increased job hazards and generated more aggressive group attitudes. These servants of the people have been taken for granted by the people themselves. Their personal needs not only in economic but also in social terms have been neglected. They have all too frequently been regarded as pawns in a political chess game played by the small number of leaders accepting the responsibility of local public office.

Because unionism has become more acceptable in American society and has been demonstrably successful in improving the lot of its members, public employees have offered a fertile ground for union organization. Their new-found strength has been applied to produce a feeling of crisis in many local government jurisdictions. As in the federal government, there is an immediate need for the adoption of policy and practice to deal constructively with the aspirations and demands of these burgeoning labor organizations. In that decision-making there needs to be an open acceptance by the public jurisdiction of certain fundamental principles to guide future relationships.

First, there should be a clear declaration that public employees have the right to join unions. This right of representation establishes the means for more effective communication between management and employees on the basis of a limited partnership where both parties accept certain obligations. The absence of this basic right has been one of the most important causes of labor disputes in public employment. No workable labor-management relationship in public employment can exist without these representation rights.

Second, when a majority in a democratic election chooses a union, that union should be recognized as the exclusive employee representative. To permit the union to perform its basic function as advocate for its membership, the employer must recognize that the union speaks for his employees in all consultations and negotiations. The steps leading to union recognition may vary, just as the definition of the appropriate unit of representation by a union may be variously specified. As a general rule, public employment is best served through the largest feasible unit for recognition consistent with acceptable negotiating conditions. This will help prevent potential distortion in public services that can occur when the negotiations are conducted by one government organization with a particular unit without regard for negotiations by other organizations under the same governmental authority. While some public employers may be reluctant to grant recognition because of certain doubts about a union's standing or capability or because of anticipated demands they are unable to grant, a policy must prevail that acknowledges the representativeness of the union that has gained the majority will.

Third, the public employer has the obligation to meet and negotiate in good faith with the union that has been recognized. While the scope of issues upon which negotiation can be conducted will be expanded or restricted depending upon the statutory authority of management, the public manager should not exclude from consultation and discussion any issues judged to be significant by union representatives. In many municipal jurisdictions the entire area of pay and benefits may be excluded by statute from negotiation, as they are at the federal level. Nevertheless, areas open to negotiation should be sought and incorporated in agreements formally reduced to writing.

Fourth, grievance machinery should be designed and installed with provision for final settlement by impartial arbitration. One of the most affirmative aspects of a union-employer relationship is that it produces a mutually agreed-upon process through which complaints that might otherwise be allowed to go unattended by management are systematically brought before those who can respond with a decision. The lack of such machinery has frequently led to disputes because employees have no alternative method of pressing their claim against real or imagined unfair treatment. There may be reluctance on the part of management to permit the outside arbitrator to render a binding decision on a grievance. But experience has shown that as long as such adjudications are within the scope of legal authority and subject to review by the courts, management will not be seriously handicapped.

Fifth, when an impasse does arise, the technique of mediation and the process of fact-finding should be applied. As we know from newspapers and television, even with the right to organize and achieve recognition and the presence of laws and court decisions prohibiting strikes, impasses are leading to work stoppages. Alternatives to the strike as a means for settling disputes must be established for all agencies of government. Threatening disputes should be exposed to the intensity of continuing negotiations among all parties until the prospect of agreement is exhausted. At that point, the recognized techniques of mediation can be applied in an effort to seek new avenues of discussion on the part of the disputing elements. The purpose of this mediation should be to avert the breakdown of communication between the parties and to provide a neutral element in what has become an adversary situation. It is important that the mediator be agreed to by both parties and that he possess a sophisticated understanding of the particular issues faced in municipal labor relations. If mediation fails, the next step should be resort to the process of fact-finding through action by the public official or a separate board removed from the dispute. Such fact-finding can be most effective if conducted by an individual or panel of experts recognized for competence and impartiality. The specific process of fact-finding should be left open to those selected. The findings and conclusions of the fact-finders should provide the basis for resumed negotiations and the ultimate yielding by one party or the other in a final agreement. Relatively few disputes should survive the process of negotiation, mediation, and fact-finding and deteriorate into a strike.

Sixth, an agency independent of executive direction and subject only to court review should be created where none exists, to assure compliance with the basic principles of the program and to administer a code of public employee labor relations.

These principles shy away from the fundamental critical question: should public employees be allowed to strike? Some experts in labor relations believe that a strike of public employees, usually excepting firemen and policemen, could be permitted, subject to a court determination concerning possible peril to health and safety. They contend that public employees should have the opportunity to strike if government authority with the decision-making power fails to accept the recommendation for settlement offered by the fact-finders. If a strike should occur under these conditions, the management would have access to the courts to seek an injunction against the strike's continuance and the ultimate determination of whether the strike constituted an emergency would be left to the courts on a case-by-case basis.

The contrary view is that employees should work on the best terms negotiated, seek redress through legislative authority, and be prohibited by law from striking. It contends that this should be a blanket prohibition to bar strikes of any and all public employees. It accepts the view that government workers are employees of the public at large, acting through elected legislators, who may delegate but not abdicate certain authority to administrative officials. In accepting government employment, the employees have committed themselves to public service not subject to interruption by dissatisfaction over working conditions. Permitting strikes disrupts the functioning of government even if the functions performed by the employees are judged nonessential.

This latter view is the more persuasive, provided the principles cited earlier are established and pursued in good faith by both parties. If the prohibitory statute is violated, prescribed penalties must be assessed with firmness and fairness without creating martyrs of the leaders or imposing undue economic sanctions on the members. Clearly such violations should at least lead to suspension of recognition and denial of the privilege of dues withholding. Such penalties have serious consequences for the offending leaders. The economic value of checkoff cannot be overestimated. Its loss will seriously handicap the future growth and effectiveness of a union.

In conclusion, the problems faced today and over the next decade in our society are and will be so complex and so difficult that no risk can be run that will diminish the effectiveness of government and its employees. The response of the government to the needs of its citizens will be effective only if government personnel have the required skill, motivation, and commitment. The challenge for management and unions in the public service will be to create new forms of joint action so that government can exercise effectively the central leadership that will be vital if the social and economic crises are to be successfully overcome. This cooperation should be based on a mutual goal: preservation of the public's confidence in the service of its government, in its efficiency, its productivity, and its responsiveness to the public will.

Balancing
of Rights
and Responsibilities
in Public Employment

11

The dissent and protest that spilled over the American landscape in the late 1960s did not flow around or away from the public service itself. Those symptoms of growing demand for personal involvement in basic decisions that appeared on the face of other American institutions also were displayed on the face of government. Civil rights, poverty, Vietnam, environmental decay, civil liberties, invasion of privacy, and other areas of American public policy or personal behavior awoke the sources of dissent even in the governmental institutions designed to deal with them.

These displays of dissent transcended the issues pertaining to working conditions and union status. They exceeded the traditional demand of employees for the right to petition Congress. They were the new manifestation of the venerable and revered rights to dissent and to protest. These rights are basic conditions available to all citizens in a free society, and they find their wellspring in the Jeffersonian doctrine that the spirit of revolution must be preserved. Our history is replete with examples of citizen dissent. They range from the acts that preceded the Declaration of Independence and the Revolution itself through to those that led to the conflict between the states over the preservation of the Union. They were reflected in every movement for reform. They appeared in the citizen drive for reform in civil service and civil rights, in the demand for equal suffrage and the rights of unions, and in the resistance to

145

conscription and unemployment. In a more contemporary form, they have been revealed in drugstore sit-ins, freedom rides, the marches on Selma and Washington, the battle at the doors of the Pentagon and on the streets of Chicago, the take-over of college buildings by students, and the creation of Resurrection City by the poor people at the foot of the Lincoln Memorial. These reactions were generated by human forces seeking change or reform. Although dissent was frustrated and dissipated in some instances, it also led to political and social progress in many areas. Some of the protest events of our times have been without precedent and have been received with mixed reactions. Where protest has escalated to violence, dissent to refusal to listen, and opposition to obscenity, the mass of the public and their representatives have tended to turn away or to seek restrictive measures to control or suppress such expressions.

Public employees have recently turned to active dissent and have caught both the government and the public by surprise. A concrete example of such action occurred in the spring of 1968, when a group of federal workers drafted, circulated, signed, and published a petition opposing the national policy on Vietnam. The sponsoring group, constituted primarily of young activists, called for massive response on the part of other employees in conveying to President Johnson, their ultimate employer, their assertive opposition to the continuance of the war in Southeast Asia. Their action prompted the extremes of forceful criticism and militant support. From one side was heard the demand: "Why don't you fire these dissidents?" From the other side came: "Don't you dare lay a hand on these conscientious people for exercising their constitutional rights!" The reason for the surprise both inside and outside government was not difficult to find: by long-standing custom, federal employees had abstained from public expression of disagreement with government policy. Most persons in government felt the same sense of obligation to their government employer that they would presumably feel toward a private employer.

There was need to assure that management's position in dealing with this form of internal dissent would be balanced with due consideration given to the employee's rights as a citizen and his responsibilities as a public servant. Clearly, the federal employee was a full citizen and entitled to express his views. Their expression might take a public form if that was his desire. But he could not proceed down the path of public dissent in perfect immunity. He was responsible for his actions, like any other citizen. And he did indeed have special obligations connected with his own role in his agency's program when that program came into question. Further, he must separate his private activities from his use of official time or government property. Last but not least, he needed to be aware of any special regulations that might bear upon his participation in dissenting activities.

The official response to questions concerning employee behavior under these circumstances was that a federal employee had the right to express his opinion on national policy and that he might do so by signing a petition or participating in an orderly assembly or demonstration. It pointed out that in applying this general rule it was essential to understand that employees of the federal government had duties and obligations toward the government as their employer and that these duties and obligations sometimes transcended those ordinarily owed an employer outside government and hence demanded extra restraint. For example, some federal employees had official duties that required them to recommend policies dealing with U.S. programs in Southeast Asia. Others had duties that required them to explain those policies, or responsibilities that required them to support operations based on them. Employees who occupied such positions were under a positive obligation to carry out the policies fixed by those charged with that duty. It would have been incompatible with their responsibilities if such employees had made public their criticism of the policies that their jobs required them to explain or implement. Their critical opposition might have impaired the value of their service.

It seemed patently unfair to remain in such employment while using against the government information which the employee had obtained only because he held an official position. At some point, a clear obligation and simple decency required the dissenting employee to leave the government if his convictions and his conscience necessitated public words or actions critical of the government's policies.

Moreover, the government, like any other employer, had the obligation to perform its operations as efficiently and effectively as possible. If the conduct of one of its employees was shown to have interfered with the efficiency of the service, then law, regulations, and custom authorized the government to take corrective action. Some agencies' regulations recognized that the government could be adversely affected in its capacity as an employer by certain public statements of its employees. For example, the Department of State required any employee to obtain the specific permission of a department official before using his name in any publication dealing with foreign policy. Under that regulation, the administrator of the Agency for International Development denied its employees permission to have their names published in connection with the 1968 peace petition. There were also general restrictions regarding the time and place that a petition might be signed or circulated; for example, such activity was forbidden on government property without the consent of the agency concerned.

Stripped to the bare essentials, constitutional provisions granted the federal employee certain basic rights in the area of self-expression. The bounds within which those rights could be exercised could be defined by law, custom, good taste, and regulations, paramount among which was the government-wide regulation on ethics and conduct as set forth in an Executive Order on May 8, 1965. Such regulations set minimum standards. Individual agencies prescribed additional standards appropriate to their particular functions and activities of the agency.

Several thousand federal employees' names were published in a Washington newspaper along with the peace petition, and the leaders of the petition group presented their dissenting views to a member of the President's staff. With the President's concurrence, no disciplinary action was meted out against the participants. No evident damage was done either to federal establishments or to employee rights. There remained, however, an unsettling concern as to what might be done to the public's concept of a professional career service, objectively carrying out policies and programs of the administration in power without regard to political or other private affiliations, if episodes of this type multiplied in magnitude and intensity.

Of different dimension but of similar perplexity during that same spring was the involvement of federal employees in the civil disorders following the assassination of Martin Luther King, Jr. For a federal employee to be arrested for criminal behavior during a civil disorder was a matter of far greater consequence than signing a petition. Neither social mores nor public laws nor constitutional rights exempted the individual from the consequences of his behavior when, in expression of his dissent, he broke the law. Immediately after the disorders that followed the assassination, news reports indicated that hundreds of federal employees, residents of the District of Columbia, had been arrested. It turned out that these early reports were grossly exaggerated and that the maximum involvement implicated only thirty federal employees arrested for serious crimes during the disorders. That was one in a hundred thousand for the total federal establishment, although it was regrettable that even one was arrested. As happens in inaccurate reports, it is doubtful whether the facts ever caught up with the exaggerations of federal employee involvement. The first reports understandably set off a clamor among members of Congress and resulted in the swift introduction of punitive legislation requiring the summary dismissal of all arrested employees. This legislation set aside the ample provisions for appropriate action in existing law and regulations against the few employees involved. The case of any employee who committed a criminal act during these disturbances should have been treated like any other case involving criminal conduct by a federal employee. Civil service regulations provided that agencies might take adverse action against an employee "for such cause as will promote the efficiency of the service." Sustaining this principle, the regulations forbid employees to engage in "criminal, infamous, dishonest, immoral or notoriously disgraceful conduct, or other conduct prejudicial to the government." Evidently these suitability standards would permit agency management to take adverse action in the face of criminal conduct. A number of reported arrests, however, were for relatively minor infractions such as unintentional and technical curfew violations, for which adverse action might not be warranted. The agencies were advised not to act precipitously against employees solely on the basis of arrest, but rather to make individual determinations based upon firm evidence of criminal conduct, such as convictions.

In periods of public alarm it is necessary to deflect the force of reaction that would create new restrictions while disregarding the available routes of recourse for fair and balanced treatment. It is also essential to remember that each case must be acted upon in terms of all relevant facts relating to the individual and his conduct in the particular event. There should be vigilant opposition to the imposition of additional rigid penalties for entire classes of offenses of varying gravity merely because they are related to a civil disorder.

The third testing ground for the balance of rights and obligations of federal employees in that fateful spring of 1968 related to federal employee participation in the Poor People's March. Large numbers of employees wished to be identified with the cause of the poor people who encamped just beyond federal offices and were frequently observed representing that cause in and around the nearby federal buildings. As a general rule, federal employees were free to participate in the Poor People's March without adverse effect upon their employment. But again, there had to be qualifications with respect to that general rule. If the march should be directed against some particular agency of government in such a way as to constitute public criticism of the agency or its programs, then federal employees, and particularly employees of that agency, were not to participate. This restriction was especially advisable if the employee occupied a position in which his official duties required him to recommend or directly support the policies or operations under fire from the marchers. For such an employee publicly to criticize policies it was his duty to formulate, administer, and support would compromise his value as an employee. But it was emphasized that the employee was responsible for his own conduct. If a disturbance broke out or an event became disorderly to the point where violations of law occurred, and if the facts established improper conduct on the part of the employee, he could be disciplined. The discipline, depending upon the gravity of the offense, could go as far as removal from the service. The mere fact that his behavior ensued from what was expected to be an orderly demonstration could be no excuse.

Likewise, there was need to underscore the view that federal facilities should ordinarily not be used to promote the Poor People's March or any similar event. Official hours were not the time for demonstrating an expression of private conviction, though vacation time might be granted when the employee could be spared without undue interruption of the agency's work. These guidelines were both workable and acceptable, and have assisted supervisors and employees alike in determining permissible conduct in subsequent demonstrations.

Certain conclusions were drawn from these three episodes, pointing the way toward new steps that could be taken to accommodate the employee's entitlement to equity and the government's entitlement to good order and discipline among the work force.

The first conclusion drawn was that the arena for dissent did embrace federal employment in an era of restiveness and an age for the activist. There was an awareness that the traditional assumption of federal employee passivity had been discarded and that further expressions of dissent by public employees in their private capacities but on public issues were to be expected.

From the experiences of 1968, the conclusion was drawn that each episode required the wisdom of careful thought and deep reflection rather than immediate action that might be magnified to overreaction dominated by emotion or panic. While in some circumstances such overcorrection may have seemed highly convenient, the medicine prescribed could be more deadly than the original illness. It was clear that the contemporary world was simply too full of issues that could become the focus of dissent for policymakers to attempt to develop detailed directions or guidelines designed to cover every situation. Each one needed to be judged on the basis of actual facts against basic principles of law and policy.

Finally and most significantly, there was a renewed belief that all parties must be scrupulous in abiding by the law and that the law is the greatest ally of all parties in troubled times.

The law can set some outer limits and provide some useful guidance through its interpretation by the courts. In recent times, the courts through opinions in individual employee cases have provided new definitions of rights and responsibilities and of relationships between management decision and employee performance. Such redefinition is illustrated in the 1968 decision on the *Meehan* case, which involved an incident that occurred during the riots in the Canal Zone in 1964. While tensions over that international event were at their highest, certain policemen publicly criticized decisions of the Zone's governor and were dismissed for that criticism. The U.S. Court of Appeals in the District of Columbia found that there were some limits on freedom of expression by federal employees in some circumstances and sustained the disciplinary action of the government. As the Boston *Herald Traveler* editorialized, "the court's ruling has not disturbed their [the government employees'] freedom of conscience, but it has denied them freedom from the consequence of their actions."

The presence of dissent on public issues among federal employees should be viewed in constructive ways and should stimulate the formulation of basic questions concerning the nature of public employment and the culture within which it is performed. Are the institutions and processes available within government so cut and dried and lusterless that the innovative and conscientious federal employee feels he must go outside the established framework in order to find expression for creative ideas? Have public managers imposed an environment that has such a stifling effect on activists and innovators that they gain no sense of constructive involvement? How can the idealism and the sense of urgency evidenced by the responsible dissenter be channeled into the government's agenda of critical actions?

Every public manager must think about these questions and set his own constructive course in a time of change when far more men march to different drummers than in the past. The public work force cannot be deaf to the tune of its times because it must be representative of the total population if it is to transmit the future hope and aspirations of that population. Animating dissent and protest is the individual's desire to count for something, to explore his full potential as a human being. Not all men share this desire at any particular point in time. Large numbers of people are more apathetic than is wise or safe. But the leavening process is in full swing. The stirrings are being felt in large groupings of minorities, among the disadvantaged, and in the ranks of the disaffected.

Society can gain or lose from the expenditure of this boundless energy. In some recent events—on campuses, in public buildings, on the streets —this energy has been used for destruction without any seeming constructive objective. Properly employed, this energy can generate the momentum to assure a better future. Society must have new patterns of participation in order to attract all those who have felt stifled in the past and to open the gates of opportunity for the positive use of their abilities and personal attributes. In this endeavor to find new patterns of participation, both in employment and in private life, those who create the employment environment and the public missions for the civil servant should be in the vanguard.

The balancing of rights and responsibilities has been measured in recent efforts to define the employee's protection from invasions of his privacy by the government employer. A convergence of new federal personnel programs in 1966 and 1967 prompted complaints on the part of many employees and their union representatives that their privacy was being violated. These complaints received a sympathetic treatment and a vigorous investigation from the Senate Subcommittee on Constitutional Rights chaired by Senator Sam J. Ervin. The complaints reflected a negative and even hostile attitude on the part of some employees toward the self-administered minority census, the enlarged program of training in civil rights, the requirement for reporting of personal holdings for certain employees under the ethics program, and a particularly aggressive savings-bonds campaign within the federal establishment. In a number of instances, these programs had been pursued with excessive zeal by individual managers or had been initiated without adequate consideration of employee reaction. Once the flow of invasion-of-privacy complaints had been given wide publicity, additional grievances, real or imagined, were reported to Capitol Hill either directly or through union channels. There were reports of excessively personal questions on medical or psychological questionnaires, political intrusion in personnel actions, supervisory favoritism or discrimination, and other acts that were interpreted as violation of the employee's rights.

From these complaints, the legislative process was initiated by Senator Ervin with a draft bill and extensive hearings. The bill soon acquired the label "Bill of Rights for Federal Employees," and it accumulated sponsors representing a cross section of views and representation in the Senate. The bill's sponsors and the union representatives believed that statutory protections were necessary to guard the employee's rights against an invading management inclined to force its will upon the employees through acts or requirements of various types. Representatives of the Executive Branch opposed the legislation on the ground that the constitutional rights of employees were protected by existing statutes and policies and that administrative means were most appropriate in dealing with instances of abuse. The proposed legislation would give exclusive emphasis to the protection of individual rights without concurrent recognition of employee obligations to the government as employer and would thereby create an imbalance. A disproportionate emphasis on the protection of individual rights without a balancing appreciation on individual obligations could result in distortion and disorder. The bill, for example, gave an employee the right to counsel whenever a supervisor wished to question him about the most minor infraction of the rules. Under such statutory restraint a supervisor would hesitate to question an employee about any form of misconduct, no matter how minor. The employee's right to counsel in any formal proceeding or inquiry was already assured in existing legislation. Under the bill, an employee would be able to file a lawsuit in a district court whenever he believed his rights had been threatened or violated. Ordinarily, recourse to the courts is permitted only when all available administrative remedies have been exhausted. The proposed process would also establish a separate board of employee rights as an additional administrative remedy beyond those already in existence in the Civil Service Commission. Such direct access to the courts would circumvent and negate existing grievance procedures, many of them the product of negotiated agreements under the labor-management program.

Although the legislation failed to pass Congress, it had a significant affirmative impact on federal administrators in their relations with employees. The complaints had called attention to certain situations which were unknown to or disregarded by agency management and which required corrective action to assure ample safeguards for employee rights. Under the prodding of proposed legislation, the Civil Service Commission completely recast its processes for disability retirement to protect against abuses that had crept into the system. The existing medical questionnaires were discarded and less offensive queries were substituted. An amendment was proposed to the Federal Tort Claims Act so that employees would be protected from private lawsuits arising from their official conduct. Another recommended bill would make it a federal crime to assault or kill an employee of the federal government. The self-administered minority census was discarded in favor of a return to the supervisory count. High-pressure tactics in the selling of savings bonds were outlawed in subsequent drives. Finally, a public complaint office was established as a type of employee ombudsman in dealing with employee complaints that could not be readily resolved within the employing agency.

The sensitive balance of employee rights and responsibilities must be subjected to constant testing and evaluation. While public officials, executive and legislative, have the fundamental obligation to measure that balance, they must heed the assessment offered by employees, individually or through union representation, to avoid giving undue weight to their own definition of public interest. The size and diversity of governmental operations should not be allowed to overemphasize institutional needs to the disadvantage of the individual worker. Occasional oversight or stupidity on the part of management, however, should not stimulate rule-making that protects the employee to such an extent that reasonable discretion in managing public programs is frustrated. This concept of balance cannot be static in a time of change, and all parties concerned must be prepared to make adjustments on both sides to assure a new equilibrium.

The

Public Servant

and Prohibited

12   Political Activity

Tucked away in one of the appendices to the annual report of the U.S. Civil Service Commission, there is always a heading "Political Activity Cases." Under this is a listing of federal and state employees who were removed or suspended during the previous year for violation of the prohibition on partisan political activity in the section of the federal code most commonly referred to as the Hatch Act. That report for 1968 reveals that only two federal employees, a Selective Service clerk in Hebron, Nebraska, who was active in a political campaign and a St. Paul postal clerk who held a political party office, were removed by commission action. An additional sixteen federal employees—postal clerks and carriers, Navy mechanics, an Air Force production-matériel expediter, and assorted supervisory personnel of the Post Office—were suspended for thirty to ninety days because of solicitation of contributions for political party fund raising or holding political party office or engaging in political campaign management. The number in violation of the statute at the state level was limited to a single case, Jerome Fishkin, an administrative analyst for the Office of Economic Opportunity in Contra Costa County, California. The name in this case is destined for judicial records because the constitutionality of the statute itself is being challenged in the courts in behalf of Mr. Fishkin. In two other state cases, the commission judged that the violations did not warrant removal.

157

These cases attracted little public notice as they made their weary way through the process of adjudication. Their small number could be cited to verify the absence of political activity within the federal service and the covered state and local services. It could be used to support the view that the enforcement of the statute is inadequate. It could be used to reinforce demands for a recasting of the statute to face more realistically the relationship between the civil servant and the political arena within which he must function. But the numbers of cases and of the columns of publicity about them are not valid measures of the impact or significance of this long-standing feature of the civil service culture.

The thread of politics runs through the entire history of the civil service in varying widths and colors. Politics became a factor in administration of government in the earliest days. Thomas Jefferson expressed his dissatisfaction in 1801 over the political activity of government officers and employees in influencing elections. Both Federalist and Jeffersonian Republican Presidents appointed federal employees from the better-educated families with no thought of a permanent, broadly representative civil service. When Jackson ran successfully for President, in 1828, there were rising complaints about an administrative aristocracy based upon wealth. During the previous administration of John Quincy Adams, public employees found themselves increasingly caught in the conflict between political parties. To the loyal party worker on either side, political success came to mean reward by public employment, on petty terms that would be intolerable to political officers and career public servants alike in recent times.

Many Presidents tried to correct the situation but it continued nevertheless. By 1865 the tide of patronage had reached a flood stage and had become a national scandal which drew an evangelical opposition from the reformers of the time. General Grant ran for President in 1868 on a platform committed to curtail the patronage system, and in 1870 asked Congress for a law "to govern . . . the manner of making appointments." Elected officials had come to realize that the promise of public employment was an illusory means in developing public support. If the party lost, the loyal workers felt they should have been on the other side. If the party won, there were never enough jobs around to reward those who claimed to be loyal.

The reforming forces found public opinion far more responsive following the assassination of President Garfield in 1881 by Charles J. Guiteau, a Republican party worker who daily visited the White House in an effort to press his claim for an appointment as U.S. Consul in Paris. The spoils system, which had cost the nation millions of dollars in governmental inefficiency, had claimed the life of a President. Although reform began in earnest with the passage of the Civil Service Act in 1883, it did not, as pointed out earlier, take place overnight. Rules were established initially to protect the public employee. Step by step, merit-system employees acquired a sense of security in their employment as they survived the administration changes instituted at the ballot box. A longer and more aggressive step was achieved through the service of a future President, Theodore Roosevelt, on the Civil Service Commission. A committed crusader and a political realist, Roosevelt waged a sustained campaign against political preferment and in support of merit principles. His feelings bubbled over in a letter he wrote on February 8, 1895: "A spoils system was more fruitful of degradation in our political life than any other that could possibly have been invented. The spoils monger, a man who peddled patronage, inevitably bred the vote-buyer, the vote-seller, and the man guilty of misfeasance in office."

President Arthur had been instructed by the Civil Service Act of 1883 to promulgate rules providing, among other things, that no government officer should "use his official authority or influence to coerce the political action of any person or any party." This was one of the essential building blocks of the civil service structure. It was intended to overcome the evil that was manifest in coercive political activity imposed upon the public servant. On the other hand, there was no intent in early legislative or executive action to limit *voluntary* political activity on the part of that civil servant.

It was not until Commissioner Roosevelt became President Roosevelt that restrictions against voluntary political activity were first imposed. In 1907 Roosevelt formulated new public policy in an amendment to civil service rules stating that while persons in the civil service could express privately their opinions on political subjects, they "shall take no active part in political management or in political campaigns."

These twin prohibitions were the guiding lights for federal employees for the next thirty-two years. The Civil Service Commission exercised its policing authority by following those two lights. Congressional attention was drawn to this issue during the rapid expansion of the federal government during the New Deal days. The combination of widespread unemployment, low salary and wage levels, the increasing numbers of federal jobs, and a swollen flow of federal dollars created new problems in political activity. Criticism was directed toward the alleged use of federal funds for political purposes in the emergency relief program, with the result that the program's director, Harry Hopkins, issued a directive in 1936 that "persons who are candidates for or hold elective offices shall not be employed on administrative staffs on the Works Progress Administration." Later that year, an amendment to the same effect was incorporated in the WPA appropriation bill.

Not satisfied with administrative and legislative prohibitions, a special Senate committee investigated employment and relief the following year and discovered evidence of widespread violation. Senator Carl A. Hatch of New Mexico, whose name became a familiar word among succeeding generations of federal employees, offered another amendment designed to prevent any person employed by the federal government in an administrative capacity and paid from relief funds from using "his official authority or influence for the purpose of interfering with or influencing a convention, a primary, or other election, or affecting the results thereof." This amendment applied the basic restrictions of the original civil service rule to all administrative personnel in the WPA. When this amendment was defeated, a special committee was requested to investigate in greater depth the alleged use of relief funds for political purposes. That committee, under the chairmanship of Senator Morris Sheppard of Texas and with Senator Hatch as a member, reported to Congress early in 1939 with sixteen specific recommendations that were subsequently incorporated in a bill. This piece of legislation was passed as the Political Activity Act and was signed by President Franklin Roosevelt on August 2. The Hatch Act, as it is always called, prohibited the coercion of federal employees to participate in political activities and outlawed voluntary employee participation in political management and in political campaigns. In the following year, a second Hatch Act incorporated into law two recommendations proposed by President Roosevelt. These extended the act to cover state and local government employees participating actively in federal programs and maintaining the exception to civil service regulations permitting employees permanently residing in the Washington metropolitan area to run for local office.

Since 1939, the American political scene has changed fundamentally. The growth of federal programs, the heavy emphasis upon technology in governmental processes, and the requirement for skilled and highly educated personnel have made obsolete many of the traditional patronage schemes whose evils the enactments of 1883 and 1939 were intended to eliminate. The importance of the public job as political currency has been depreciated. The political organizations, at least at the national level, have designed other forces to sustain the viability of the political party. The merit principle and impartial administration in government programs have been accepted as integral parts of contemporary federal management.

Under the Hatch Act, the Civil Service Commission has functioned successfully in maintaining high standards and integrity in public service consistent with the need for voluntary and desirable political activity by government employees. The average public employee desires the protection from coercive political activity afforded by the act. The problems and disagreements arise over the placement of the line between permissible and forbidden political conduct. The dynamic conditions of the government environment, and the changed size and nature of government activities have shifted the position of that line. To some extent, employees determined to avoid even the most limited political responsibility have hidden behind the Hatch Act barricade even while complaining about their "Hatched" condition. With the growth of federal unions and their involvement in political activity, there have been rhetorical blasts about the alleged second-class citizenship imposed by the Hatch Act. In all fairness, employees were faced with considerable difficulty in ascertaining what the statutory restrictions really meant. The decisions of the Civil Service Commission in individual cases received only limited circulation and were not readily available to rank-and-file employees. Interpretations of the statute were offered by only a small cadre of legal experts. New forms of political activity necessitated the drawing of inter-pretative lines. For example, in the 1964 campaign the distribution of paperback books attacking each of the presidential candidates became a major campaign weapon. Was the distribution of such documents by a federal employee judged to be active participation in political manage-ment or in political campaigns?

More than 4.5 million public employees at federal, state, and local levels had become subject to the provisions of the Hatch Act by 1966. As a result, a large portion of the adult population was severely limited in its exercise of political rights while those in private employment were not restricted in any way even if the primary source of funds for their employer came from the federal Treasury. Public employees, for exam-ple, might attend political conventions as spectators, but "may not take any part in the convention and must refrain from any public display of partisanship or abstrusive demonstration or interference." A public em-ployee "may not publish . . . with any newspaper generally known as partisan" a signed or unsigned letter to the editor. "It is not required that a publication be regarded as the organ of a political organization or that it have an official connection with any political organization or party . . . the objective behind this restriction on activity in connection with publications or newspapers is prohibition of political activity of a parti-san character through the medium of the public press by a person subject to the statute and the rule." Other interpretations of this nature have narrowed the sphere of voluntary political activity on the part of public employees. With the ever-spreading embrace of federal funds into state and local governments, the potential restriction of interpretations of this type and the potential jeopardy of public employees will continue to have far-reaching and expanding implications.

There has always been a serious question as to how seriously Congress wished to have the Hatch Act enforced. Ever since 1940, Congress has placed an expenditure limitation upon the Civil Service Commission's enforcement activities. The appropriation for the fiscal year 1967 limited these expenditures to an amount of not to exceed $98,000. With more than 4.5 million employees subject to the provisions of the act and with the commission the only enforcement body, this meager appropriation has clearly inhibited the enforcement process. It has necessitated the conduct of enforcement largely through response to complaints, the investigation of such complaints, the issuance of charges where investigation indicates violation, the adjudication of such charges, and the general educational function of publicizing permissible and prohibited activities and providing interpretations. This circumscribed degree of activity has undoubtedly allowed certain violations to occur without restraint and has inhibited certain legitimate political activites because of misinterpretation.

The heavy financial burdens placed upon political organizations through the increased cost of political campaigns, largely attributable to the massive use of television, have necessitated a continuing growth in fund-raising activities. Testimonial dinners, high-priced luncheons or cocktail parties, theatrical benefits, overpriced barbecues, and myriad other schemes have been devised by ingenious fund raisers to pay off the debts from the previous election and to build a campaign warchest for the next. Public employees are a natural and attractive target for these forays. Since the political officer is usually the ultimate boss of the public servant, he tends to look upon these men and women as his supporters and as immediately available prospects for ticket purchase to fund-raising events. Inevitably, what has been described by some as an opportunity for the voluntary purchase of such tickets has been condemned by others as solicitation of political contributions. Particularly in politically sensitive Washington, the annual fund-raising dinner for the party in power is productive of complaints of political coercion in the sale of tickets. With its limited resources, the Civil Service Commission has been unable to patrol the corridors or the offices of the agencies where the alleged coercion may take place. Those offended by the practice file their complaints with a friendly newspaper reporter or a member of Congress, not with the enforcement agency. Thus the impression of widespread arm twisting is conveyed to the general public and the integrity of the no-politics restrictions and the public service itself are placed in jeopardy.

When reports of pressure tactics appeared in the Washington newspapers at the time of Democratic fund-raising dinners in 1962 and 1963,

President Kennedy expressed concern not only about these presumed violations but also about the entire policy and enforcement of rules covering political activity. He had received continuing complaints from his political advisers concerning the supposedly excessive restraints, real or implied, upon the permissible political activities of federal employees. To give a better-balanced picture of activities permitted and prohibited, the educational poster released by the Civil Service Commission to inform employees about the Hatch Act had been modified to list the permissible activities in space and type equal to those tabooed. The President had read the chronic complaint of federal union leaders about the second-class citizenship imposed upon federal employees by the Hatch Act. But before his concern could be converted into action, he was no longer President and Lyndon Johnson was obliged to pick up this piece of unfinished business.

The need for a new evaluation of policy in this area was further emphasized in the debates concerning the political activities of beneficiaries of the new programs authorized by the Economic Opportunity Act. As in the days of the New Deal, there was early apprehension that these funds distributed to individuals and organizations across the country would be diverted into political channels. In many cities the federal money was distributed to organizations that were beyond the control of local governments. In fact, it frequently went to individuals who were politically antagonistic toward the incumbent mayor and city organization. The immediate tendency was to extend the restrictions of the Hatch Act to employees of these private organizations.

Rather than propose new legislation in this general policy area, President Johnson chose to support a comprehensive study by a statutory commission with bipartisan representation. Any presidential recommendation for reform, particularly if those reforms liberalized existing restrictions, would be interpreted as an effort by the President to gain political advantage through increased activity on the part of federal employees. Congress, accepting the idea of the study commission, in October 1966 created the Commission on Political Activity of Government Personnel to investigate and study federal laws which limit or discourage the participation of federal or state officers and employees in political activity. The new commission was directed to report to the President and Congress by the end of 1967 with recommendations for legislative changes.

This commission, appointed by the President, the Vice President, and the Speaker of the House, was chaired by Arthur S. Flemming, former Secretary of Health, Education and Welfare and former Civil Service Commissioner, and included bipartisan membership from Congress (Senator Daniel B. Brewster, Democrat of Maryland, Senator George Murphy, Republican of California, Representative Arnold Olsen, Democrat of Montana, and Representative Ancher Nelsen, Republican of Minnesota), two representatives from the Executive Branch (Roger W. Jones from the Bureau of the Budget and Frank M. Wozencraft from the Department of Justice), and five other public members (Charles O. Jones, Malcolm C. Moos, Frank Pace, Jr., Austin Ranney, and Robert Ramspeck). At the outset the commission sought the views of all three of the Civil Service Commissioners at both formal hearings and informal conferences, and it heard testimony from representatives of government employee unions, local political leaders, political scientists, representatives of interested organizations such as the American Civil Liberties Union and the National Civil Service League, and directors of state merit-system offices. In response to an open invitation to the general public, the commission received testimony from individual federal employees on their own behalf. In order to secure more than the Washington point of view, the commission held hearings in Atlanta, Dallas, Chicago, Boston, and San Francisco.

Faced with the difficult task of ascertaining the true view of public employees, the commission undertook a major survey of both federal employee opinion and the views of state employees and party chairmen. For the survey of federal employees, the commission used the services of the Survey Research Center at the University of Michigan, an organization that has been conducting political surveys since 1952. The survey's starting point was a statistical sample of approximately one-tenth of all federal employees, from which 1,108 employees were drawn for interviews during July and August 1967 that resulted in 980 opinions about the Hatch Act. The findings from this research indicated an awareness on the part of federal employees of the Hatch Act but widespread confusion about its specific prohibitions. There was no support for the impression of extensive arm twisting: only 2 percent indicated they had ever been encouraged to buy tickets to political dinners and only 1 percent had been encouraged to contribute money to a party or candidate or to distribute campaign material. There was no apparent reluctance on the part of employees to report political-activity violations if they knew of any. They took no serious exception to the existing penalties or to the restraints on political activity. By and large they did not favor changes, nor did they know what changes should be made. Where changes were suggested, they centered on more participation in general political activity or on permission for activity in support of a candidate. Sixty percent advised that federal employee activity would stay about the same if they were allowed to do more things in politics.

The survey of state employee opinion was based upon nearly 3,000 responses, which in general were similar to those from federal employees. A slightly lower proportion of them were aware of the regulations. More than a fourth stated frankly that they were unable to describe even the general purpose of the Hatch Act. There was a marked tendency to extend the prohibitions into such permissible activities as placing political stickers on cars, running for nonpartisan school-board positions, and becoming actively involved in local issues such as taxes and civil rights. Although many indicated a desire to have a greater scope of political activity, two-thirds of the respondents said that they would be no more active if the permission were granted.

The commission identified the overriding problem of public policy in this area as a reconciliation between constitutionally assured political expression and the fundamental protection of the public service. Some conflict was inevitable between these two desirable objectives. The national need was to strike a balance between employee participation in the democratic process and protection of an impartial public service built on integrity and efficiency. The commission eloquently and effectively expressed these two goals:

"First, a democratic society depends for strength and vitality upon broadly based citizen participation in the political processes of the nation, and governments are responsible for granting their citizens the constitutional rights of free speech and association.

"Second, to assure the honest impartial and efficient transaction of the public's business, a democratic society equally needs a government that functions with a permanent system of employment under which persons are hired, paid, promoted and dismissed on the basis of merit rather than political favoritism."

In seeking this balance, the commission paid special heed to constitutional considerations as set forth in the opinions of the Supreme Court. The Hatch Act itself had been challenged in its early days by appellants who questioned the constitutionality of the prohibition imposed on federal employees with respect to taking "an active part in political management or in political campaigns." In this case, *United Public Workers* v. *Mitchell,* the court in 1947 rejected the claims of unconstitutionality by a narrow 4–3 decision. The court found that the fundamental human rights involved under the Bill of Rights were not absolute but subject to proper regulation, and that the task of the court was to "balance the extent of guarantees of freedom against a congressional enactment to protect a democratic society against the supposed evil of political partisanship by classified employees of the government." Pointing out that Congress and the President "are responsible for an efficient public service," the court concluded that "if in their judgment efficiency may be best obtained by prohibiting active participation by classified employees in politics as party officers or workers, we see no constitutional objection." In a companion case, *Oklahoma* v. *U.S. Civil Service Commission,* the court upheld the prohibition relating to state and local officers and took the position that while the United States has "no power to regulate local political activities as such of state officials, it does have power to fix the terms upon which its money allotments to states should be disbursed."

Although these decisions have stood for more than twenty years, more recent state-court cases relating to political activity have called for a more compelling demonstration of governmental interest in imposing a restriction on First Amendment rights. The California Supreme Court had held the state's "little Hatch Act" invalid because the statute was too broad in its specification of prohibited political activity. Consequently, the Commission on Political Activity of Government Personnel recommended new legislation in which the prohibition restricting political activities would be drawn as specifically as feasible. The restriction should be no more extensive than was necessary to protect the merit system and the integrity of the public service.

There was strong unanimous support for protection of the public employee from political coercion and intimidation. Although the employee survey produced little evidence of coercion, the commission concluded that any evidence was a serious matter and that existing administrative sanctions against coercion should be applicable to federal, state, and local employees as essential protection. Beyond that, the commission called for new provisions to encourage reporting of violations, promoting greater dispatch in processing cases of complaints, and providing for more equitable enforcement. The commission proposed a new approach in specifying prohibited and permissible areas of activity and recommended that all activity be permissible except in those areas specified by Congress in the statute to protect employees against actions that would threaten the integrity of the public service.

There was a call for a uniformity of statutory coverage and exemption, for greater latitude in imposing penalties. In a major recommendation for change, the commission proposed the withdrawal of federal control over state and local employees where states brought their own standards within the scope of prohibition specified by the federal government. This step would permit policing of those standards by the states without federal intervention as long as standards were maintained.

In addition to recommending additional funds for enforcement of the new statute by the Civil Service Commission, the Commission on Political Activity recommended that consideration be given to the creation of an office of employee counsel to which public employees could come to seek information and advice on activities prohibited by the statute. Such an office would serve as the means for protecting the privacy of employees and the confidential nature of complaints about mismanagement of federal funds or activities.

In the area of distinguishing between partisan and nonpartisan political activity in local government, the members of the commission found agreement impossible. Whereas existing prohibition did not apply to public employees who sought or held local public office on a nonpartisan basis, a majority of the commission recommended abolishing any distinction between the two and specifying a prohibition on candidacy by federal employees on the basis of the specific office and the duties to be performed. This recommendation reflected the views of some commission members that federal employee participation in local government should be restricted to the absolute minimum and that most such activity did not constitute a threat to the efficiency of the federal service. These members found existing and proposed definitions or demarcations arbitrary, difficult to administer, and relatively inconsequential. Others believed that participation in partisan political activity, even on the local level and in minor public office, would erode the impartiality of the federal service and might lead to friction between politically ·involved employees and their political superiors in the federal government. The more liberal view was expressed in a final recommendation calling for consideration of a voluntary bipartisan contribution system that would permit financial participation by public employees in the functioning of their party without coercion or suspicion concerning their objectivity.

Unfortunately, the significant progress of this commission in formulating a new and more equitable approach to prohibited political activity has failed to receive strong support from the presidency or Congress. Political leaders are decidedly reluctant to engage in the revision of existing requirements without more forceful demonstration of public need. There is no clamor from any source for change at this time. Employee unions are able to engage in meaningful political activity without violation of the existing law. The great mass of public employees have no burning desire for more extensive political activity. In fact, many of them quietly applaud the mistaken extension of prohibition because it provides a convenient excuse for avoiding legitimate political responsibility. There is a genuine concern, not supported by evidence, that presumed liberalization of prohibition will lead to a greater politicizing of the bureaucracy. The out party is always suspicious of any move that might strengthen the political resources of the in party. If the prohibitions on the employee's rights for freedom of expression are to be defined in narrower and more specific terms the pressure for change will in all likelihood come through the judiciary system. In view of recent Supreme Court definitions of individual rights in other areas and state-court decisions in this area, it is not unreasonable to expect that the Hatch Act, or certain provisions of it, may be judged unconstitutional and thereby force a new chapter in the relationship of the public servant to political activity. This chapter cannot come too soon. The growth of government under the existing breadth of prohibition has inhibited public employees at the very time when dissent and protest are heard in the land against restraints on the citizen in changing established institutions. While the public employee should be protected against coercive involvement in the country's political life, he should be permitted to engage in those activities which are the right of all citizens unless the exercise of those rights has a demonstrably bad effect on his performance of the public's business.

Training

and Education

for

Public Service

13

Shortly after World War II, training in and for public service went into limbo. The manpower shortages of the mobilization and wartime periods had necessitated an extensive investment of funds and resources in the training of men and women for public assignments, both in uniform and mufti. When hostilities ceased and the manpower supply was considered plentiful, the budgets for training were the first to be cut, in the private sector as well as in public service. There was a return to the prevalent peacetime belief that the labor market should provide ready-made the knowledge and skill required for the performance of any available jobs. This view was particularly dominant in the public service, where the belief prevailed that a competitive examining system should function in such a way as not only to meet the skill qualifications but also to pick the person best equipped with the skills. In order to protect a minimum of funds for essential training, the War Department purged the term "training" from its organizational and budgetary presentations and substituted the politically more palatable term "manpower utilization."

This did not mean that no training was provided for public employees. Rather it restricted the development of training institutions within the government or the use of training facilities outside government for the greater development of employee talents. New employees were exposed to orientation training. On-the-job guidance was conducted by supervisors. Apprentices and interns were put through their paces to learn their chosen craft or profession. Certain agencies had special statutory authority to use universities or industrial plants as a training ground for specialized work. Most government agencies maintained a small staff to conduct those training sessions which could be managed most effectively at a central point and to assist managers and supervisors in the organization of training efforts that would facilitate their particular operation. Concurrently, administrative officials in the Executive Branch sought to devise a legislative proposal that would give the training function a more affirmative charter and would expand the permissible resources for application in public service training.

Through the years there had been a growing realization of the need for educational preparation prior to public service. University courses in the social sciences began to extend branches into political science, government, and public administration. The impetus of the New Deal, with its idealistic attraction to the college generation of the depression, created a student demand for more instruction and research in the workings of political institutions. The demand of cities for city managers and other experts, the rapid multiplication of federal functions, and the growth of new functions in state government stimulated an unprecedented demand for education in public service. Syracuse, Princeton, Harvard, California, Southern California, Chicago, Wisconsin, Michigan, and other universities had created graduate schools specializing in the field. The early Syracuse program gained such prominence in the late 1930s that many in the federal government assumed that you had to be one of the "boys from Syracuse" to advance up the bureaucratic ladder. These institutions were also available to provide training for those in the public service who required advanced education or exposure to new knowledge in order to perform effectively in positions of higher responsibility. There was a growing belief that the return to the intellectual stimulation of the university would significantly enhance the future potential of executives and professionals in government. These benefits were obviously not limited to schools of public administration but could be secured in virtually every field of study—law, medicine, science, engineering—because the government required professionals in all of these fields. Also, more and more scholars recognized the beneficial impact upon curriculum and teaching that came from the participation of public servants in the teaching and research conducted on the university campuses.

With the changes in needs and attitudes came increased support for legislative authorization for training. The realization gradually spread that employee training was in the public interest as much as in the individual's interest, and that money spent upon such training was not a contribution to the employee receiving the training but an investment in future government performance that could pay tangible dividends. This growing realization, combined with increasing professionalism in government programs, culminated in the passage of the Government Employees Training Act in 1958. This statute, proposed by the Eisenhower administration and with bipartisan support in Congress, marked a watershed in the acceptance of training and education as continuing ingredients in a dynamic public service. Under its terms, Congress gave authority to federal agencies to provide needed training for their employees, both within the agencies and at outside institutions. It opened the way for many different kinds of employee development. It authorized the development of interagency training by the Civil Service Commission to promote improved performance in areas of knowledge or skill requirements that transcended individual programs. It provided authorization, under certain time and dollar controls, for agencies to use nonfederal institutions in the conduct of necessary training, permitting new patterns of collaboration between the universities and the federal government in the development of training experience. The effect was to legitimatize and expand training opportunities within the management structure of all governmental organizations.

With the passage of the training legislation, the federal government gave more comprehensive and intensive attention to career development. For the first time, it was possible to incorporate training and educational experiences within the scope of a federal career. With such objectives in mind, four basic approaches were defined as the bench marks for individual development in the federal service:

1. Individual self-development—the efforts made by the individual on his own initiative to become better prepared for present and future responsibilities. These efforts were identified as the most important evidences of the individual's trainability. Although agency management might encourage such activities through the availability of training courses on government time or in government quarters, the primary motivation must come from the individual. This motivation was manifest in after-hours courses and in personal participation in the activities of professional societies.

2. Intra-agency training—training activities conducted by a department or agency for its own employees. This type of training could range all the way from totally unstructured guidance given to the employee by his supervisor to elaborate institutional training provided by the agency. There was no denial of the fundamental necessity for continuing training on the job. This mode of learning was re-emphasized in the executive implementation of the 1958 act's provisions.

3. Interagency training—training conducted by a department or agency that may be attended by employees of the federal government at large. Although the Civil Service Commission exercised the lead in planning programs of this type and gave wide publicity to available offerings in other agencies, the bulk of this training was pursued and organized by agencies with program responsibility in particular fields.

4. Education and training in nongovernment facilities—training conducted by universities, professional societies, or other institutions outside government. This was the training approach that assumed new possibilities under the Training Act. While individual agencies worked out training arrangements with individual universities, collective activities were also promoted through a variety of connections between the government and university worlds. This approach was not limited to the institutions of higher education. Many hours of training were provided by nonprofit organizations such as the Brookings Institution, by professional societies such as the American Society for Public Administration, by industrial

training centers such as those in the aerospace industry, and by vocational schools in certain technical skills.

Fostering exchanges of views with university representatives, the Civil Service Commission convened meetings at Princeton (1961), Berkeley (1962), and Bloomington, Indiana (1965), to explore new approaches to collaboration. Out of these meetings emerged a number of experimental efforts in full-time, long-term educational experiences as a part of a systematic career-development plant.

One of the most significant experiments was based on the value of a university experience for persons in mid-career. This form of continuing education placed a new responsibility upon individual universities to adapt their curricular and instructional patterns. A pilot program was undertaken through a grant from the Ford Foundation for the establishment of a career-education awards program. The grant was presented to the National Institute of Public Affairs, the nonprofit organization that had originated the government intern program in the 1930s, to plan, promote, and administer an academic year for fifty young careerists with high potential in graduate study at several leading universities. The first group of nominees were screened by the institute in 1962 and a full complement was selected for an academic year at Harvard, Princeton, Virginia, Chicago, or Stanford. The participants were encouraged to select an academic program that would broaden their background with study in disciplines related to their own. A portion of the time was reserved for a core seminar on major public policy issues among the awardees themselves and for individual research. The program was subjected to frequent evaluation that led to changes in the line-up of the universities and in the conduct of the selection and preparation process prior to the experience. In planning for this university sojourn, the participants were encouraged to look upon this segment of their career as a time of stimulation in the development of new ideas. Not every participant gained the full range of benefits contemplated in the program. Not every agency assigned the returning awardee to work that took advantage of his added educational strength, but more of them became conscious of the professional assets among these younger professionals.

The consensus about the program's possibilities were expressed in these terms:

1. At the university they were exposed to new knowledge. It was new to them, whether or not it was in a larger sense old or new: new knowledge produced through research or through the development and application of ideas to ways of doing things; knowledge about new technology; facts about the world in which they lived, which, meeting other facts of which they were already aware, would produce new understandings about the nature of the world in which they must make official decisions.
2. They undoubtedly experienced a personal re-examination of values, including those relating to the bureau in which they served. They were inevitably challenged to question what they had been doing and what the government was doing in this reassessment.
3. They were exposed to disciplines and methods of thought requiring the application of economic or mathematical analysis to problems and circumstances previously treated as verbal abstractions.
4. They were obliged to face the discomforting experience of examining contradictory observations, theories, or phenomena in an abrasive collision between social science disciplines, from which they may have been sheltered in the isolation in federal programs.
5. They admittedly faced tensions and new environment, new relationships, and new ways of measuring personal success and failure. They encountered problems of adjustment to intellectual pursuit of vigor and responsibility.
6. There was the opportunity to stimulate the idea-creating processes through analogies drawn from the arts and sciences and the humanities. The exposure to music, art, literature, and philosophy offered new analogies for their examination of their own present and future in the cultural setting they had selected for a career.

At the end of five years of this program, it was possible for the National Institute to withdraw its participation and for the Ford Foundation to terminate its funding because the government was sufficiently convinced of its value and committed to its continuance to take it over and sustain it under its own auspices as one of the career-development options.

But the use of the authorities in the Training Act tended to be uneven —extensive in some ways, very limited in others. Interagency training was widely used, growing in variety and enrollment with each passing year. It had many obvious advantages, including lower cost, better quality, and reduction in duplication of training effort. A total of 65,000 federal employees participated in the courses offered on an interagency basis in 1966, of whom nearly a third enrolled in courses conducted by the Civil Service Commission. Courses were conducted not only in Washington but also by expanding training units located in the commission's ten regional offices, which had assumed training leadership as a major responsibility in the federal community everywhere. But even with the encouragement of the act and the success of such pilot operations as the Career Education Award program, there was relatively limited use of the authority for training in nonfederal facilities and institutions. As late as 1966, 71 percent of the federal employees who received outside training for periods in excess of 120 days were in science and engineering.

In recognition of this condition, President Johnson in a speech at Princeton on May 11, 1966, gave public service training a new impetus: "The public servant today moves along paths of adventure where he is helpless without the tools of advanced learning.

"He seeks to chart the explorations of space, combining a thousand disciplines. . . .

"He has embarked on this planet on missions no less filled with risk and no less dependent on knowledge.

"He seeks to rebuild our cities and to reclaim the beauty of our countryside. He seeks to promote justice beyond our courtrooms, making education and health and opportunity the common birthright of every citizen. And he seeks to build peace based on man's hopes rather than his fears. These goals will be the work of many men and of many years."

The President went on to announce the creation of a task force to survey federal programs for career advancement and to "study an ex-

panded program of graduate training which, with the help of the universities, can enlarge our efforts to develop the talents and broaden the
horizons of our career officers."

At his specific request, the task force was formed of government,
university, and industry representatives under the guidance of the chairman of the Civil Service Commission to address its efforts to a critical
review of postentry training and educational programs for federal employees in professional, administrative, and technical occupations. It was
given the responsibility for recommending action that would make the
maximum use of the best methods for individual learning and for personal renewal in a time of continuing change. Its study included a review
of training and development activities not only in government but in
industry and universities as well. It found that federal agencies had much
to be commended in their training of employees but that much improvement was still needed. It also found, not surprisingly, that in this huge
complex of diversified, decentralized organizations called the federal
government, there were vast differences in the amount, kind, and quality
of training, ranging from exemplary to virtually nonexistent. While
recognizing that much variety in training programs was necessary in
order to serve the needs of widely varying agency missions, the task force
concluded that there should be a new government-wide policy on training, clearly stated by the President and applying to all agencies.

The task force at the outset asked the basic question: Why train? The
answers given at that time are relevant to the design of future training
efforts. The Government Employees Training Act of 1958 places the
basic responsibility for an employee's own development on the initiative
of the employee himself and makes all other training supplemental to
those efforts. If the employee wants to learn, and to advance, opportunity
should be at hand to help him; management has an obligation to create
a work environment that fosters such motivation. Once motivated to
seek them out, he should then receive guidance from management.
Where management adds to the motivation to learn, develops training
programs, provides texts and other materials, and answers questions as
they arise, the learning time is greatly reduced. Training accelerates
learning. At the same time, it lets employees share management's view-

point on the work at hand, what should be done and where and when and how, to make training most productive. Such insight into management thinking helps prepare specialists who may eventually advance to management responsibility.

The task force discovered that agencies train for a variety of purposes. They may train to attract better-quality recruits and to prepare employees for more responsible work. They may train to foster employee understanding of agency goals, to promote the best use of the employee's abilities, and to develop new skills and knowledge. They may train to improve the quality of the work done or the quality of supervision and managerial effectiveness. They may train to cultivate excellence. They may train to instruct in new methods, procedures, and technology. While all of these constitute good reasons for investing in training, some are more significant than others. The final purpose, that of instructing in new methods, procedures, and technology, has a particularly dramatic current impact and can be applied to employees in virtually all occupations and grade levels. This age of constant and conspicuous changes places special demands on employees to keep up with it. Professional and technical employees, and the executives who must bring knowledgeable administration to their fields, are affected daily by change. Indeed, they themselves are responsible for continuously creating it. The threat of obsolescence in knowledge without advanced education is supported by these facts presented by the National Commission on Technology, Automation and Economic Progress:

- Half of what an engineer has learned today will be obsolete in ten years.
- Half of what he will need to know ten years from now is not available to him today.
- Eighty percent of modern medical practice was discovered in the last twenty years.
- Knowledge is now accumulating at such a rapid rate that it will double in the next fifteen years.

Obviously, management-sponsored training for employees involved with this change must be thoroughly planned and precisely carried out. Haphazard support for professional, administrative, and technical learning can only be wasteful of valuable time and invaluable skill.

The task force found a need within federal agencies to distinguish more clearly between education and training that should be government-conducted and that which should be obtained in universities. There was support for the general policy that federal facilities should be used whenever adequate and economical, but there was a need for further definition. Government is best suited to provide specialized training dealing with specific government programs, in techniques closely related to work performance, and in frontier areas such as space technology, where a federal agency is the prime source of advanced knowledge. Universities can meet the training requirement more effectively where knowledge is sought in academic disciplines, where there is preparation for a professional career, where broad learning about society as a whole is desired, and where horizon-expanding courses can be offered to selected career officers.

Except in very special cases, employees should obtain undergraduate education at their own expense. The task force deemed it essential for all government-supported training and education to further agency missions and management needs. For the nation as a whole, the demand for graduates with bachelor's degrees in the natural sciences, social sciences, humanities, and related professions will increase by 68 percent in the ten-year period ending in 1976. Moreover, the number of master's degrees will rise to 83 percent and doctorates 94 percent in that same period. These demands measure the heavy burden under which the universities must function without any supplementary demands from public service for advanced education of its professional personnel. But government and industry have a common need: to update professional, administrative, and technical personnel during their working lives. Unfortunately, most university courses as now offered are directed to inexperienced persons. If the universities are to serve in this vital capacity, they must continue to create new types of academic programs for the mature.

If the Act of 1958 marked the birth of modern employee training in the government, that training came of age when President Johnson declared on April 20, 1967:

"Today I have signed an Executive Order which will strengthen the most important resource of the federal government—the federal employee—through improved training and educational opportunities.

"In America we are fortunate to have the finest civil service in the world. It is well trained, experienced, and dedicated. Its skills are unsurpassed. But there is room for improvement.

"The tasks facing the government employee are increasing in complexity each day. He is challenged by the problems of outer space and urban blight, of national security and crime in the streets, of economic development abroad and manpower shortages at home. To each task, he must bring the best advanced technology can provide. . . .

"But to fulfill his responsibilities as a public servant he must be equipped to respond quickly and effectively to new demands and new conditions. His skills must be continually upgraded. He must be able to adopt and use the most advanced techniques and equipment available."

The Executive Order, supported by the findings of the task force, begins with this clear statement: "It is the policy of the government of the United States to develop its employees through the establishment and operation of progressive and efficient training programs, thereby improving public service, increasing efficiency and economy, building and retaining a force of skilled and efficient employees, and installing and using the best modern practices and techniques in the conduct of the government's business."

It directs the Civil Service Commission to expand its central staff services in training to promote the development of new programs, to assist departments and agencies in improving existing programs, to encourage more appropriate use of nongovernment training resources, and to develop a training-information system to provide data essential to sound planning and evaluation. Under this mandate the commission created for the first time a Bureau of Training with adequate staff resources to give government-wide leadership in the training field.

Under the terms of the order, each agency head is expected to create a work environment in which employee self-development is encouraged by opening up opportunities for training where the employee is stationed and by giving special recognition to improvement in performance resulting from such training.

The order recognizes the essential alpha and omega of all training programs: the initial systematic determination of training requirements and the subsequent critical evaluation of training results. Agency heads are instructed to provide for periodic reviews of training needs as related to program objectives and for evaluation of training results in terms of the same objectives. In addition, as a part of inherent management responsibility for training, the agency manager is advised to budget the use of funds and man-hours in accordance with training priorities. There is no longer any justification for hiding or mislabeling the funds for this administrative purpose.

In that same statement of April 20, 1967, the President directed the Civil Service Commission to establish a Center for Advanced Study for executives in the highest grades of the civil service. He proposed that the center should call upon leaders in the academic community and other fields to assist in providing top executives and professionals with the highest quality of training and with primary focus on three vital areas:

- The major problems facing American society and the nature of the government's response to them.
- The adequacy of the existing structure of government in relation to today's problems.
- The ways in which the administration of federal programs could be improved.

The creation of this new governmental institution, to be named the Federal Executive Institute, was the culmination of many years of study and debate concerning the character of such a training facility for those at the very top of the career service, the capstone of the government's executive development structure. Several years earlier the Civil Service Commission had successfully founded two Executive Seminar Centers at Kings Point, New York, and Berkeley, California, for residential training experiences for administrators in mid-career, specifically for the tier just below the top. Through the two-week seminar sessions of these centers had passed hundreds of career officials who in the course of their advancement had received little if any training exposure on the broader issues and environment that related to their work. The new institution, with a longer residential period and with a diversified staff of university and government professionals, would complete the executive training structure of the federal government.

The Federal Executive Institute opened its doors to the first group of participating executives in the fall of 1968. A site had been selected in Charlottesville, Virginia, adjoining the campus of the University of Virginia and a two-hour drive from the nation's capital. A staff had been recruited from government and academia by the institute's new director, Frank Sherwood, former dean of the School of Public Administration at the University of Southern California. A unique curriculum of seminars, lectures, project groups, and individual work had been organized to afford a special learning and renewal experience for these officials. The institute was dedicated to executive preparation for continuing change with these words of challenge from the Chairman of the Civil Service Commission:

"The mission of this new Institute is to stimulate these managers of change to new heights of public performance and personal achievement. It is intended to provide a new and continuously innovative experience in advanced learning for the government's leadership potential. It is a thoughtful refuge from the tyranny of daily operations, a congenial place for penetrating thought, provocative conversation and broader program vistas. It is a center for the exploration of the forces of change and for the trial formulation of strategies for the mastery of change. It is a hilltop from which the total public landscape can be observed in all its motion and contrast, its problems and its promise.

"This is a mission worthy of the Jeffersonian tradition and the challenge of tomorrow's world. May what we start here today match the tradition and challenges in both 'the promotion of the general welfare' and 'the improvement of the quality of American life.' "

It is still too early to assess the contribution of this new institution to the stature and performance of career leaders. It has successfully survived the transition from one administration to another. This was clearly evidenced when President Nixon received all members of the third residential class, key Civil Service Commission officials, and the institute's staff in the White House Rose Garden in April 1969. Whether it will fulfill the lofty goals set for it upon its dedication can be measured only in the decision-making and the performance of the senior executives in the federal government.

Intergovernmental
Cooperation
in Public Service
Development

14

Whether it be called "the new federalism" or "creative federalism," the essential interrelationship at the several levels of government in the United States must be not only recognized but strengthened to a substantial degree if contemporary problems of government are to approach solution. The commonality of purpose on the part of federal, state, county, and local public servants has been all too clearly demonstrated in administering programs for housing and welfare, law enforcement and education, and civil defense and public health. Outpourings of assistance from the federal government in new programs and new funds will be meaningless unless the intended service reaches the people for whom those programs and funds are meant. That goal can be achieved only by those who work for local government. Grants-in-aid are not enough. There must be "grants-in-people"—federal assistance in staffing with skill and talent the public services at the state and local levels that directly serve the people. Such grants are a vital ingredient in creating a more effective partnership at all levels of American government.

In his State of the Union message in 1967, President Johnson pointed out that in the three preceding years about $40 billion had been returned to state and local government in federal aid. In 1967 alone, 70 percent of all federal expenditures for domestic social programs would be distributed by state and local government. Some 170 separate federal aid programs, representing more than $17 billion, are being administered by about 25 federal departments and agencies. Some of these programs overlap but 50 different programs can be identified for aid to general education, 57 programs for vocational and job training, 35 for housing, more than 10 involved in transportation, 27 for utilities and services, 62 for community facilities, 32 for land use, and 28 for cultural and recreational facilities.

Obviously, the long lines of administration from Washington to the statehouse and the city hall must be cleared and strengthened to assure maximum program effectiveness. These lines should not become political bonds to force dependence by states and municipalities upon the national government. The financial contribution is a response to the staggering burden under which these jurisdictions presently labor. Unless the professional and administrative personnel are hired, motivated, and trained, this burden will crush the very institutions and people they were created to serve. By a conservative estimate, state and local governments will require an estimated average increase of 290,000 administrative, professional, and technical personnel each year for the foreseeable future. These governments are ill equipped to compete in the contemporary labor market to overcome this deficit and improve the capacity of the staffs already on their payrolls. A recent report of the Committee on Economic Development noted: "Positions in states and cities requiring knowledge of modern technology are frequently occupied by unqualified personnel. Except in large cities, most department heads are amateurs. The spoils system still prevails in many parts of the nation and has deep roots in many local governments. Pay scales are usually too low to attract competent professional applicants."

Starting in 1967, the responsibility of the federal government to provide grants-in-people was increasingly recognized as a corollary to new programs and funds growing from federal legislative action to solve critical national problems. Without infringing in any way on state and local jurisdictions, the federal government can contribute much to improve the supply and development of quality personnel at local government levels. Federal assistance in personnel and manpower can be extended without relieving state and local government of any of their responsibilities but rather strengthening them so that they can play their full role in the complex social and economic programs. This assistance can be offered in three main areas.

The first area is the training and developing of state and local government employees. Federal agencies could arrange to admit them to regular federal employee-training programs. Such commingling of government personnel from different jurisdictions could be mutually beneficial and strengthen the total training experience. Federal agencies might administer grant-in-aid programs to provide special training courses for state and local employees principally engaged in these programs, or make training grants from funds available for training purposes. Certain grant-in-aid programs already have training components, but these are not uniform and they frequently overlook such essential areas as program administration. The federal government could authorize grants to state and local governments for training and educating their employees in their own organizations, thus augmenting the financing of in-service training already undertaken or contemplated by states and municipalities. To take advantage of available university graduate study, the federal government could fund fellowships for state and local personnel, perhaps as a counterpart program to the Career Education Awards in the federal government with many of the same university resources used by both programs.

The second area is strengthening state and local personnel administration. In this area the approach of the federal government might well include any or all of the following:

1. The establishment of merit standards of personnel administration for programs financed in whole or in part from federal funds. Here again, some grant-in-aid programs already require the development of merit service standards to become eligible for federal funds. But civil service systems with broader coverage and with no vestiges of the spoils system would decidedly enhance the reputation of state and local government and presumably would attract larger numbers of well-qualified candidates.
2. Authorization of grants to state and local governments for

strengthening their staffs in methods of personnel administration. In many states and cities, both the personnel staff and the methods they employ do not match the needs of the programs they administer. Federal assistance would be entirely justifiable in expanding the capacity of personnel organizations to meet the new demands for program staffing.

3. Cooperative recruiting and examining activities with state and local governments by the federal Civil Service Commission, to save expense and to share the competitors attracted by this combined operation.

4. Technical advice and assistance in personnel management from the federal Civil Service Commission, on request by state and local governments. This type of advisory support might profitably be contributed in such areas as labor-management relations, wage and salary determination, research in tests and measurements, and the design and administration of in-service training programs.

The third area might deal with the mobility of federal, state, and local employees between jurisdictions. Here the intent would be to encourage assignment for periods up to several years, to state and local governments of federal employees equipped with the skills and experience needed by those governments while protecting their job rights and benefits at their federal home base. Similarly, the movement of state and local employees to temporary assignments in federal agencies would be facilitated. The long-term functioning of this type of interchange would permit the design of intergovernmental careers in a number of program areas where combined federal-state or federal-local operations are essential for successful administration. Two very tangible benefits can result from such mobility: the broadening of the employee's capacity by exposing him to new challenges and alternative ways of solving familiar problems, and the ability to call on an expert from some other level to perform an urgently needed task. The federal government would benefit greatly from the firsthand, practical experience of state and city administrators and technical experts in the formulation of national policy and in the development of administrative standards.

These proposals for intergovernmental training and personnel activities were embodied in two legislative proposals and submitted to the Congress in the spring of 1967. The first proposal, entitled the Education for Public Service Act of 1967, was designed to increase the number of qualified students choosing careers in government by providing fellowships to students who wanted to embark on the adventure of government service and by providing support to universities seeking to enrich and strengthen their public service education programs. This bill ran the legislative course of the Congress and was enacted into law in late 1968. Responsibility for administration of the statute was assigned to the Office of Education, where through lack of adequate funding no significant implementation has been possible. There has, however, been an opening up of federal training programs to state and local employees. Combined training experiences of this type have been particularly useful in courses covering financial management, computer technology, personnel management, and the executive seminar programs.

The rest of the suggested provisions were incorporated in the proposed Intergovernmental Manpower Act of 1967. This bill has passed the Senate twice, in 1967 and 1969, only to languish in the House Education and Labor Committee. The bill's provisions were modified in the Senate, some of whose members had reservations about imposing a merit system on state and local governments by federal authority. These reservations were based less on a desire to perpetuate existing practice than on doubts about the capability of merit-system administration to meet the operating needs of state and local agencies. There was an understandable apprehension that federal money would result in federal dictation in administering public personnel programs. The advocates of the bill endeavored to provide reassurance through flexible systems adapted to meet program needs and employing the most modern methods within the framework of equal opportunity and competition on the basis of appropriate qualifications. There was an effort to overcome the impression that civil service would undermine the executive authority and discretion of the governor or the mayor, in that personnel assistance would be extended to the chief executive officer and not to an independent personnel agency or to individual program agencies receiving federal aid.

There was debate over the size of the state or local contribution to any matching program for personnel assistance and the relationship between state and municipal governments in the provision of grants for the cities. To accommodate both points of view, a compromise process was evolved along these lines:

1. The state government would, if it desired, have the option of presenting a coordinated state-wide plan covering its own employees and those of its local governments, in order to encourage state-wide planning and coordination rather than fragmentation city by city.
2. On the other hand, no state government could exercise a "pocket veto" on city plans for training or personnel improvements, merely by failure of the state to present a suitable plan. In some instances, especially in the larger cities, the state and the city concerned might prefer that the city submit a plan directly to the federal government.
3. If within one year a state government did not obtain approval of a plan that included participation of local government, any city of 100,000 population or more could submit a direct proposal. The waiting period would be waived if within a specified time, say ninety days after enactment, a state indicated that it did not intend to submit a plan.
4. Cities of 50,000 or more could apply for grants in special circumstances resulting, for example, from their location in an area of rapid urbanization, in a metropolitan area, or in a transportation corridor.

No opposition was offered to the proposal for the temporary assignment of personnel between the federal government and state and local governments. But if and when this authority is granted by law, it will require an unprecedented degree of collaboration among governmental jurisdictions in order to install a meaningful plan. There are natural hesitations about this form of cooperation. State and city managers are reluctant to allow their best people to lead the seductive federal life for any extended period of time, fearing that they will never return. Except for a few of the larger states and cities, the federal government offers better salaries, fringe benefits, and working conditions, and it enjoys a more favorable employment status among the general public. Also, the rising career professional within the federal government has little incentive to interrupt his climb with a lateral move to a state or city. Still, career-development plans must be constructed to offer incentives for such diversity of experience. For example, some federal-state programs might require that certain high-ranking berths would be open only to those who had gained firsthand state experience. Since these interchange assignments would be temporary, the usual obstructions to mobility would be overcome. There would be no need to meet the civil service qualifications of the receiving governmental level, nor would there be a loss of vesting time in the retirement system in which the individual was accruing benefits. Under some personnel systems there might be a loss of seniority, but a genuine desire to have a plan of mobility function effectively could effect the necessary modifications. At some future date a cooperative plan for transfer of retirement credits should be worked out so that no pension plan would become a block to long-term mobility, because if the temporary-assignment process is at all successful it should include career planning involving extended tours of municipal, state, and federal service.

A bill containing these compromise measures cleared the Congress late in 1970 to give these modes of intergovernmental collaboration the force of law.

New legislation and new executive direction are not prerequisites to more effective intergovernmental performance. Additional steps can be taken to interrelate federal, state, and municipal services available to the individual citizen. Today even the most sophisticated political scientist faces serious difficulty in finding the appropriate level of government and the responsible governmental agency to which he should go to conduct his business with government. Changing agency titles, confusing acronyms identifying programs, and multiple locations for related services combine to make government at the citizen's level a perpetual puzzle. If the services are intended for disadvantaged citizens with limited education and from an isolated environment, these difficulties in

dealing with his government are almost insurmountable. Some preliminary and limited steps have been directed toward simplified and rational
approaches to the public. In a number of large cities the federal government has established a single federal information center from which the
citizen can obtain immediate answers to the more common questions and
reliable referral to federal offices where more complex and specialized
answers can be delivered. These centers also explain that certain desired
information can be secured only from state or local offices, whose address
or phone number they furnish. The value of this obvious form of service
has been demonstrated so fully that necessary funding to establish centers in every major city should be forthcoming as soon as possible. It is
all too easy for those regularly engaged in government operations to
forget their accountability to each and every citizen.

With the rapid expansion of federal services to the cities, it became
increasingly apparent that the federal government was not organized so
as to achieve lateral coordination of related programs in dealing with the
cities they were endeavoring to assist. Each department or agency had
a different regional and field structure, different delegations of authority
to field managers, different administrative processes through which
grants must pass, different reporting and accounting procedures, and
little in common with each other except the basic mission of improving
the quality of life in American cities. To overcome these differences to
the greatest degree possible, committees on critical urban problems were
formed in each of the Federal Executive Boards, the presidentially designated assembly of key officials in each of fifteen major cities, to attempt
a more uniform approach to the cities within their combined responsibility. It was soon discovered that these committees could achieve little
without greater coordination of planning and operations in Washington.
As a result, officials of Under Secretary status in each of the agencies
involved met regularly to formulate more common standards of administration. Early in 1969 these sessions led to a realignment of the principal
departments into common geographical areas for regional administration and to substantially simplified and expedited procedures for handling municipal grants. President Nixon's creation in 1970 of a Domestic
Council with a policy staff and the reconstitution of the Bureau of the

Budget as an Office of Management and Budget should contribute new and more forceful leadership in the formulation and coordination of federal programs that have direct relationships with the states and cities. It is a matter of highest urgency to rationalize these points of connection between levels of government engaged in the same program functions.

The ultimate in intergovernmental collaboration at the local level has occurred in the one-stop state service centers, where federal, state, county, municipal, and private agencies have set up shop under a single roof. The prototype for this type of center has been constructed in East Los Angeles to serve a population of 228,000. Of these, 39 percent are 25 years of age or older and have less than an eighth-grade education. Some 23 percent of the families earn less than $4,000 a year. The Spanish-surnamed population has increased during recent years from two-thirds to three-fourths, while the black population has declined to about 2.1 percent. Many of the newcomers have flooded into this section of Los Angeles as refugees from agricultural employment now supplanted by mechanization in the rich central valleys of California. Many are unable to speak the language of the city or to learn its ways. Government is a remote complex of public buildings in downtown Los Angeles, a long journey into a strange world where everything is costly and complicated. Many of those who have the courage to make the trip tell horror stories of visits to one impersonal office after another in a vain attempt to receive the help desired. The East Los Angeles state service center has brought these people to a one-door, one-roof government. Sympathetic men and women who speak their language welcome them at the reception desk and try to lower the barriers of suspicion. The services covered under that one roof involve welfare and health, employment and child service, Social Security and immigration counsel, drug treatment and consumer advice. It is truly a kind of neighborhood government where the lines of separation between governments and units of government are obliterated in the interest of solving the problems of the citizen who is dependent upon government. The center has brought government into a community where it has been suspect and has demonstrated its desire to help those for whom life has become even more of a burden to themselves than to the taxpayers. Similar responsiveness could be created in thousands of communities without more legislation, without more funds, and with the public servant performing his mission with compassion and efficiency in a face-to-face relationship with the citizen.

Pay

Isn't

15   Everything

A cynic once commented, "Pay isn't everything, but I don't even know what's in second place." Although public officials and the employees who work for them would probably put the principle of service in second place, their dedication to the public interest does not dampen their ardor for adequate pay and fringe benefits. In recent years the pay issue has dominated discussions of public personnel policy. It has contributed to the increased momentum of public employee unions. It has occupied more and more of the time of public administrators and legislators. Many other issues of personnel policy are directly or indirectly linked to this fundamental theme of adequate employee compensation.

The traditional mythology about the public service propounds the thesis that public employees should be satisfied with wages or salaries lower than those prevailing in similar occupations in the private sector. The conventional belief has been that service to the public carries an intangible form of psychic income in the opportunity to serve the public and avoid the competitive atmosphere of private enterprise. Employment security in the form of tenure has been assigned a value which presumably offsets higher dollar compensation elsewhere. Idealism has been equated with modest income. For years, teachers and policemen, government clerks and tax collectors, were viewed as necessary public servants who performed their tasks after swearing a vow of poverty. In some circles the view was offered that competitive salaries might make a government too strong and too efficient, or that there were always opportunities for public servants to acquire income on the side.

The revolt against this mythology is at the root of increased militancy by public employees at all levels and in all occupations. This revolt is occurring at the very time when rational and more competitive pay systems are being installed by more and more governmental bodies as a result of determined executive and legislative action aimed at improvement. But such improvements, rather than producing an atmosphere of satisfaction, have engendered hopes for even better conditions.Through collective bargaining or legislative lobbying, the increased involvement of employees and their representatives in the determination of compensation rates has contributed to the present state of ferment.

A brief review of recent federal compensation reform will demonstrate not only the progress that has been made but also the necessity for further improvement if government is to attract and retain the necessary capabilities from the national labor market.

In the twenty-fourth annual report of the Civil Service Commission presented to President Woodrow Wilson in 1917, the following depressing note was sounded:

"The increase in the number of employees, due to the war, has been accompanied by an increase in disparity in salaries paid for the same kind of work. Very much of the Commission's work goes for nought by reason of the large number of declinations of appointment because the salaries offered are insufficient. . . . This is a matter which Congress alone can remedy, as appropriation acts usually prescribe the salaries to be paid and the classification of salaries remains unchanged since 1853. . . ."

No change in basic salaries for federal employees in sixty-four years! No wonder that their World War I recruitment was not satisfying prevailing needs. Even so, the federal government was not prompt to act. It was 1923 before the federal Classification Act became law and federal employees in the white-collar occupations had a solid framework for the pay they received. This fundamental statute was to pay administration what the Budget and Accounting Act of 1921 was to financial management in the federal government. It is historically ironic that these two fundamental reforms, long overdue during the periods of more liberal leadership in the presidency, were enacted during the discredited administration of Warren G. Harding.

The Classification Act was formed on the basic principle that a position structure based on job evaluation should serve as the pay framework for most federal positions. It established the rank-in-position doctrine as a principle to ensure that equal pay was provided for equal work no matter where the tasks were performed. It necessitated position descriptions that would spell out duties and responsibilities. These descriptions could be matched against written job standards that would place the position in a particular occupational classification and at a particular grade level in a fifteen-grade scale. Each grade had a number of steps to permit merit and seniority advancement in pay without a fundamental change in job content. It defined in statutory language various levels of difficulty or magnitudes of responsibility for each of the fifteen levels. The pay schedule was then constructed on the basis of the grade levels and the steps within each grade, with a pay differential between grades to provide a progression from the lowest to the highest rate. Although the position classification structure was to remain stable, the rates of pay assigned to that structure could be altered from time to time by statutory action.

From 1923 to 1945 the initial salary schedule in the Classification Act changed little except during 1933 to 1935, when the Economy Act reduced all rates by 15 percent and it took more than two years to have rates restored to the June 1932 level. In the climate of today's government, resort to this form of governmental economy is utterly incomprehensible, just as other aspects of the great depression have assumed an aura of unbelievable fantasy. The durable pay scale of this twenty-two-year period started at $1,080 per annum for the lowliest messenger and ascended to a munificent $8,000 for the top career executives and professionals in the service.

A totally different sequence of pay actions marked the post-World War II period. In 1945, even before the conclusion of hostilities, a bill was passed that provided a 15.9 percent average increase. This action blew the lid off wartime salary controls and provided the first step in the

long march toward federal salaries comparable to those in the private
sector. The following year, Congress authorized an additional 14.2 percent increase, much of which was negated in the inflationary price rise
of that time. These increases, however, placed a $10,000 ceiling on the
maximum salary. The same limitation was maintained when a flat $330
increase was authorized in 1948. Then in 1949, Congress enacted the first
major revision in the Classification Act, authorizing structural improvements in the classification system and extending the top of the scale
through the addition of three grades in a consolidated general schedule.
This measure produced a new maximum salary of $14,000 a year that
applied to only twenty-five positions, thus introducing into the federal
jargon the term "supergrades" as an identification for grades GS-16,
GS-17, and GS-18. In the process of revision, the pay scale received
another upward push averaging $140 per year.

Between 1950 and 1960, salaries were increased four times. In 1951
the increase was by 10 percent, with a minimum of $300 and a maximum
of $800, the average working out to $358 a year; this adjustment raised
the minimum rate at grade GS-1 to $2,500 and the maximum at grade
GS-18 to $14,800. In 1955 there was an across-the-board increase of 7.5
percent, with the maximum remaining static. Then, in the congressional
election year 1958, another across-the-board increase, this time for 10
percent, was authorized. In 1960, a presidential election year, an increase
of 7.5 percent, ranging from $225 to $1,235, was passed over President
Eisenhower's veto. This raised the span to from $3,185 to $18,500.

Although these increases had served to place the federal government
in a more effective competitive position, there was a growing dissatisfaction with the entire process of salary setting. Except for the increase in
1955, each salary bill had been primarily the product of collaboration
between the employee unions and the congressional committees, with
virtually no guidance from the Executive Branch other than resistance
to the amount and rationale in each increase action. The preference for
across-the-board percentage increases with a maximum ceiling and with
a minimum advance in the lower grades had produced a condition of
serious compression between the lower and the upper grades and inadequate pay differentials between various levels of responsibility. No crite-

ria had been developed by which the amount of increase could be justified. In some years the argument for the increase was based upon the upward spiral of the Consumer Price Index. In periods when that measure was reasonably stable, the brief was grounded upon the need for an improved standard of living. References to competitive rates in the labor market tended to be selective in order to demonstrate dramatic contrasts between federal and private salaries. Throughout that decade and many years before, the postal pay schedule had been adjusted separately with proportionately higher results for postal employees in the clerk and carrier jobs. The substantial political weight of the postal unions resulted in the congressional committees' giving first attention to the postal schedule, with the adjustments in the Classification Act schedule coming later. The process of salary setting was basically political. The amount authorized by Congress was the most the traffic could bear and tended more and more to be enacted during an election year.

All these conditions generated increasing discontent in the Executive Branch, where the impact of the salary increases constituted an abrogation of executive leadership and produced budget pressures, salary inequities, and a failure to meet salary competition in the middle and upper grades. This discontent rose to the level of Cabinet discussion in 1957, when a thoroughgoing study of civilian compensation was assigned to an interdepartmental committee under the chairmanship of Rocco Siciliano, President Eisenhower's Special Assistant for Personnel Policy. That study group endeavored to formulate an action program to improve pay fixing for civilian employees and to establish a sound relationship among the various pay systems. At that time, the 2,275,000 federal employees were compensated under sixteen major statutory pay systems, with the Classification Act covering 950,000, the Postal Field Service 440,000, the Foreign Service 12,400, the Veterans Administration and Medical Service 20,000, the Atomic Energy Commission personnel 6,500, and the Tennessee Valley Authority personnel 6,400. The remaining 770,000 were covered by sixty-one different wage-board pay systems for blue-collar workers that will be outlined later.

The study committee found serious deficiencies in all salary systems, with these general conclusions:

- Salaries fixed by statute had not been adjusted in a timely and adequate manner in response to general changes in nonfederal salary levels.
- In general, federal statutory salary rates were below nonfederal salary rates for comparable positions.
- Statutory salary increases had lagged far behind adjustments for blue-collar employees compensated in terms of local prevailing rates.
- Statutory salary pay systems did not provide adequate rate ranges for all grades, a large enough money differential between grades, or appropriate recognition of individual merit performance.

Also, there was inadequate coordination among federal pay systems, resulting in unequal pay for like work in the same localities.

To correct these inadequacies, the committee proposed an overhaul of the basic Classification Act structure to permit meaningful pay *differences* between pay rates of successive grades, a proper number of grades, adequate and uniform rate ranges in each grade, and within-grade advancements on merit as well as service. But the recommendation on pay *determination* was the most significant change proposed, forecasting the pay actions of the 1960s. Pay determination was based on nationwide schedules, adjusted periodically on the basis of nonfederal rates and with comparability assured through the use of benchmark positions. These proposals could not be activated in the time remaining to the Eisenhower administration but funds were allocated for the extension of the Bureau of Labor Statistics' salary studies to encompass the collection of data on salaries paid in eighty metropolitan areas by private employers for certain benchmark jobs that had federal counterparts. The findings from that survey were made available to the new administration in 1961 and formed the centerpiece of the Kennedy plan for salary reform in the following year.

The Federal Salary Reform Act of 1962, signed by President Kennedy on October 11 of that year before a large assemblage of congressional leaders, union officers, and executive appointees in his office, set for the first time a definite policy for determining and adjusting federal salaries. It incorporated in a single statute the pay schedules under the Classification Act and the Postal and Foreign Service pay statutes and for the medical personnel in the Veterans Administration. It delineated a policy based on two principles: alignment and comparability. The alignment principle provides that there shall be equal pay for substantially equal work, with pay distinctions maintained in keeping with work and performance distinctions, while the comparability principle mandates that federal salary rates be comparable with private enterprise salary rates for the same levels of work.

Although the alignment principle had long been the governing standard under the Classification Act, compression of the salary schedule over the years had effectively nullified the policy of pay differences in proportion to differences in levels of work and individual contributions. The comparability principle was totally new to the statutory salary systems. Together with a plan for annual salary review, it established a continuing competitive relationship with salaries paid in the private sector for similar jobs. It assured equitable salaries for federal employees, consistent with general salary levels in the national economy on a basis that was fair to the taxpayer and provided an objective yardstick for future adjustments. The procedure for regular salary reviews introduced a regular rational adjustment device. Each year the Bureau of Labor Statistics would survey salaries in business firms. The Bureau of the Budget and the Civil Service Commission would prepare a report comparing federal salaries with BLS findings in private enterprise, whereupon the President, after seeking the views of employee organizations, would recommend to Congress any changes in salary schedules or policies that he believed desirable.

The extension of the two principles of comparability and alignment to all four statutory salary systems supplied for the first time a means of coordinating salary levels among them. The Classification Act's comparability salary schedule was produced directly from the BLS findings on salaries paid by private employers. The salary schedule of each other system was tied to the Classification Act schedule at a few key grade levels. For example, the key Level 4 in the Post Office system, which included all of the clerks and carriers, was linked to Classification Act Grade GS-5; and to complete the linkage at higher points, Classification Act Grade GS-11 was equated with Postal Grade 11 and Classification Act Grade GS-15 with Postal Grade 20. Thus, future adjustments could be readily made in other schedules whenever the Classification Act was adjusted.

Most importantly, the statute recognized the responsibility of the President for salary administration as a part of the general management of the Executive Branch. From that time on, the President was obligated to initiate the salary-adjustment processes through his recommendations to Congress on changes necessary to preserve comparability between federal and private rates.

Needed improvements in the pay structure along the line of those recommended by the interdepartmental committee in 1957 were incorporated in the statute. So that the government could compete for well-qualified personnel under all circumstances, the President was authorized to set special rates when exceptionally high private salaries for a particular occupation or at a particular location handicapped the government's recruitment. The Classification Act system was strengthened through the establishment of percentage intervals between salaries at successive grades on a regularized basis, with more uniform salary ranges within grades, thus permitting more meaningful within-grade increases. As an incentive and reward, additional within-grade increases were permitted for top-quality performance. Salary administration was improved by assuring an increase on a grade-to-grade promotion equal to at least two within-grade increases. An increase was authorized in the number of positions in the three "supergrades," and numerical restrictions were removed completely for positions in critically short occupations. The improvements made in the Classification Act structure were also applicable to the other systems, thereby spreading the benefits of uniformity and greater discretion in salary administration.

The first serious test of the statute occurred the following year, when the first action to maintain comparability was undertaken. In a message forwarded to Congress on April 29, 1963, President Kennedy reasserted his commitment to the comparability principle and recommended adjustments in salary schedules in accordance with new levels in private enterprise. In this message the President identified two problems already appearing within the new system. The first problem related to the restriction imposed upon comparability in the higher salaries as long as no action was taken to increase executive and legislative salaries. This ceiling produced congestion and almost total lack of differential among the jobs at the very top of the career scale. In passing the act the previous year, Congress had imposed a $20,000 ceiling on grade GS-18 instead of the $24,500 rate recommended by the President. To secure advice on the appropriate levels for executive and legislative pay, the President designated an advisory panel from outside government chaired by the industrialist Clarence Randall.

The second problem was revealed in the comments provided by the employee unions on the proposed pay adjustment on the basis of the comparability data. The employee representatives had expressed great concern over the time lag between the BLS findings and the enactment of adjustments based on those findings by Congress. The President shared this concern and advised Congress that "the spirit of the comparability principle and natural considerations of equity require that the lapse of time be held to the minimum possible." This particular problem continued to plague the operation of the system and produced contention that threatened the regularity of adjustments.

Because federal salaries lagged so far behind comparable salaries in industry at the time the 1962 act was passed, the statute provided for a three-phased adjustment to bring about equivalent rates. But stretch-out in time accentuated the lag already built into the system. This problem and that of top-level pay frustrated any further pay action in 1963. The Randall panel recommended much higher executive and legislative salaries than even the President and the Congress could accept. The President released its report to Congress as a basis for further study of the sensitive salary question at those highest levels. Congress hesitated to face up to the issue of raising its own salaries, an act which was essential if the comparability and alignment principles were to be applied as the 1962 measure intended. President Johnson called public attention to this delay in acting upon the salary issue shortly after he took office. In a memorandum to heads of departments and agencies on November 30, only eight days after his assumption of presidential authority, he discussed management goals for the Executive Branch and pledged himself to "support salary scales for civil servants, military personnel and policy officials which will enable the executive branch to retain and recruit talented, energetic and imaginative employees." In his first budget message he forcefully reinforced his position with this endorsement:

"Although this budget is deliberately restrictive, I have concluded that government economy could be best served by an upward adjustment in salaries. In the last year and a half the federal government has taken far-reaching steps to improve its pay practices. The Federal Salary Reform Act of 1962 and the Uniformed Services Pay Act of 1963 established the principle of keeping military and civilian pay generally in line with pay in the private economy. This is a sound principle, and it is reinforced by the sound procedure of annual review. This principle is fair to the taxpayer, to government employees and to the government as an employer."

But these statements were unavailing when Congress took up its responsibility and was faced with the awesome political task of raising its own salaries while conforming to the 1962 principles. In an unexpected vote the pay bill was defeated on the floor of the House in March 1964, throwing all pay considerations in disarray. Once again the President assumed the initiative, writing to the Speaker to urge early reconsideration. In strong terms he spelled out the consequences of failure to act. Referring to the broad coverage of necessary pay action, he stated that "failure to act would undercut the principle and promise of comparable pay—federal career pay scales comparable to those in private enterprise —adopted by the Congress just a year and a half ago in the historic Federal Salary Reform Act of 1962." With this expression of executive necessity, congressional wheels began to turn. The House Post Office and Civil Service Committee recast the original bill, the House acted favorably, the Senate committee opened its hearings and passed the reported bill, differences between the two chambers were compromised in the conference committee, and the completed bill was signed by the President on August 14, thereby contributing a second reform statute that reinforced the 1962 edition. This new legislation adjusted schedules so as to set the minimum of grade GS-1 at $3,385 and grade GS-18 at a single rate of $24,500. The other schedules followed the Classification Act through the points of linkage previously established. The unfinished business of 1962 was completed when congressional salaries were raised from $22,500 to $30,000 (no member who voted for the bill suffered thereby at the hands of his constituents in the election that year), a new executive salary bracket of five levels was established with Cabinet officers moving from $25,000 to $35,000, and lesser executives were increased by proportionate amounts and specific executive positions were listed in the statute in accordance with the existing levels.

In succeeding years, annual pay statutes were enacted with the 1962 principles serving as the principal guideline. Each enactment tended to increase salaries at the lower end of the scale by more than the amount indicated by the survey of private rates and to limit those in the upper levels to a point below comparability. The threat of inflation and the constant pressure of budgetary restrictions forced upon the system certain arbitrary limits of increase—3.6 percent in 1965 and 3.2 percent in 1966. The process of achieving these adjustments was never truly simplified. Arguments developed between administration spokesmen and union leaders on the validity of the system by which comparability was measured, and there was no reluctance on the part of these leaders to seek much greater increases through independent negotiations with the congressional committees. The postal unions challenged the basis for the linkage between the Classification Act and the Postal Field Service, and various devices were adopted to increase the postal pay beyond what was justified for the rest of the federal service. It was always tempting for those advising the President on fiscal matters to recommend a delay in the effective date of comparability to defer increased expenditures. The attractiveness of such action was enhanced when legislation on military pay was linked to civilian adjustments on the comparability principle. By 1967, every percentage-point increase in combined civilian and military pay would raise the federal budget by $400 million. Since no upper adjustment was ever less than 3 percent and there was always a need to catch up on the time lag, the average increase was likely to be nearer 5 percent.

The private market reacted in different percentages of increase at different levels and in different occupations. It was exceedingly difficult to transfer these differences to the federal pay scale because they would usually result in lower percentages at low levels and higher percentages at the upper levels where fewer employees were covered. As a result there tended to be across-the-board percentage increases on the basis of the average increase in the private market.

A third significant statute was enacted in 1967, when Congress provided an immediate increase of 4.5 percent for most salaried employees and 6 percent for postal employees and scheduled two additional increases in July 1968 and July 1969 that would completely close the gap between federal salaries and comparable rates on the outside as shown by the 1968 BLS survey. The three-stage increase eliminated the necessity for separate pay legislation in 1968 and 1969 and authorized the President to take action on his own motion to install appropriate schedules for effecting comparability. This was a particularly significant move in that it carried presidential initiative to the point of actual salary determination. It also gave added validity and support to the comparability principle while insisting on more extensive consultation with union representatives in the final development of the comparability schedule.

The Congress adopted in the 1967 act a provision, recommended by the President in 1965, for regular adjustment of controversial executive, legislative, and judicial salaries. It called for the creation of a commission made up of members appointed by the President, the President of the Senate, the Speaker of the House, and the Chief Justice of the United States on a quadrennial basis. The first such commission was to meet in fiscal 1969 to review the basic salaries of the members of Congress, members of the judiciary, and top officials of the Executive Branch. The commission would report to the President, who in his budget message would present his recommendations as drawn from those in the report with the proposed rates taking effect after thirty days if not disapproved by either house of Congress. This process was followed in fiscal 1969, when President Johnson, joined by the Vice President, the Speaker, and the Chief Justice, named a nine-man panel under the chairmanship of Frederick Kappel, a former chairman of AT&T.

That commission made its recommendations to the President, who agreed with them in part but made certain adjustments in accordance with advice from members of Congress. He did adopt the Kappel Commission salaries for the top officials of the three branches, with a rate of $62,500 for the Chief Justice, $60,000 for the Associate Justices of the Supreme Court, and $60,000 for members of the Cabinet. He pointed out that congressional compensation posed the most difficult problem of all. He believed that the $50,000 congressional salary recommended by the commission could be justified, but after consultation with congressional leaders he reduced the figure to $42,500. On the basis of that determination he modified other salaries, linking the second level of executive positions to the congressional salary at $42,500 and following with salaries of $40,000, $38,000, and $36,000 for the succeeding three levels. Since the salaries of the Vice President, the Speaker of the House, the Majority and Minority Leaders of the House and Senate, and the President pro tem of the Senate were not covered by the Kappel Commission charter, he submitted separate recommendations through the legislative route to provide $62,500 for the Vice President and the Speaker, and $55,000 for the Majority and Minority Leaders of the House and Senate and the President pro tem of the Senate. Independently, President Johnson recommended that the salary for the President be increased from $100,000 to $200,00 for his successor, who would be inaugurated a few days later.

The thirty days ran out on February 14, 1969, and all the new rates went into effect. There was some complaint in Congress about the new salary levels, and in subsequent pay controversies over the proper rates for public personnel there were reminders of the percentage of increase enjoyed by top officials. The durability of this process for setting top level salaries will not be ascertained until the time comes around in 1972–73 for the next round of adjustments. By that time executive and congressional attitudes may have so altered that a new process must be designed, or there may be a return to the old hesitancy and uncertainty dominated by political considerations. By any standard of comparability or equity, the 1969 roster of top level salaries is not out of line. The responsibilities exercised by the officials in these positions have virtually no counterpart in the private sector even in big industry, where six-figure salaries are not uncommon. When the Kappel Commission was conducting its review, it discovered that General Motors alone had twenty-three executives receiving salaries in excess of the President of the United States.

With these improved salaries, the President particularly can insist on high quality among his appointees because the salary differences can no longer be serious deterrents to public service. Members of Congress should suffer no embarrassment from the $42,500 salary level even if they come from constituencies where high salaries are rare. A member of Congress faces heavy expenditures in carrying out his obligations. He can no longer spend significant portions of the year at his home base nor can he legitimately pursue other income-producing activities. In fact, the higher level salary should destroy the argument that members are justified in continuing outside pursuits that detract from the time they can devote to their congressional duties or give reason to question the true objectivity of their decision-making on public issues.

In most western democracies, decisions with respect to public service salaries are assigned to the executive, with the legislature exercising control through the appropriations process and periodic review and evaluation. In recent years the American system has been moving in that direction at an accelerated rate. Such a division of responsibility has definite benefits. It would let the President exercise full management responsibility with respect to the employees in the Executive Branch. It would permit the development of objective and measurable standards for the determination of rates. It would substantially reduce the time lag in making adjustment because it would eliminate the most time-consuming step of all, the legislative cycle in Congress. The necessary congressional control can be exercised through action on appropriations, through periodic reporting to substantive committees, and through open hearings at which executive decision-makers could offer and defend the basis for the most recent annual adjustment. Periodically the entire system, including standards and process, could be thoroughly scrutinized by the appropriate congressional committees or by citizen panels. The assignment of greater responsibility for the setting of salaries to the President might open the door to meaningful collective bargaining between the real federal management and recognized unions. This could have a salutary impact on the pay system and eliminate the extra arena of political lobbying in determining pay levels. A legislative body is not equipped to bargain, to act promptly, or to reflect management judgments in reaching these determinations.

More than a century ago, in 1862, Congress ceded control of the pay-setting authority for a significant number of federal employees when it authorized the determination of wages for trades and craft workers in the naval shipyards on the basis of local prevailing rates in the communities where they worked. That authority has been used, as amended by the Classification Act, which excluded these positions from the classification structure, by all departments and agencies with blue-collar workers. By 1967 the total was more than 700,000 workers employed in more than 200 different localities. These rates have been adjusted on an annual basis following surveys of comparable jobs and rates among the private employers in the specific locality. The adjustments are authorized by the head of the department or agency, and the necessary funds to support these increases have been appropriated almost without question.

In administering these rates, it has not been difficult to secure adjustments or to keep pace with the private sector. With a regular rhythm, they have risen at an average annual pace of 3 to 5 percent since World War II. Between 1951 and 1957, for example, they advanced 35 percent, while Classification Act salaries advanced 17.5 percent. The problem instead was a multiplicity of individual agency systems with inconsistencies and inequities among them. The federal government had become several employers rather than a single one in many localities. The differences in system produced substantial differences in rates for the same job in the same locality depending upon the employing agency. Any kind of unification was resisted through the years by both agency and union leaders. Informal efforts were made in the Eisenhower and Kennedy administrations to eliminate overlapping in wage surveys and to promote voluntary cooperation in identifying common jobs and common locality boundaries. These improvements failed to eliminate the fundamental problem, and in 1966, following an extensive review by the Budget Bureau and the Civil Service Commission, a new consolidated wage-setting operation was proposed. In protracted negotiations, first with agency representatives and then with union representatives, neither of whom agreed totally among themselves, the Civil Service Commission developed a plan that President Johnson approved on December 1, 1967, for a new coordinated federal wage system so designed that blue-collar workers performing similar work in the same local wage area would receive the same rates of pay in all federal agencies.

Although agencies and unions still had reservations about the system's details, they accepted the plan subject to further consultation on the implementation steps. This coordination represented a triumph in achieving a unified federal pay system, improving interagency collaboration, and strengthening labor-management relations between the government and union members working under exclusive recognition agreements. The executive agencies and labor unions cooperated in the development of the large body of standards, policies, procedures, and instructional material needed in order to begin operation. Occupational definitions were cut in half, from about 1,600 to 800. Job-rating standards were slashed from about 1,300 to 200. The more than 300 wage areas were narrowed down to a more manageable 150. A combined group of agency personnel officers and union representatives met with the chairman of the Civil Service Commission to advise on the formulation of policy and processes in the administration of this coordinated system. This advisory method proved time-consuming and full of friction as long-standing practices were modified to accommodate a unified system. It was a totally new pattern of union participation, which suffered from stresses and strains in early determinations. The ultimate form or success of the process is still unpredictable. Its tensions may not be accommodated and a new form more nearly related to collective bargaining may be the ultimate answer. Already there is growing interest on the part of some union leaders to cast this system, or an alternate generally resembling it, in legislative form, but members of Congress have been reluctant to move away from the 1862 policy position and the administrative modifications that at least assure its workability in the 1970s.

The federal pattern in wage and salary administration has been followed or improved upon in some state and municipal jurisdictions.
Where genuine collective bargaining has been established, the more formal job-evaluation system has been modified and the legislature plays a
lesser role in the determination of rates. The rate of improvement, however, is still sluggish. Salaries have been allowed to lag too far behind the
market. Too many wage and salary structures are out of date in relation
to modern management practices and the rapidly changing job market
and occupational definitions. Too often, upward adjustments have been
authorized at the entry level of certain career fields without proportionate increases up the line, so that salary compression is produced and the
career configuration is flattened out. Certain pay schedules are too
tightly geared to credential requirements; this is particularly true in
teachers' salaries. These requirements tend to become pro forma as a
means of promotion, with limited improvement in performance demonstrated at higher levels of pay. In many public jurisdictions, pay scales
are not designed to provide a meaningful incentive for higher productivity or improved performance. The differences between salary levels are
too slight, and all too many increases are based exclusively on length of
service rather than quality of performance. These narrow differentials are
particularly noticeable between various levels of supervision, where some
qualified persons are unwilling to accept the added burdens of increased
responsibility for the limited increase in compensation. The workings of
income-tax and other deductions can actually result in a reduced take-
home pay following a promotion.

Each and every jurisdiction would be well advised to conduct a penetrating and objective evaluation of the pay structure and pay-setting
practices of its various operations. Citizen participation and advice based
on objective pay information collected throughout the market area can
be a forceful combination in demonstrating the need for significant
changes in compensation.

The subject of compensation, however, concerns more than pay.
Fringe benefits have become important. While wages and salaries were
frozen during World War II, the compensation escape hatch was the
fringe benefit. More leave, improved pension benefits, life insurance and

health plans, and other nonpay compensations, fully or partially provided by the employer, became a decided influence on the total compensation the worker received for his services. In some of these benefit areas the public sector has been out in front. This is particularly true in vacation and sick leave, where liberal policies were established in the 1930s and were even cut back in the federal service to bring them more into line with private enterprise. Today there is greater comparability in these leave privileges, but in all likelihood government employees still enjoy an advantage.

Retirement systems are a universal factor in public service, and they have grown and accumulated more liberal benefits since the federal statute was enacted in 1920. The provision of deferred compensation in the form of annuities for the retired employee or of benefits for his survivor has become a treasured fringe benefit for the longtime employee and a costly obligation for public jurisdictions. The systems are under constant pressure in support of benefit and coverage liberalization and in opposition to increased funding. In the federal government a series of liberalized benefits, along with the impact of pay increases for active employees, pushed up the unfunded liability of the Retirement Trust Fund to the $50-billion mark and raised the prospect that annual appropriations of $3 to $4 billion would be necessary in a relatively few years in order to meet the obligations to those expecting earned benefits under the program. This funding issue was long a playground for political gamesmanship. To avoid increasing current expenditures, one President after another failed to request funds to cover the government's contribution to support the retirement program. Not until 1956 did government payments match those contributed by the employee through a percentage deduction from his salary. Not until 1969 did the amount of this contribution move up to a point where anticipated benefit levels would be covered, namely at 15 percent of payroll.

As in private enterprise, federal pension plans should be closely related to Social Security benefits and should be largely supplemental to retirement compensation flowing from that source. This is already true for most states and cities, but in the federal government the retirement statute preceded the Social Security Act by fifteen years and several of the Social Security benefits had been incorporated in the Retirement Act. Over the years the sweetening of the retirement plan has made coordination with Social Security less and less attractive even though such an interrelationship has been strongly recommended by retirement experts, Executive Branch officials, and the advocates of Social Security.

In a recent liberalization, the annuity benefits under the federal plan were shifted to a computation base of the three highest salary years rather than five. This change will mean even higher benefits upon retirement, particularly in view of the prospect of annual salary adjustments. This underscores the financial impact of salary increases on future retirement liability. This impact is frequently overlooked at the time the costs of pay increases are measured or the long-term financial obligations of retirement liberalization are being studied. Those with public responsibility must consider that the gross compensation increases whenever pay or benefits are being increased, or else some future public manager will find dollar overruns in his payroll that will surpass those periodically recorded for new weapons systems.

Two other fringe benefits of common acceptance and major importance to employers and employees alike are group life insurance and group health coverage. These benefits were added to the federal package in 1954 and 1959 respectively, and they have proved to be substantial elements of economic security for employees and their survivors. Both plans are contributory with the employee carrying the major portion of the cost. There are recommendations that all the costs should be carried by the government for all employees, or at least for those at the lower end of the pay scale. The unions are demanding that the full cost of health insurance be met from the federal treasury. Such liberalization can certainly be defended on social grounds and increasingly in terms of comparability with private practice. But the costs must not be overlooked when the combined fringe benefits already amount to more than 25 percent of the payroll. The life-insurance program was liberalized in 1968 to place a floor of $10,000 on coverage for federal employees and to permit the voluntary purchase through payroll deductions of additional insurance at the favorable group rate. With the rapidly rising costs of health care, the premiums for group health plans have risen with such rapidity that the government's share of the total payment has fallen off because of a mandated ceiling on its contribution. Adjustments in these plans can be accomplished only through legislative action and only at infrequent intervals. Additional executive discretion might be desirable if there were assurance of adequate funding to cover increased expenditures.

Public managers need to plan changes in pay and benefits on a combined basis with respect to costs and to their competitive position in the market. It is necessary to make choices as to where investment of additional resources will have the maximum benefit to the public interest and to the employees. While a further liberalization of the pension plan may appeal to older employees, the equivalent investment in salaries may be attractive to a larger number of younger employees and may improve the ability of the agency to compete for high-quality personnel in the labor market. With tight budget strictures, it may not be possible to advance on all fronts simultaneously. It may even be necessary to defray higher salaries by reducing the number of employees. This course is always distasteful, but it may be preferable to deferring a required increase and thereby weakening government's competitive position in the market and possibly breaking faith with the employees themselves.

The Quest

for Leadership

in

Public Service

The large numbers of employees, the multiplicity of governmental jurisdictions and agencies, and the massive public funds appropriated to meet payrolls should not obscure the vital importance of high quality and strong dedication in the leadership ranks of public service. Those who carry public responsibility as top managers and professionals set the tone. They determine the patterns of administration to carry out the legislative mandate. It is through their offices that proposals for new or revised programs must pass to initiate public progress. It is their planning and their acts that enter the record upon which Presidents, governors, and mayors must go to the people. Within government, they set the style of vigor and imagination and efficiency or they deflate those qualities among their subordinates.

First let us consider those leaders who are a part of the continuing bureaucracy, whose capacities have developed in the course of a career. These men as a group have long been scrutinized and studied. David Stanley, one of the most perceptive writers on the subject, claimed in 1967 that they had been subjected to more research than juvenile delinquents. Starting with the personnel report of the second Hoover Commission and running through successive studies by Ross Pollack and Paul David, Marver Bernstein, John Corson, Paul van Riper, and David Stanley himself, to say nothing of the CED report of 1964, there has been a general conclusion that the quality of the men in these positions has been remarkably good, probably better than can be found in the private sector, but that the system under which they live is too rigid, not sufficiently rewarding, deficient in training opportunities and until recently inadequate in compensation. These evaluators have identified a tendency in government to apply egalitarian principles to such an extreme that special measures to meet the needs for leadership development are resisted.

The second Hoover Commission, reporting in 1955, explicitly recommended the creation of a senior civil service constituted of the career officials in the top three grades—the supergrades—and subject to assignment from a central agency to any post for which they might qualify. This particular recommendation was among those most strongly advocated by former President Hoover. Key administration officials, including White House staff chief Sherman Adams, were deeply involved in the efforts to translate this proposal into specific action. There was, however, strong opposition from a number of sources. The presumed beneficiaries of this program used subtle devices to frustrate it; they were fearful of the uncertainty that might follow changes in assignment and control of their future by some unknown central body. Department and agency heads were not particularly enthusiastic because it would eliminate their appointive authority for top positions. Union leaders, though not directly affected, detected possible erosion of civil service tenure. And members of Congress, particularly those in the opposition party, viewed the proposal as a political move, despite all reassurances that senior civil servants would be political neuters, or as an indirect means of undermining the stature of the bipartisan Civil Service Commission. This accumulation of opposition was exasperating to the efficient Mr. Adams, who was heard to say that for no other program had his efforts been more completely thwarted.

The President did designate an advisory panel of administration executives and distinguished public citizens to formulate a plan within existing statutory authority pointing toward the formation of a senior civil service. This modest beginning never proceeded very far because it failed to gain the support of the House Post Office and Civil Service

Committee and subsequently was denied funds by an appropriation rider.

This record of failure deterred all but the researchers and writers on this subject for the next several years. With regularity the Civil Service Commission journeyed to Congress to justify additional authorizations for supergrade positions, which it proceeded to allocate to department and agency claimants on the basis of priority needs and without regard to any government-wide system of selection for the positions to be filled. Meanwhile, the commission recognized the need for initiative within the Executive Branch for special consideration of the leadership element in the government. It sought to design a new system within the limits of existing statutory authority—one that would not prove as threatening as the senior civil service concept, that would emphasize high quality in filling key positions through carefully drawn standards and extensive search for candidates, and that would encourage a government-wide outlook by those in the system and presumably a greater degree of assignment experience in various parts of the government. The existing authority was well established in the commission itself through the requirement that it allocate most of the top positions and approve the qualifications of most of the people appointed to those positions. Further, the commission had been designated by President Eisenhower as the body to determine which of these positions should be excepted from the career service because of their relationship to a policymaking official or to the process of policymaking itself; these were so-called Schedule C positions, which could be filled without reference to competitive civil service procedure but nevertheless required the commission's approval of the proposed appointee's qualifications. President Johnson prodded the commission in its search for improvement with a promise in his 1966 State of the Union message to "restructure our civil service in the top grades so that men and women can easily be assigned to jobs where they are most needed and ability will be both required as well as rewarded."

The President fulfilled his promise in the establishment of the Executive Assignment System in an Executive Order signed on November 17, 1966. The system was extended to cover all employees in the Executive Branch occupying supergrade positions and provided a foundation for an expanded personnel program to meet executive manpower needs in the federal service. The system had three primary objectives: to make available the most capable executives from within and outside the federal service for staffing top-level positions; to provide expanded opportunities to career executives to use their talents throughout the government; and to help bring about greater identification of career executives with the over-all purposes of the federal government.

The characteristics of the program had been cleared in advance with agency personnel officers, representative career executives, union officials, congressional committee members, and researchers and writers in the field. The plan was reasonably well received by most, although some felt it did not go far enough in giving separate status and broader flexibility to this particular group of officials. Others doubted that the Civil Service Commission would have sufficient strength in the executive hierarchy to give such a plan the stature, meaning, and force to influence the key officials in the administration. They believed that such a system could succeed only if it were more closely identified with the President himself and located in the White House or the Executive Office of the President.

The system covered about 4,000 positions in the federal service and had an indirect bearing on another 5,000 positions under special salary systems in the Executive Branch. There were two major types of assignments within the system, career and noncareer. Career Executive Assignments were in the competitive civil service and must be made through merit staffing procedures. Noncareer Executive Assignments originated outside the competitive service and were not subject to merit staffing requirements, much like Schedule C appointments. Both types of assignments, however, would be filled in conformance with qualification standards tailored for the particular job, which was to be filled jointly by the commission and the agency concerned. Thus there was opportunity for the commissioners and the staff of the new Bureau of Executive Manpower to meet with the department and agency heads to review plans for top-level staffing in the immediate and more distant future. These meetings concentrated on the importance of high standards and the thorough search, not only within their own organization but elsewhere in the government and outside it, to find the person best qualified for the post. In the course of such discussion, previous and anticipated problems could be aired in confidence, and frequently the Commission was in a position to aid the agency head in some phase of this staffing. Cooperative manpower planning produced plans for staffing these positions and brought new executive emphasis to bear on the selection and development of its most valued personnel.

An automated executive inventory, containing biographical data on over 25,000 federal employees in grades GS-15 through GS-18 and others at comparable salary levels, was established. This inventory became the primary vehicle in assisting agencies in finding promptly the right man for the job. It also facilitated executive manpower planning by creating a solid basis for estimating the pertinent manpower resources available and for projecting future recruitment and development needs. From the data in the inventory, a 1967 profile of the top executives in the federal service revealed some salient characteristics:

- Fewer than 25 were under 25 years of age. One-third of the executives had reached the age of 55 and thus were eligible for optional retirement.
- About 4 percent were over 65 and thus were within five years of compulsory retirement age.
- Two-thirds of the executives had more than 20 years of federal service, and only 12 percent had less than 10 years.
- Only 535, or 2.4 percent out of the 25,000, were women. Of that number, more than one-third were medical officers.
- 30 percent of the women and 21 percent of the men had entered the federal service in the past 15 years. About 7 percent of the women and 3 percent of the men had 5 years or less in the service.
- 20 percent of the executives were classified as serving in the administrative occupational field, with 16 percent in engineering, 16 percent in the medical field, 9 percent in physical sciences, and 7 percent in law.
- About 85 percent of the group had at least one college degree and more than one-half held master's or higher degrees. The educa-

tional differences between those in grade GS-15 and those in the supergrades were very slight. Nearly 40 percent of those who had entered government service with less than a doctoral degree subsequently completed significant amounts of education, with 20 percent gaining a master's or higher degree and 6 percent having completed doctoral degrees. Of the approximately 5,000 who had entered the government without a college degree, 37 percent earned at least one degree and 15 percent earned multiple degrees.

- More than one-half of the executives first entered the federal service below grade GS-9. Nearly one-quarter entered below grade GS-5 and almost 20 percent came in at the upper-middle level grades, GS-13, -14, and -15.

- Among the reasons cited for entering the federal service, the most common was that it offered the best opportunity for pursuing a chosen profession. Only 1 in 8 executives under 45 and 1 in 20 under 35 reported that they had accepted a federal job because it was the best offer they had. Among all respondents, 19 percent did report that it was the best offer they had.

- More than one-half of the executives had spent their entire government career within a single agency. Most of the mobility that occurred came comparatively early in the executive's career.

- Over one-half of the executives who had worked in only one agency were willing to consider changing jobs, with 46 percent stating that they would prefer not to change at the time interviewed. Those who had worked for more than one agency were more willing to change than those who had passed their entire career in a single agency.

- When queried on the training they desired, more than half of the physical scientists and engineers expressed a need for advanced or refresher training in their technical or professional fields. They showed less interest than other occupational groups in such areas as government policy and operations, public administration, and political, economic, and social problems.

- 58 percent had received awards from within their agency on the basis of their performance and 23 percent had received awards from outside sources.

Special boards and panels were established to assist in locating high-quality talent from outside the federal service to supplement that covered in the inventory. An increasing shortage of executive talent in the nation at large underscored the necessity for well-planned efforts by the federal government in seeking executive talent from outside.

The system ultimately will need to be supplemented with special government training and educational facilities to help in the further development of those persons already serving in executive assignments as well as for those in lower level positions with potential for ultimate selection into executive posts. The Federal Executive Institute should serve as the primary center for training of this type and for continuing research with respect to executive performance, attitudes, and behavior.

The system in no way changed the tenure status of those with career assignments, which could not be accomplished without new statutory authority. In all probability the functioning of the system will show the need to change this and other areas of policy and practice in order to promote more effective executive development in the federal service. There is need to provide greater flexibility for the President and his department heads in achieving reassignments of career personnel and to exercise discretion in filling the positions that clearly should be outside the career service. The existing system has too many different categories of jobs and different measures of control. Increasingly there is serious doubt whether a completely job-related method for pay determination is appropriate at the top levels. In posts of such magnitude and significance, the nature and scope of the assignments are so substantially determined by the quality of the individual himself that job descriptions possess little meaning. The strict dependency upon Congress for the authorization of additional openings for certain top positions leads to distortion and undue delay in staffing new and frequently critical programs. Congressional overview could be exercised through periodic reporting or more general limitations than those presently applied. Serious consideration should be given to a salary range without grade designation or rates for top positions, with individual salaries determined by multiple executive judgments on the basis of qualifications and performance.

In the first week following his State of the Union message in 1971, President Nixon sent to Congress a comprehensive proposal dealing with many of these further needs. He boldly sought a change in the tenure system for top career officials through the institution of three-year contract terms. He would create by legislative action a Federal Executive Service of these 7,000 managers and professionals, encouraging their assignment across agency lines. Under this new system the coveted supergrades would be changed to a salary range with greater discretion in setting and adjusting individual rates. He would also seize the initiative in creating new top-level positions while leaving Congress the opportunity for veto within a limited time. Such a long step forward will require skillful congressional footwork, but it is in the right direction and will overcome existing limitations in the program installed in the 1960s.

The other segment of top leadership is composed of the officials appointed by the Chief Executive at his discretion to join him in directing the administrative organs of government. These are the posts where the men and women selected will shape the character and effectiveness of the administration of Presidents, governors, or mayors. While these positions have generally been described as political, they can no longer really be used primarily as currency in a system of political rewards. Each Chief Executive will turn to those he knows or has worked with in the past to fill some positions, but even a political leader of long experience and wide acquaintanceship must reach beyond his own circle to select the talent necessary to make his administration successful. On the federal scene, the President has only about 800 appointments with which to build his administration. Each appointment decision he makes will add to the composite of personalities that forms the picture of his administration in the eyes of Congress, the press, and the people themselves.

Each President organizes his White House staff to suit his own temperament and style of operation. He may prefer a tightly organized staff system under a chief assistant, as President Eisenhower did. He may prefer a more informal cluster of advisers on a variety of policy issues, as President Kennedy did. The same discretion will undoubtedly be exercised in his search and selection of appointees for top positions. He may wish to divide up the task among several advisers on the basis of fields of interest or he may elect to centralize the function in one person. He may choose to set up a large organization at the beginning of his administration for an extensive sweep of possible candidates and then scale down the activity or disperse it. He will usually realize that although the immediate drive for talent is massive and intensive in the period between election and inauguration and immediately thereafter, this function cannot be abandoned: vacancies do occur, appointments do expire, and new organizations with new positions are created.

During the Kennedy-Johnson years, a special unit was organized to give the President a continuing service in the search and evaluation of potential candidates for vacancies. This function had its origin in the experience encountered a year or so after the initial staffing of the administration, when it was necessary to search out replacements and to maintain presidential initiative in later appointments.

Following the Kennedy election in 1960, a recruiting task force was established under Sargent Shriver, with assistance from Ralph Dungan and Adam Yarmolinsky, to seek out in a systematic fashion well-qualified candidates to present to the President for his consideration in filling Cabinet and sub-Cabinet posts, agency-head positions, and vacancies on major regulatory bodies. From comprehensive information describing the basic functions of each post, they collected qualification information on men and women throughout the country who appeared to be best equipped to join the President in the development and administration of his programs. Extensive evaluation sheets were prepared on each potential candidate from information gathered by the task force from trusted sources, largely over the telephone. As a roster of candidates for a particular position was completed, it was delivered to the President-elect in Georgetown, Manhattan, or Palm Beach for his review, evaluation, and interview with the preferred candidate. One by one, these selected appointees were announced and introduced to the public as members of the New Frontier.

The process followed in filling the subordinate presidential positions varied significantly. In the State Department, where the President had named certain of the Assistant Secretaries prior to his selection of Dean Rusk as Secretary, the task force continued to conduct its search with only occasional consultation with the Secretary. The process was quite different in the Department of Defense, where the former president of the Ford Motor Company, Robert McNamara, had accepted appointment with the understanding that he would select his own subordinates. McNamara closeted himself in a hotel room for several days and pursued his own personal search, with the result that he was able to present a complete list of prospective subordinates to the President well before inauguration day.

The task force continued to function after the inauguration, with important posts with lesser public visibility ultimately being filled by late spring 1961. At that point the recruiting group was disbanded and its members moved into active posts with the administration: Shriver became the first director of the Peace Corps, the Kennedy administration's most innovative institutional development; Yarmolinsky became special assistant to Secretary McNamara; and Dungan joined the White House staff with a substantive assignment in international affairs and only a minor concern for recruiting. But within twelve months it was clearly evident that the President's responsibility for sustaining a leadership group in his administration could not be pursued on a part-time or casual basis. Consequently, Dungan moved with the President's strong support to form a special White House unit, staffed with professional rather than political personnel, to concentrate all of its time and energy in filling the constant need for executive talent. To head the unit, he selected Dan H. Fenn from the Harvard School of Business Administration. Upon inspecting the executive recruitment machinery of the highest office in the land, Fenn described it as a manifestation of BOGSAT, which he translated as a contraction of "a bunch of guys sitting around a table," scratching their heads, looking off into the distance, and endeavoring to think of someone they knew who could fill a particular vacancy. Seeking a more constructive and affirmative approach, Fenn turned for assistance to the Brookings Institution in setting up a nation-wide network of persons considered leaders in their fields or in communities to whom he could go for information and evaluations on candidates for future vacant positions. The Brookings staff arranged meetings around the country with leaders in various disciplines to talk with Fenn and his professional staffers. From these meetings an initial roster of potential and reliable sources of talent was created. From these sources, numbering several hundred, came biographies and opinions, both solicited and unsolicited, for future use.

This new approach recognized that the filling of a vacancy was a two-step proposition. The first step related solely to the job itself. The search process, consequently, began with the construction of a qualifications profile of a particular position to be filled at a particular time. The development of this position profile was the responsibility of the White House staff, with the involvement of the President himself and the head of the department or agency if the position was subordinate to him. Each executive position was looked upon as a unique and complex array of responsibilities where the primary focus of the job might change from time to time depending upon a variety of factors: the nature of the leadership of the head of the department, the qualifications of the other presidential appointees, the program emphasis at the particular time, the specialized character of the program to be administered. For example, in seeking candidates for an Assistant Secretary of Commerce, should primary attention be given to successful business experience, to professional background in economics, to skill in executive-legislative relationships, to managerial capacity, to an area of specialty experience such as foreign trade, business statistics, or research and development, or to previous experience in developing the concept of new programs or in the realignment of existing missions? Since it was assumed that those accepting positions would do so for no less than four years, the present requirements were modified by a projection of future requirements.

With the profile in hand and in mind, the search staff went to work. First it utilized the biographies and evaluations of the candidates considered to be qualified to fill the vacancy in terms of that profile. The President received in due course the individual folders, in which on one side he could read the statutory authority and the profile for the position and on the other side the background of the candidates considered most appropriate for the post. The President reacted to the recommendations, indicating his choice or choices for personal interview. These interviews were conducted by the President himself or by the staff, depending on the importance of the post. Relevant background investigations would then be pursued if the candidate cleared the interview hurdle and the President wished to carry the selection to the final point of decision. If the background investigation revealed no questions requiring further exploration, the President would either make the appointment or, as required, nominate the candidate to the Senate for confirmation.

Under the leadership of Fenn and his successor, John B. Clinton, this process developed slowly into a professional clinical approach to executive recruiting. Fenn fell victim to his own search process when he was nominated by the President for a term appointment to the Tariff Commission. Before he took the oath, he had built the first systematic means for continuing assistance to the President in his responsibility for leadership selection.

Shortly after the assassination of President Kennedy, however, an unexpected problem started to develop. The Kennedy staff had built a strong resource of talent in their files as critical support for the new system, and a presidential tradition had to be modified to retain that resource for the benefit of his successor. It had been traditional to assume that all White House papers were the personal papers of the incumbent President. When he departed from the White House all these papers would be removed overnight, with the result that a new incumbent was faced with empty file cabinets. Since, however, most of the Kennedy staff who had been selected for professional rather than personal or political reasons remained at the White House in this recruiting area, they retained these files for use by President Johnson until early 1965, when they were transferred to the custody of the Kennedy Library.

Immediately following the election in 1964, President Johnson appointed Ralph Dungan ambassador to Chile. In another break with the traditional way of doing things, President Johnson called upon the chairman of the Civil Service Commission to expand his responsibilities by taking over the management of the recruiting function and the professional staff that had developed during the Kennedy years. The Johnson approach was that if the civil service philosophy and method could successfully fill lower-level jobs, the same technique of evaluation should be applicable for higher positions if they were to be filled primarily on the basis of merit. Consequently, to the recently initiated professional approach he added the personnel-management experience that had been the hallmark of the Civil Service Commission. The new team leader inherited the talent files and the contact network, and on the recommendation of the inherited staff, he sought to have the files indexed for maximum utility.

While supporting a continuation of the evolving process inaugurated by his predecessor, President Johnson set forth certain general criteria to be applied in seeking all candidates for his administration. He placed a high premium on evidence of intelligence; a Phi Beta Kappa key, a Rhodes scholarship, or some other symbol of intellectual achievement was an important factor in his selections. Although no age bracket was specified, there was a special emphasis on seeking younger men and women. The President took particular pleasure in announcing the youthful age of many of his appointees. A premium was also placed upon previous success in government, leading to the appointment of many career officials through promotion to these noncareer assignments. It also meant that the biographies of those considered from industry, education, law, and other outside fields were scrutinized for previous governmental service, whether federal, state, or local. The President wanted evidence of professional success in the field of a particular appointment. More and more, a background in scientific research, financial management, systems analysis, large-scale procurement, international affairs, or legal specialization became a prerequisite.

From the beginning, the President proclaimed a lack of interest in party affiliation. He would describe with relish how he was unaware of John Gardner's party affiliation until two or three minutes before his appointment as Secretary of Health, Education, and Welfare was announced. (He was a Republican.) But among the criteria set by the President there was a related standard: the candidate's support for the President and his programs. In the early days of the search, this standard was relatively easy to meet, but as the dissensions brought on by the Vietnam war increased, the standard reduced the available field.

The White House Executive Biographic Index became an essential tool in the expanding search process. This index was an absolute necessity in extending the memory of the professional recruiters beyond the recollection of names and qualifications conjured up in sessions around the table. As designed and installed, the index provided a means for storing and retrieving biographical information that eventually grew to 16,000 entries. From computer files it was possible to obtain information on incumbents and presidential positions in such a fashion as to meet the constant need for public information and for advance warnings about vacancies through term expirations. The staff received assistance and guidance from all the major computer manufacturers in the design phase of this system. The computer-service and programming assistance was provided by the Office of Emergency Preparedness.

At the same time that the computer systems were being developed, the structure of the staff also was changed. Rather than the entire staff working on the vacancy list in total, the vacancies were divided between international positions and domestic positions, with a desk officer and an assistant for each area. This procedure allowed the two teams to concentrate their energies and gain in-depth experience in two distinctly different kinds of executive recruiting. The original list of contacts was enlarged over the years to a total in excess of 600 by the end of the Johnson administration. It was in no sense a static list. It changed as the recruiters were better able to assess the contact's ability to identify high-quality persons for specific vacancies and to evaluate the professional and attitudinal characteristics in a candidate with sensitivity and perception in response to presidential requirements.

With the Executive Biographic Index, the staff did not forget names in the file. The computer provided them with catalogues listing biographies cross-referenced by skill, providing an effective means of producing a large number of names for any vacancy. In addition, the staff utilized the roster information available on federal career people—civil service, foreign service, and even the armed services—to seek out potential candidates within the government itself. From all these sources an initial list of qualified persons was developed for evaluation of each candidate by three or four knowledgeable persons in the network of contacts and thorough checking of all biographical sources, including material written by or about the candidate. Through this evaluation process, the number of candidates was reduced to a manageable two to six and a descriptive memorandum was prepared for the President's review. These memoranda, which became part of the President's regular "night reading," contained a description of the profile for the position, a brief history of previous incumbents, and an assessment and biographical summary on each of the candidates presented. Each memorandum contained a ballot for ready expression of the President's view following his study of the material. Almost invariably, on the following day, he returned the memorandum with a choice on the ballot checked or with an independent opinion offered. The verdict might be: "Obtain additional information on candidates #2 and #4"; "none of these appeal to me"; "determine availability of #1"; "approve #5." In most instances, further research and evaluation were necessary before the availability of the preferred candidate was ascertained. Further checking might eliminate the candidate but in most cases it strengthened his qualification for the position. As the staff gained experience in working with President Johnson, they came to realize that evaluations from strangers did not fully meet his needs, and so the evaluation process was extended to seek out persons who were known to the President for their judgments on the individual. These additional evaluations in the memoranda helped him to make his choices.

Wherever it was possible, the availability of preferred candidates was ascertained through third-party sources before an appointment was proffered. The response to the inquiry concerning availability was helpful in determining the degree of motivation the candidate might bring to the appointment. This advance determination eliminated the delay and potential embarrassment that might occur if the candidate said "not available" upon receiving a direct invitation from the President.

Mr. Johnson devoted substantial time to the reading of any and all material provided to him on individual candidates. His personal storage and retrieval system performed with remarkable reliability in producing biographical details in conversation weeks and even months later. In most cases, the President put through a personal call to the individual he finally selected to proffer the appointment. He took particular delight in these conversations and would frequently request the individual to come to the White House for conversation before inviting him to join the administration. All such invitations were subject to field investigations by the FBI, whose reports were usually reviewed by the security officer at the White House in addition to the recruiting staff. In one or two appointments, negative information was revealed that necessitated an interview with the individual by a White House staff member. The knowledge that such an investigation would be conducted reduced the possibility of subsequent embarrassment. Frequently it was necessary to check additional information about the candidate that did not normally show up in the FBI investigation. This was particularly true of the individual's previous business and financial involvements that might have some future relation to a potential conflict of interest or an embarrassing controversy.

In selecting his executive appointees, President Johnson had the choice of promoting career appointees or of selecting persons from outside the government. Statistics on the background of his appointees from 1965 through 1969 indicate that 44.8 percent came from within the government while 18 percent were recruited from business, 17 percent from law, 12.4 percent from the universities, 6.5 percent from state and local government, and 1.3 from the ranks of organized labor. Obviously the President was not limited to the names provided by his specialized staff; he received suggestions and evaluations from a great variety of other sources—from leaders in his party, from members of Congress, from business and labor acquaintances, and countless other individuals and groups. But for the first time a President had a system to serve him and to give him a wide range of options in selecting his executive subordinates. With an average of eleven new vacancies each month, the need for organizing a professional and systematic recruiting effort, backed up with the best in management information systems, was clearly confirmed. More than 600 appointments were made to a complete array of top-level responsibility and from a cross-section of talent, drawn from every state and a great variety of professions. The success of this approach can only be gauged by the historians. One historian-commentator, James MacGregor Burns, observed that Lyndon Johnson might well be best remembered for the high quality of those he picked to positions of major responsibility. Many of the elements of this system were carried over into the executive search and selection processes followed by his successor in 1969. But with each President there will be differences in approach and differences in system, coupled with an abiding need to exercise extreme care and critical evaluation in staffing the leadership element for the support of the presidency.

The American
Public Servant
Beyond
17   the Borders

More than a quarter century after World War II, American civilian payrolls still carry the names of more than 58,000 men and women who pursue their government's service beyond the borders of the country. During this quarter century of accelerated change, the American civil servant has taken up residence, usually for a short period of time, in virtually every country on the globe to perform the overseas tasks of the United States government.

Where in the late 1930s American representation was confined to a relatively small number of diplomatic, consular, and support personnel under the direction of the Department of State, today the overseas employment is in a far broader range of professions and occupations under the direction of twenty-nine federal agencies. While more than 58,000 American citizens serve in foreign lands, more than 150,000 foreign nationals join them in carrying out American functions in their own countries. With the passage of time these foreign nationals have been trained to replace the overseas Americans who cost their government so much in salary, benefits, and services when they are employed in service abroad. In Germany and Japan the local labor market is supplying the bulk of the skills required by the American employers. An intricate array of employment agreements has been worked out with various government authorities, specifying the conditions under which the men and

233

women of the host country will be compensated and supervised. An entire new form of personnel management has been developed to administer these agreements and to assure that the visitor-employer treats his host-employee in a manner equitable by American standards but not disruptive of or offensive to local employment practices.

For the Americans themselves, employment conditions are a patchwork of policies and practices—more an improvised extension of domestic personnel standards than a consistent pattern for all Americans working in a given locality. There is the regular Foreign Service of the State Department, with its career officers and its staff corps functioning under a set of precise conditions set forth in great detail in the Foreign Service Act and implemented by the Director General of the Foreign Service. This group, relatively small in size, is committed to a long-term career with extended periods of service outside of the United States. By intent, design, and its own admission, it is an elite corps that has carried the burden of political representation for the United States throughout history and, in the modern phase of American overseas operations, takes on the over-all leadership responsibilities. It is from within this group that the great majority of ambassadors are selected, and it is in the person of the ambassador as chief of mission that whatever coordination of U.S. operations has been sought is achieved.

During much of the postwar period, the United States has been committed to a vast program of economic, technical, and military foreign assistance, administered and supervised by country directors and specialized staffs recruited by the Agency for International Development (AID), or one of its alphabetic predecessors, to serve a limited tour overseas as Foreign Service reserve officers. Because of the presumed impermanence of the foreign assistance agency and program, Congress has never seen fit to authorize a continuing personnel system for these activities. Without a doubt, this agency has suffered the most battering personnel history of any federal agency. It has been rapidly expanded, precipitately cut back, periodically evaluated and then reorganized, chronically attacked for everything from malfeasance to overstaffing, regularly berated by congressional committees, and virtually unloved by its own government and the governments it was created to assist. In such an environment it is a miracle that the agency was able to attract or retain any people of ability. But some very competent professionals with deep personal belief in the program's objectives have survived this ordeal ever since the early days of the Marshall Plan in the late 1940s. Others have clung tenaciously to their risky jobs for too long and remain after their time of skilled contribution. For many years, from 1956 to 1966, the agency was never staffed to its intended level and vast recruiting efforts were pressed to discover technicians already in short supply at home who were willing to serve abroad in underdeveloped countries under difficult conditions. Often after such a search was successful the individual assigned would prove unable to adapt to the foreign culture or his mission might be cut back or even eliminated.

The foreign information activities, sometimes highly publicized and sometimes quietly functioning out of the public view, have employed substantial numbers of Americans in libraries, exhibits, and cultural-affairs and information centers throughout the world. In 1967, after a determined drive to reduce the overseas employment of the United States Information Agency, it still had more than 8,000 agency employees abroad. The personnel system for this group had also been largely based on an assumption of impermanence, although successive directors since the destructive days of the McCarthy era of the early 1950s had endeavored to design a career system to give continuity and progress to the work of these specialists. Finally, in 1968 Congress authorized the creation of a career corps of these officers on a basis comparable to but separate from the Foreign Service itself. In contrast to AID, the USIA has experienced little difficulty in attracting media specialists for work overseas; there usually has been substantial competition for entry into available posts.

The largest employer of personnel throughout this period has been the Department of Defense. More than three-quarters of the total personnel employed abroad by the United States are civilians working for the Army, Navy, and Air Force. The great majority of these are foreign nationals in Europe and the western Pacific. But there are also significant numbers of Americans in positions considered sensitive to national security and in specialized skills not available in the indigenous labor market. Since 1955 these Americans have been included in the regular civil service. The argument advanced for this decision was that these employees are not engaged in work directly related to the foreign country to which they are assigned; instead it is an extension of activities pursued within the domestic military establishment. If their employment conditions were made roughly comparable to those in the home service, periods of overseas duties could be viewed as segments in a continuing career. There are adjustments in compensation, benefits, and working conditions that relate to the overseas environment, but matters of appointment, pay structure, promotion, and the like are the same as for persons performing similar functions in the United States.

The incorporation of overseas tours within a civil service career has been only moderately successful. Only a limited number of Defense civilians have been willing to risk a tour of duty far from familiar supervisors and tasks and clouded with uncertainty concerning the next assignment after their return. To make the foreign time more attractive, statutory assurances of job rights back home had to be enacted in 1959 —another instance of the low interest in risk-taking and in mobility on the part of secure civil servants.

The contrary situation—where a civilian overseas did not wish to return stateside—produced different but nevertheless difficult management problems. Longtime employees at certain foreign locations had "gone native" or had discovered decided income advantages overseas. Newly arrived commanders would be bound by a network of well-entrenched civilians who knew the local ropes and operated their own intelligence system. Colonies of expatriate civil servants could thrive on new military bases in Japan, the Philippines, or Germany. The acquisition of a native spouse further dampened interest in domestic assignments. Since there was no compulsion to return, little management action could be applied. A move to set a maximum tour length was opposed by union representatives.

Changing conditions abroad frequently invalidated past benefits, such as cost-of-living allowances, but resistance was met whenever adjustments or eliminations were sought. Many were continued after they became anomalous or excessive, not because of oversight but because of congressional or executive unwillingness to deal with the few employees who enjoyed the windfalls. A prime historical example was created in the Panama Canal Zone, where three generations of American colonials have lived and worked under special pay and benefit conditions justified during the Canal's early days but long since superseded by better transportation, sanitation, and services.

No review of contemporary overseas Americans would be complete without a special mention of the new nongovernment types, the Peace Corps volunteers. In a frank effort to counteract past American behavior abroad, these generally youthful volunteers endeavored to establish constructive person-to-person relations in host countries that requested them. They taught in schools, aided local government, advised on health and food problems, designed and built public works, and, most important, conveyed an American spirit, outside official bounds, aimed at the betterment of all mankind. Although they were supported by government staff and supplies, they stoutly maintained their independence, frequently to the discomfort of the U.S. ambassador and the host country, and they refused to become a part of an American "compound." They frequently boasted of their lack of special benefits while serving in remote and primitive regions. They volunteered for two years of service and accepted duty wherever the Peace Corps assigned them. Many signed up for additional tours or joined the staff in Washington and abroad. A positive effort was directed, with backing from Presidents Kennedy and Johnson, to attract the returning volunteers into other federal service, at home or abroad. But it was not very successful. Many volunteers found the bureaucracy unattractive after their more individualized Peace Corps experience. Many returned to the universities for further study and new career directions. While with the Peace Corps they had gained an invaluable experience for themselves besides contributing to the welfare of those they served and to the understanding of America's desire to help the developing nations on a truly personal scale. While the Peace Corps volunteer and his experience abroad unquestionably injected a new and fresh set of attitudes and conditions for future American service beyond the borders, many have more recently turned against further public service because of strong opposition to the war in Vietnam and other foreign policy actions of their government.

The interrelationship of these several systems to eliminate conflicts, to remove inequities, and to better serve the President and the Secretary of State has been a perpetual challenge for concerned administrators in the Executive Branch over the past decade. There has been a sustained dissatisfaction with the individual systems and with their interplay. Intended reforms have either fallen short of a desired objective or failed to produce change rapidly enough to meet current requirements. Presidents Kennedy, Johnson, and Nixon have all evidenced exasperation with the foreign-policy establishment at home and abroad. While highly commending individual performers in foreign operations, they have found the total system sluggish and unresponsive in serving the President in his range of world-wide responsibilities. As a consequence, an ever larger staff of foreign-policy advisers has been assigned to work within the orbit of the White House under the successive leadership of McGeorge Bundy, Walt Rostow, and Henry Kissinger. With the communications revolution, the President has been able to bring heads of state within the range of his telephone or hot line and is less dependent upon the extended lines of communication that follow the diplomatic channels.

Dean Rusk, who generally supported the professional Foreign Service, was openly critical of the organization of the department he headed, particularly of its inability to coordinate the multiplicity of American operations in individual countries abroad. Early in the Kennedy administration he worked with the President in the development of a letter to each of the chiefs of mission, advising them that they were in fact to be the President's representative in the country to which they were accredited and that other American officials pursuing missions assigned by other departments and agencies were responsible to the ambassador. The doctrine set forth in this letter led to the creation of the country-team concept, with the ambassador serving as captain and the other American personnel assigned by AID, USIA, the military, and other agencies working in close harmony with him. There was no intention on the part of other Cabinet officers with overseas programs to bypass the Secretary of State and the chiefs of mission, but individual foreign programs frequently took on lives of their own with specific objectives that could run counter to the principal American approach to the host country. The separate personnel systems tended to foster this separatism and complicate the conduct of coordinated operations. In the interest of interdepartmental policy and operational coordination at the national level, various organizational devices were evolved to secure high-level consultation and decision-making in both substantive and geographical terms. Such machinery, however, necessitated heavy time commitments by departmental Under Secretaries and Assistant Secretaries who were all too frequently burdened with the daily manifestations of crisis management in foreign affairs. As a consequence, decision-making was frequently allowed to descend to a lower and less persuasive level of coordination.

Early in his presidency, Lyndon Johnson commented derisively on the large number of Americans he had observed in visits to U.S. operations abroad. He urged more determined efforts by the responsible department heads to reduce the magnitude of the American presence and to improve the efficiency of American performance. The President's discontent reflected the inadequacy of overseas manpower planning. Staffing requirements on a country-by-country and agency-by-agency basis were not formulated in terms of specific program needs. The career mix in the Foreign Service, both in skills and in rank distribution, did not accurately represent the true staffing requirements for tight operation. All too frequently there appeared to be a surplus of personnel awaiting assignment if an appropriate berth could be found instead of a well-organized search for the proper combination of abilities to fill a demonstrated need in an overseas program. Once a substantive program was initiated and the supporting staff was assigned, it was exceedingly difficult to terminate that program even if its purpose had been fulfilled or it was considered no longer necessary and the personnel had been laid off. Congressional investigative reports and the studies of outside panels echoed the criticism advanced by President Johnson. Even the Secretary of State was inclined to admit that the overseas establishment was overstaffed.

A computerized determination of manpower requirements for overseas operations was undertaken but abandoned when it appeared to impose additional administrative controls on the operating program directors. A consultant expert in systems analysis was employed to assist the departmental management in the development of a planning, programming, and budgeting system that would lead to a more systematic formulation of personnel requirements. But when faced by obstructive opposition in securing the required information, he abandoned the assignment without any apparent evidence of progress. These failures, however, should not be allowed to foreclose further analytical study of the relationship between overseas program commitments and the staffing necessary to carry them out. In the meantime, individual ambassadors should be offered the incentive to reduce rather than expand the staffs assigned to them. When Ambassador John W. Tuthill evaluated the staffing of the embassy in Brazil and concluded that a 30 percent reduction could be achieved, he received plaudits all the way up to the President. His action prompted pressure to reduce by some degree all overseas personnel. This process, though unscientific and arbitrary, may be the only way in which to slim down the American presence abroad.

The Foreign Service personnel system itself has been the target of frequent study during the past generation. Shortly after World War II, the original Foreign Service Act of 1924 was amended to give greater prestige and independence to the Foreign Service corps. The process by which the Foreign Service officers maneuvered this legislation through Congress without significant participation by the Secretary of State or the White House is a casebook example of the functioning alliance between the career service and friendly members of Congress. The inadequacies of the amended act soon became apparent as the State Department substantially increased in size when war-born foreign activities were transferred from their temporary organizational locations into the department. This growth injected into the traditional system, based upon the skillful generalist with his career objective set on diplomacy, a variety of professional practitioners essential to the expanded scope of foreign operations. Economists, attorneys, research analysts, information specialists, and many others came under the enlarged umbrella of the department. These specialists were for the most part Washington-based without overseas experience, and yet to retain their services it was necessary to pay them at the same level as the more senior Foreign Service officers. Many of them had no desire for or expectation of over-

seas service except on a short-term and sporadic basis. Others had become so enamored of foreign affairs that they sought lateral entry into
the career service, a move that the service itself opposed on the ground
that it would lower standards and introduce greater competition for the
relatively few positions at the top. In other words, it would dilute the elite
corps.

After a couple of false starts in attempting to apply the recommendations of advisory panels, the department, during the regime of John
Foster Dulles, underwent what has been characterized as "Wristonization" in honor of Henry Wriston, the former president of Brown University and one of the architects of the original Foreign Service Act in 1924,
who chaired and aggressively led a distinguished panel that reviewed the
Foreign Service in 1953. With Wriston applying steady pressure, the
department undertook a massive lateral entry of specialists into the
career service. The results were mixed. Many senior Foreign Service
officers have described them as disastrous; others believe that the step did
go too far in admitting many who were unprepared to accept life outside
the country; and others view it as the salvation of the service through
the new blood injected into the system. The mass lateral entry more than
doubled the numbers in the Foreign Service and spread the scope of
qualifications to a much broader range.

Even if Wristonization is judged a success, it left a residual problem
that continues to haunt the foreign-affairs establishment in Washington
to this day. Long after the lateral-entry process of the mid-1950s, there
are still large numbers of State Department employees, many of them in
critically needed professional skills, who are not available for overseas
duties and who have continued to be covered by the regular civil service
system. The Wriston Report had called for more frequent tours of duty
in Washington for Foreign Service officers to permit a home break in
long-service overseas stations. The report revealed that some officers had
been on continuous overseas assignment for thirty years and that it was
not unusual to find officers with a series of foreign assignments that kept
them away from Washington for more than a decade. Under the reform,
officers would be expected to rotate back to Washington for repatriation
and for exposure to the formation of foreign policy at the seat of govern-

ment. This rotation meant the posts of most significance in the department hierarchy were occupied by returned Foreign Service officers and the professional civil servant was forced to perform his functions under an arbitrary career ceiling. In some instances, the returned officer would be assigned to a specialized post where he was unable to function without the immediate availability of the civil service specialist. This situation could readily lead to double staffing in the administration of certain programs. Both the morale and the utilization of these Washington-locked specialists deteriorated. There were murmurs of complaint to the effect that the civil service employees of the department enjoyed only a second-class citizenship.

These deficiencies led the Johnson administration to seek legislation for the establishment of a unified and flexible career Foreign Service. The proposed bill contemplated a single foreign-affairs personnel system, fully responsive to presidential requirements and to changing conditions in foreign relations. It would be a system broad enough to accommodate the personnel needs, domestic as well as overseas, of all agencies engaged in foreign affairs. It did not attempt to include the large number of overseas employees of the Defense Department. Under the bill there would be free interchange of personnel among foreign-affairs agencies, and between these agencies and the other agencies of the Executive Branch. Maximum flexibility would be the goal for the assignment process to enable management to meet unique requirements and crisis conditions with maximum efficiency and at minimal cost. It proposed to achieve increased coordination with the civil service system by closer liaison with the Civil Service Commission on various personnel matters. It preserved the merit objective of the existing systems by prescribing appointments, promotions, and "selection-out" of personnel on the basis of competitive evaluation.

But the presumed extension of the selection-out principle, which had become an essential and desirable feature of the Foreign Service career system, generated a storm of protest over the prospect of its application to those not then subject to it. Emotional discussion of this issue distorted the objectives of the bill and obscured its benefits and positive objectives. Essentially the proposed system was intended for getting people *in,* not

out. Selection-out had become a necessary part of a rank-in-man personnel system. Its extension did not forecast a return to a new era of political
spoils. It was pointed out in testimony supporting the bill that good
administration of foreign affairs required a plan of uncomplicated movement of personnel from overseas to headquarters and back again, and
that under existing conditions such movement was clearly hampered by
the incompatible rules of the two systems. The civil service system, while
highly effective in itself, had been designed primarily to meet domestic
needs, which can be decidedly different from overseas requirements. The
situation had become further complicated by the fact that the Foreign
Service personnel system had three separate facets of its own: the Foreign
Service itself, the foreign reserve, and the foreign staff corps, each with
different conditions for personnel serving the same department. The
coexistence of the foreign and civil service systems had produced many
problems in addition to that of appropriate assignment. It tended to
breed competition, if not jealousy, between groups of employees. There
was a sensitivity about violations of rules and an exaggerated concern for
rights and not enough concern for duty. Despite all these factors, opposition to the changes prevailed. The legislation was blocked in the Senate
Foreign Relations Committee in response to pleas from some Foreign
Service officers, from government unions, and the veterans' organizations, which feared erosion of the veterans' preference principle. Whatever improvements were to be made must be limited to those possible
through executive action.

An Executive Order was signed by President Johnson to facilitate
interchange of personnel between the Foreign Service and civil service.
The actual application of that authority was very limited because there
was no strong motivation for anyone in either system to make the move.
A tentative start was made in the direction of domestic assignment for
Foreign Service officers on duty in Washington outside the State Department in other foreign-affairs agencies, in the Department of Defense, and
even in the Office of Economic Opportunity. The civil servants remained
in the subordinate support posts at the department headquarters, with
the prospect of little change in their condition but with the knowledge
that their civil service status had been preserved to give them a hunting

license for transfer into other federal establishments in Washington.

The rank-in-man principle, which is the dominant theme of the career Foreign Service, has been subject to frequent critical analysis. It has the benefit cited earlier of assignment flexibility and of promotion decision without reference to duty assignment. It permits the relative evaluation, on a periodic basis, of all officers in the same rank and with the same period of service. It affords the selection-out route as an honorable entry into retirement for those who fail to be promoted after several evaluations. (In actual fact, this exit route was used infrequently for many years and is followed only with great hesitancy.) On the other hand, the system lacks the discipline of position-based assignments and contributes to overstaffing and to assignments which do not permit the officer to perform at the highest level of capability. The functioning of the promotion process has increased the population in the upper ranks without reference to the number of top assignments, so that the career system is distorted. Many officers of the same rank are serving in posts that vary widely in difficulty and authority. Young officers are discouraged over the prospect of long delay before advancement. Traditionally, political or diplomatic assignments have been given greater weight than those which are predominantly administrative or specialized. For this reason, officers are apt to compete for political reporting assignments where they can qualify themselves for future diplomatic work. This tendency in turn has narrowed the diversity of experience, particularly in foreclosing management assignments, as the officer prepares himself for greater responsibility.

For many years the Foreign Service enjoyed a higher prestige among the ablest college students of the nation than any other form of public service. In college recruiting forays a federal representative would usually find a larger number of students raising questions with respect to Foreign Service careers than about any other public experience. This high level of interest was evidenced in a large volume of applications for the annual Foreign Service examination. It was not unusual for more than 50,000 applications to be received and for 60 percent or more of that number to show up for the difficult examining session. Those who cleared this written hurdle would be further examined orally before a panel of

Foreign Service officers and outside experts. Those who were finally selected and admitted to the service had been thoroughly tested and were judged to be of the highest quality the nation had to offer. Although the Vietnam war and general student disillusionment with American commitments abroad have reduced this number in recent years, there still is a far larger volume of applications than there are career entry posts for the competitors. In most years, no more than 200 new appointees take the oath of office as Class 8 Foreign Service officers. It has not been unusual for some of the competitors who were not selected to seek temporary State Department jobs in the hope that their name would be ultimately reached. Even when they fell short of final selection, they constituted a valuable reservoir of young talent for other forms of public service. It was never possible, however, to convince many of these candidates that service in the domestic civil service would ever match the glamor, fascination, and rewards of service on the international plane.

Young Foreign Service officers, with their strong motivation and high potential, receive orientation and language training and are prepared for their initial assignments as American representatives abroad. Coming as they do fresh from the stimulation of the campus, they are convinced that they are qualified to give immediate advice directly to the Secretary of State on the formulation of foreign policy. Naturally it is a matter of disappointment to them that they rarely advise any senior departmental officer. Instead their assignments are largely routine and clerical or call for low-level reporting. If their career runs true to past form, it may be ten or fifteen years before they are assigned any type of supervisory responsibility. Although they may be stationed in exotic countries, they will in all likelihood sample the hardship posts and be subjected more to boredom than overwork. These early experiences either result in the loss of promising officers to other work or in the deadening of their ambitions and talents. There is need for a more determined drive on the part of Foreign Service management to create posts of interest and stimulation at the earliest possible career stage and to allow the outstanding young officer to break out of the lockstep of the promotion system and even move ahead of his superiors to accept greater responsibility. His counterparts in the civil service are frequently able to achieve this recognition in certain programs without any special preferment or added advantage. If such liberalizing steps are not taken, the attraction of the foreign career will wash away. This is a distinct possibility in these times when the committed student is directing his attention to the problems of race, poverty, and environmental decay in his own country.

The ultimate goal of every Foreign Service officer is to receive the credentials from his President for an ambassadorial appointment. If Napoleon's corporals carried marshals' batons in their pack, American Foreign Service officers carry draft credentials as chiefs of mission in their attaché cases. Only a limited number of officers can expect to rise to this ultimate attainment, although the chances have been decidedly enhanced by the rapid growth in U.S. representation around the world as colonies assume independence. Today there are more than 120 ambassadorial assignments. It has been traditional for each President to fill a significant percentage of those posts with noncareer appointees. Until recent times the major embassies, notably in Paris, London, Rome, and Tokyo, were reserved for men of wealth who were known to and had served the President. The career officers have been limited to the posts of lesser prestige and in locations marked by more substantial hardship. In the past decade, however, career officers have been appointed to the major embassies and have occupied an ever larger percentage of the total number of ambassadorial posts. In 1968, career officers constituted 70 percent of the ambassadors; in 1956, 63 percent; and in 1940, 47 percent. The competition for ambassadorial appointments is always keen, even without the added pressure of noncareer appointments. In the top three ranks of the service (career ambassadors, career ministers, and Foreign Service officers Class 1), which constitute the prime source in the Foreign Service for ambassadorial appointments, there are nearly 400 officers for approximately 90 to 100 career ambassadorships. In addition, there is a source with only a little less experience and no less ambition—400 Foreign Service officers in Class 2. With the prospect that over the coming years ambassadorial appointments will not exceed 40 a year, the degree of anticipated competition is obvious.

During the Johnson administration, rough criteria were developed as indicators of the qualities the President sought in selecting ambassadors.

These measures were drawn from the actions and words of the President in deciding upon the men and women for these important appointments.

First, the President desired ambassadors who were both good diplomats and good managers. The emphasis on modern management and the importance of government executives taking an active part in such managerial tasks as planning, programming, budgeting, and various aspects of personnel management was a common objective in the selection of top officials.

Second, the President desired ambassadors who had the quality of mind to be creative, and the strength of courage to develop and advance creative ideas as far as good sense and organizational discipline permitted. While clearly respecting history and tradition, he was aware that the evolution of daily existence was proceeding at a faster pace than were current abilities to organize and manage international efforts.

Third, he wanted ambassadors who would give the President and the Secretary of State the fullest measure of loyalty and devotion. This meant that he wanted men and women who would go anywhere and perform any mission that their government requested. He wanted people who would give their best advice, without reservations for personal or organizational reasons. He wanted ambassadors who would act in the name of all of the people all of the time.

Fourth, he desired an ambassador who would be able to get around the country to which he was accredited to tell the story of the United States—not just the good parts but the problems and what was being done to solve them.

The President recognized the changed relationship of the ambassador in diplomatic communication and the degree to which that change had made it increasingly essential for the ambassador to be truly the President's representative. The President could talk to chiefs of state on the telephone, he could see them and their ambassadors and their foreign ministers on their frequent jet visits to Washington and when he visited other world capitals. But he could not even in this time have intimate daily contact with the masses of people around the world except through his ambassadors and ambassadorial staffs around the globe.

Performance in the Fish Bowl with the Spotlight on It

18

The public servant must serve the citizens in the full glare of public scrutiny. In accepting his public responsibility, he must recognize that he accepts a special code of conduct and a special set of ethical standards. Not only must he obey statutes and regulations that relate to his performance as a public servant; he must also avoid any behavior that creates the appearance of violation of the code or the standards or will undermine the confidence of the public in his impartiality, objectivity, and integrity. He must bring to his public performance a set of personal values that transcend his own success, satisfaction, or advancement. He must be prepared to apply a moral measure in the public interest to every act or decision. He must remember at all times that his duty is to the Americans affected by the service that he was hired to provide. He must recognize that his existence in his public position is determined by the people he serves.

In covering the activities of government, the investigative reporter is always seeking to uncover instances in which the civil servant has violated his trust to further his own personal gain. It is the aberrational or unethical act of the public servant that makes the headlines, not the record of achievement. This is as it must be in a democracy with a free press where all who work for government are responsible to the people who elect and sustain that government.

From time to time there have been complaints about the necessity for these standards of service. More numerous now than in the past there are those who claim that public employees are forced to forfeit too many of their rights when they enter government service, that too many statutes and regulations are built on negative and adverse assumptions, and that behavior requirements place the public employee apart and above acceptable practice in the rest of the society. While there must be constant vigilance against excessive demands or controls, it is not unfair or inequitable to expect higher ethical conduct on the part of those who work in the public interest. In this area as in others already discussed, the search must be for that precarious balance between the individual's rights and his obligations to the public.

The trend of legislative and executive action in the past decade has been toward reform of past limitations while specifying in greater detail what government expects of its employees—a determination to modernize and to dispel doubt and confusion about expectations of performance.

Shortly after his inauguration, President Kennedy designated three distinguished lawyers, Judge Calvert Magruder, Dean Jefferson B. Fordham, and Professor Bayliss Manning, to review existing conflict-of-interest laws and regulations and to recommend the necessary statutory reforms. This panel was only the latest version in a series of study groups to focus on the outmoded collection of statutes and regulations that had grown up over the years. The panel reported to the President within ninety days and provided him with the basis for a congressional message dealing not only with conflict of interest but also with the problem of ethics in government generally.

The message opened with this declaration of policy:

No responsibility of government is more fundamental than the responsibility of maintaining the highest standards of ethical behavior by those who conduct the public business. There can be no dissent from the principle that all officials must act with unwavering integrity, absolute impartiality and complete devotion to the public interest. This principle must be followed not only in reality but in appearance. For the basis of effective government is public confidence, and that confidence is endangered when ethical standards falter or appear to falter.

I have firm confidence in the integrity and dedication of those who work for our government. Venal conduct by public officials in this country has been comparatively rare—and the few instances of official impropriety that have been uncovered have usually not suggested any widespread departure from high standards of ethics and moral conduct.

The President cited the complexity of the ethical problems confronting public servants; while admitting that no statute or regulation can deal with "the myriad of possible challenges to a man's integrity or his devotion to the public interest, formal regulation was required to lay down clear guidelines of policy and to provide an ethical tone for the conduct of public business."

Urging statutory reform of the conflict-of-interest statutes, many of which antedated 1873, he proposed a bill that would close gaps in regulations and eliminate existing inequities. It offered special standards for part-time consultants whose skills were needed by the government without requiring the severing of regular employment obligations. It proposed administrative means more appropriate as enforcement devices than past reliance on criminal measures. Avoiding a pitfall of sensitivity, the President limited the coverage of the legislation to the Executive Branch, commenting that regulation of the conduct of members of Congress and congressional employees should be left to congressional judgment. Congress moved slowly on this bill but it was ultimately enacted in 1963 to provide a new and modernized framework in which to govern potential conflicts of interest.

Turning to policy areas with which he could deal directly, in 1961 President Kennedy issued an Executive Order prohibiting outside employment or activity incompatible with the discharge of official responsibility, outside compensation for any activity in the scope of official duty, compensation for lectures, articles, or public appearances dealing with government work or based on official information not yet a matter of general knowledge. He also prohibited gifts to government personnel whenever the employee had reason to believe that the gift would not have been made except for his official position or whenever the employee had reason to believe that the donor's private interests were likely to be affected by the actions of the employee or his agency. This prohibition dealt with a chronic problem that had plagued government officials who were the beneficiaries of gifts from persons who directly or indirectly did business with their organizations. The order eliminated any doubt about the objectionable nature of accepting such gifts. The President promised to apply government-wide standards to the continuance of property holdings by appointees in the Executive Branch to ensure that all appointees lived up to the highest standard of behavior. To enforce these standards, the President instructed each Cabinet member and agency head to issue regulations designed to maintain high standards within his own organization. He requested that in the administration of such regulations each agency establish an ad hoc committee to serve in an advisory capacity on ethical problems as they arose. To ensure consistency in agency regulation and to coordinate government-wide compliance, he designated a White House staff member as his representative in carrying out the program.

The only problem that arose subsequent to the issuance and enforcement of these policies related to part-time consultants. Certain scientific advisers to government agencies had built an intricate three-way relationship that at least gave the impression of conflict of interest. While employed by a university and engaged in research supported by the government, these scientists had advisory associations with private research-and-development or production organizations which, in turn, were under contract to government agencies for weapons systems or other development. To complete the triangle, the same scientists were called upon by the government agency to advise on the ultimate decision on the weapons-system contract for which the firm with which they were associated was a competitor. When this elaborate and conflicting relationship was pointed out in a press story, the Attorney General promptly issued a memorandum identifying the conflict-of-interest statutes and calling for their more vigorous application in cases of this type.

Aside from a case where a presidential appointee used his official stationery in connection with a transaction involving his previous employer, the Kennedy years were virtually free of ethical problems. Although exclusive credit cannot be given to the executive initiative in enunciating policy, clearly it had a marked influence on subsequent behavior throughout the Executive Branch.

When President Johnson assumed the presidency, he called for an internal staff review of these policies with the objective of establishing an ethical tone for those who would be serving with him. In an Executive Order issued in May 1965, he prescribed standards of ethical conduct for government officers and employees that codified, clarified, and strengthened the standards of ethical conduct issued by his predecessor. In his accompanying statement he reiterated this policy in this fashion:

Government personnel bear a special responsibility to be fair and impartial in their dealings with those who have business with the government. We cannot tolerate conflicts of interest or favoritism—or even conduct that gives the appearance that such actions are occurring. It is our intention that this does not take place in the federal government.

Although the overwhelming majority of federal employees experience absolutely no problem in this regard, there are some whose duties on occasion place them in difficult or awkward situations, and thus the Order issued today lays down general guidance and standards of conduct as clearly as possible. In large measure, the special problems faced by federal employees lie in the area of judgment, propriety, and good taste. Obviously these cannot be legislated or prescribed by Order or regulation. . . . every effort has been made to take into account the rights and privileges of federal employees and, on the other hand, the right of the public to have confidence in the fairness and integrity of government personnel.

Because of the necessity for individual judgment with respect to behavior in difficult and complex situations, this Executive Order encouraged individuals faced with problems involving sensitive judgments to seek counsel. The chairman of the Civil Service Commission was requested to work with each department and agency head to designate within his organization qualified persons who could provide guidance and interpretation in specific situations. The order assigned central responsibility to the commission for issuing government-wide regulations implementing the order and for reviewing supplementary agency regulations covering their special situations. The commission, always consulted for advice on such matters, gave added weight to this objective and endeavored to assist agency management in the development of standards appropriate to their particular program activities.

While most of the provisions in the Johnson order reiterated the prohibitions specified four years earlier in the Kennedy order, it had one important addition that broke new ground in the enforcement of ethical standards. It required all officials appointed by the President and reporting to him and certain other federal officials and employees to file statements of their financial interests. These statements were to reveal the property holdings of all personnel in these top positions. The statements were filed with the chairman of the Civil Service Commission who reviewed and evaluated them. Where a question of conflict or propriety was revealed, he consulted with the individual and advised on any changes that might be indicated. The reports were to be filed within ninety days after the signing of the Executive Order and were to be amended quarterly in order to keep the statements fully up to date. To set an example in the enforcement of this requirement, the President himself filed a complete statement of his real-estate and security holdings through the trustee who managed his affairs during his term in office. No serious problems arose from this feature of the policy, but as described earlier, the extension of it to large numbers of employees by agency action contributed to the cries of "invasion of privacy." It was apparent that some agency managers were overly zealous, or misinterpreted the requirement, or opposed it and extended its coverage beyond the point of necessity. Below the level of presidential appointees, the requirement was intended to assist those employees who were engaged in contract administration, auditing, regulation of nongovernment activities, and other sensitive work where conflict was a possibility from possible inadvertent difficulties in conforming to the ethical standards. It was obviously not intended for sweeping application to those whose work responsibilities were far removed from potential relationships of this type. The actual number of conflicts avoided or embarrassing appearances averted will never be known, but the mere process of preparing a declaration of holdings brought the attention of the employee to the possible relationship of his personal holdings to the obligations of his public responsibility.

During the transition between the Johnson and Nixon administrations, the declaration-of-holdings form was picked up by the incoming from the outgoing administration and used to check the potential conflict-of-interest vulnerability of prospective Nixon appointees. The Johnson order in this area of public policy has continued to stand and has become a part of the continuing personnel policy of government.

Inquiries with respect to the application of the standard were limited in number. They were primarily directed toward the application of the prohibition on income from lectures or articles, on the acceptance of gifts, and on attendance at social events given by private persons with whom the government official did business. In the course of his responsibilities many an official was requested to address professional societies or trade associations that either offered an honorarium or extended hospitality in the form of hotel accommodations or restaurant credit. It had been customary in certain situations of this type for the public official to accept without question these gestures of courtesy, and it was difficult to reverse the practice without seeming to be offensive. Nevertheless, the officials were urged to make the change to avoid the possibility of future embarrassment; the necessity for the change in no way implied past influence in government decisions through the acceptance of such hospitality. In the Civil Aeronautics Board, the board members and certain key staffers had customarily been invited to fly, by courtesy of the airline involved, on the inaugural flight on new routes. This practice was cited as necessary to conform with the mandate of the basic act "to promote the development of civil aviation." It was decided that civil aviation would continue to develop without the dubious lift it would receive from the presence of public regulatory officials on a gala inaugural flight.

The regular practice in private industry of distributing bottles of whiskey, hams or turkeys, or fruitcakes to favored customers had carried over into government, and some officials found it difficult to return such gifts without incurring the hostility of the donor. The Civil Service Commission suggested that the gift be returned to the donor with an explanation of the President's policy on this subject and with the request that the practice be abandoned in the future. This counsel avoided the difficult determination of what size or rate of consumption would be permissible for gifts under these standards. During the deep-freeze and fur-coat controversies of the 1950s it was seriously proposed that a gift was acceptable if it could be consumed within twenty-four hours. This apparently would make a single bottle of whiskey acceptable but not a full case, and a ten-pound turkey but not a twenty-pounder.

State, county, and city governments have exhibited far less determination in establishing standards of this type. Bribes of police officers, real-estate operations on the part of zoning officials, procurement purchases from friends and relatives, and other breaches of public faith frequently find their way into the public prints and erode public confidence. Although the federal standards are by no means ideal and must be re-evaluated frequently to assure that they match the requirements of the times, they do constitute a valid starting point for other jurisdictions. Such standards can emphasize for the benefit of the public the strong intention of the public administrator that the affairs of government be conducted openly, honestly, and impartially.

The Impact

of the Computer

in

Public Service

19

The computer, that Kilroy of inventions, was a constant companion of the public servant in the 1960s. Succeeding generations of these marvelous devices facilitated the maintenance of Social Security records and the collection of income taxes, served as a critical research and development device in government laboratories, provided massive storage and retrieval facilities, and participated directly in the search, selection, and advancement of the civil servant himself. In some quarters, the computer was viewed as a threatening opponent that would eliminate the necessity for jobs and needed to be outlawed, or it was an accumulator of vital statistics that no government could possibly harbor without a malignant purpose. But for good or ill, the computer was there. It was not only there but it was advancing in numbers and in functions performed. The federal government had created him and now he was being put to work on an ever broader range of tasks.

Starting at the earliest stages of the employment process, automated examinations assured the ultimate protection of the applicant's response to the questions asked. It could be truly stated that the only eyes ever to fall upon an applicant's civil service test would be his own. Even if the test was forwarded across the continent, graded, and compared with papers of other competitors, even though he might be hired and then entered a lifetime career on the basis of this test, nobody else needed to see it after he had completed it. Such processes were criticized as depersonalizing, but mass-examination scoring never was a very personal activity. Automation of this clerical type of work served to increase the time that managers could give to the problems requiring human attention.

During fiscal 1966, the Civil Service Commission's computer automatically scheduled more than 700,000 applicants into 1,000 examination points throughout the country, computed the scores of those who took the nation-wide examination, and notified applicants of the results. For any one of those 700,000 who applied for an automated examination, the initial action on his part was simple and easy. He filed only a small card form. In due course he received an admissions card that told him to report at a specified date and hour at an examination point convenient to him. His examination had been scheduled by machine, the time and location had been printed automatically. In the examination room, the competitor marked his answers to the questions by shading the appropriate block on a set of test answer sheets. When the sheets were returned to the commission, computers performed the rest of the task. The final output included a letter to the competitor notifying him of his test results.

Automatic data processing in federal personnel administration became a way of life about 1960, but the roots of this plunge into automation can be traced back to the 1880s. There is evidence that the entire development was initiated by an invention of an enterprising young employee of the Census Bureau who was submerged by the mountain of paper work necessary in the 1880 census enumeration. This civil servant of ninety years ago was Hermann Hollerith, a young engineer who put together a tabulating machine that he called his "statistical piano." It did in fact resemble the old-style player piano in that it employed a roll of punched tape to feed instructions into the machine. Apparently his machine was an instant success, because in the census tabulation ten years later Hollerith was credited with saving two years of work and more than $5 million, at 1890 price levels. Later this new mechanism became the wellspring of a phenomenal business and the origination of the company that now bears the call letters IBM.

Government research also generated the development of electronic data processing. One of the first completely electronic computers was called ENIAC, for Electronic Numerical Integrator and Calculator. Shortly after World War II, the War Department and the University of Pennsylvania developed this process to solve problems in ballistic research. The first commercial model, UNIVAC 1 (Universal Automatic Computer), was operable in the Census Bureau three years prior to the first private installation. That first UNIVAC served its government well; when it was retired to the Smithsonian Institution in October 1963, it had run up a record of more than 73,000 operating hours.

By the early 1960s the computer had outgrown its role as a large and fast calculating machine and started its service as the centralized source of personnel-management data. In a program called MODE (Management Objectives with Dollars through Employees) the Department of Agriculture built a large-scale computer operation that retained records and reports and issued paychecks for its 100,000 employees across the country. Within five years twenty-two agencies of the government had automated personnel systems covering more than 1.5 million employees with new systems to cover an additional 500,000 under development.

These developments have not been achieved without difficulty. Nearly every installation timetable has proved to be overly optimistic. Enthusiastic salesmen and programmers have frequently claimed capability which could only be achieved after long lead-time and equipment adjustment, staff training, and programming operations. A common response in a beleaguered payroll or personnel-records office was that "you will have to wait a bit longer because we now have that information on the computer." With accumulated experience, early claims of staff economies through computerization evaporated because new and higher skills were required and the computer system was soon utilized at full capacity to provide information and performing operations that originally were not contemplated.

The Civil Service Commission first entered the computer field in its administration of the government-wide retirement system. Through an automated procedure, 750,000 retirement accounts were maintained with an annual increase of 45,000 annuitants. In 1962 Congress authorized a 5 percent monetary increase in all current annuities, thus necessitating the recomputation of each annuity for each person on the retirement rolls. An earlier accomplishment of this task had required months with added work load caused by a flow of inquiries about delays in receiving the higher retirement checks. But in 1962–63, with the computer in full operation, 630,000 annuities were recomputed in ten days and checks were being distributed to the annuitants before the complaints and inquiries began accumulating. On the basis of a management study of future retirement and insurance operations over the next decade, it was estimated that more than $3 million could be saved through further automation.

In the forefront of federal computer utilization has been the Social Security Administration, with its massive records for millions of American workers in the ever broadening coverage of its program. With the advent of each generation of equipment a new timesaving Social Security application has been adopted, with the result that administrative operations are at a lower unit-cost level than those recorded in the highly efficient insurance industry. Only through this advance in computer processing has it been possible to absorb such added benefits as Medicare within the Social Security system.

More than any other technological development, the growth of automatic and electronic data processing has challenged the capacity of government to recruit and train large numbers of employees in new and frequently changing skills. From the basic typing and clerical skills for the more routine operational jobs up through the programmers and systems analysts, a veritable army needed to be deployed in the computer rooms of the government offices and laboratories. No other training requirement received more intensive treatment by the Civil Service Commission and the agencies. Multiple-tier training programs were organized and continued year after year. The demand was so great that the commission established an Automatic Data Processing Management Training Center in Washington, which more than 2,300 federal employees attended in a year's time. Even the top executives found it necessary to acquire an expanded degree of computer knowledge in order to use effectively the information generated by the new system for their exercise of decision-making responsibility.

The haunting fear of employee displacement by automation has not proved valid. With intelligent planning, agency managers prevented hardship for employees whose work was transferred to the computers. An outstanding example was furnished by the Internal Revenue Service, which did an exemplary job of minimizing the impact on employees in its extensive ADP conversion through planning that forecast the nature and extent of staff changes for five years in advance and engaged in intensive retraining and placement efforts for all employees affected. In this and other instances, many an employee had his skill advanced through training to participate in work of greater difficulty in the computer field. Likewise, the drudgery of many a manual task was eliminated by shifting the function to the machine. It is true, however, that the computer obviated the need for a massive expansion of clerical forces to meet work loads that expanded in response to population or business growth. More than any other factor, the computer converted public employment from a predominantly clerical nature to a more technical and professional work force. A future generation of computers may well complete the liberation of the public employee from a life of paper processing. Instead of dehumanizing work processes, the computer may free the human mind for more worthy purposes than clerical decisions. The computer may well have placed a premium on man at his best and not degraded his worth or enslaved his initiative.

Already the presence of the computer in government has heightened the need for more imaginative and innovative managers who can readily grasp ideas in the most complex forms, think in broad, philosophical terms, and apply such terms in decisions that advance the public welfare. It has forced a finer degree of quantitative precision in executive judgment. It necessitates a higher level of analytical capability and eliminated arguments that merely plead conclusions without analytical substantiation. It has given greater intellectual scope—and demand—to leadership positions. It has opened the way to creativity in administration.

But the emergence of automated operations in the public sector should not be accepted without asking searching questions about what these systems are actually doing in the personnel field itself. Automated personnel systems installed during recent years have been primarily intended for record-keeping and reporting. But it would be a serious mistake to think of personnel functions primarily in terms of records and reports. Personnel administration is principally concerned with finding the best-qualified people to fill vacancies, ensuring maximum utilization of manpower resources, and improving working conditions and thereby improving work. It is also concerned with providing equal employment opportunities to all citizens, not only at the point of entrance into the service but through training, promotion, and full career development. Seen from this perspective, the use of automated personnel operations is still at a threshold stage.

The basic question in terms of these objectives is: What parts of the job can a computer do better and which can men do better? Although few managers may be willing to admit it, a large part of management is actually clerical decision-making, often dignified as "judgment." It requires the identification of relevant facts and the selection of predetermined actions on the basis of those facts. This process can be done beautifully and uncomplainingly by the computer. In scheduling civil service examinations, for example, the computer makes "decisions" of this type by the thousands. Why should the time of a man or woman be devoted to this type of clerical work with less accuracy and less satisfaction? This man or woman can perform other phases of the work in a far superior fashion by using the data resources of computers. Such computer-supported work involves the decisions of personnel planning, the matching of men and jobs, the forecasting of manpower needs, the evaluation of employment experience, and the important decisions of career planning.

For proper decision in these areas there must be an integrated information system. This requires the use of information across organizational lines. To make such a system function, it is necessary to standardize symbols and codes and to assure compatibility among the computer installations in various organizations. Direct tape-to-tape feeding of data from one department to another and into a government-wide system is well within the system's ability for the future. The computer's ability to search its perfect memory and pick out records of individual and specific characteristics has already been applied in the search for candidates for high governmental posts, as explained earlier. The computerized file can become a talent bank with an automated retrieval system that broadens the scope of candidate consideration for those making critical appointment decisions.

For all its affirmative contributions, the computer as a means of storing and retrieving personnel information constitutes a source of concern. There is more than a slight Orwellian shadow in the existence of this almost human piece of equipment filled with vital information concerning large numbers of people. If the presence of dossiers formed from investigative reports is a potential threat to individual liberties, how can automated records be immune from such suspicion? Can the possessors of such detailed and voluminous information about other human beings be trusted to utilize such information in the interests of the individuals so recorded and the public at large? How can the insatiable desire for more and more information, with the presumed objective of making better and better decisions on the basis of such information, be subjected to standards of ethics as well as tests of necessity? With the best intentions, the Census Bureau, equipped with the ninth generation of Hollerith's equipment, expanded the list of desired data to be collected from the citizens in the course of the decennial census in 1970. This deeper probe for more facts about the more than 200 million Americans was greeted with rising concern that produced demands for safeguards on the information collected and a reduction in the number of requests for information. In the interest of efficiency and economy, the Bureau of the Budget proposed a consolidated data center for the government. But instead of receiving the applause of Congress, the entire system was subjected to penetrating congressional inquiry and funds for its ultimate development have not been authorized.

The computer's mysterious capacity for collecting, filing, and regurgitating data about persons must be programmed with care and discretion. Multiple judgments should be brought into play before new sources of information are tapped or additional personal data are incorporated. The loss of privacy or dignity would be too high a price to pay.

Incentive

for Improved

Performance

in Public Service

20

If serving the public interest is not in and of itself a sufficient incentive for higher performance and greater productivity, what can the public manager offer in order to ensure those goals? Is there incentive in tenure and protection through an elaborate set of guarantees and the complicated course of due-process protection from arbitrary dismissal? Can the promotion, that basic lubrication of the career system, serve as the driving thrust for more significant performance? Will more skillful and sympathetic supervision draw out the best in the people assigned? Can extra compensation directly related to more substantial achievement or higher rates of production kindle the fires of greater effort? Can recognition in cash or public identification motivate the individual to new heights? Will changes in assignment, new training experiences, and altered environment prove to be the stimuli that make the difference between the good and the excellent?

The answer must be that every incentive device should be applied and tested as a part of public managers' efforts to create an environment in which the employee will wish to do his best. The behavioral scientists and the sociologists have some guidance to offer but it is fragmentary and speculative. More research needs to be conducted. More of the devices and processes employed need to be critically studied to determine their actual effect.

265

There is reason to believe that the granting of tenure and the commitment to longtime employment may be a reverse incentive. Once the protection offered by this benefit is obtained, risk and uncertainty are removed and the individual will slip into a comfortable routine where the status quo is defended and where new displays of original or creative work are not required. One of the perpetual complaints from administrators about the civil service system is their seeming inability to remove, reassign, or demote veteran employees who are unable to meet the standard of performance. In virtually any discussion of managerial problems, the question of how to get rid of the person who has passed his peak or is deadwood ranks high on the agenda. It is not enough to delineate the procedures for taking adverse action against such an employee. Those processes are long and complicated, designed to give the employee the benefits of due process in an action that if carried to its conclusion will grievously stigmatize him. It is not enough to establish specific standards of performance and to evaluate performance against those standards. It is all too easy for the manager to resort to the more mechanistic adjective rating, which has little meaning as an evaluation device. It is not enough to encourage the manager who makes the promotion decision to take special care to seek out not only evidence of past performance but demonstrable indicators of ability to succeed in higher responsibilities. The manager must convince himself that he will not be a promoter of the Peter Principle—that in any organization a person may rise to a level in which he is incompetent. Many a manager who has complained about the failure of a particular employee has been subsequently embarrassed when reminded that he initiated the promotion. The continuity and stability produced by tenure should be exploited to assure that those conditions activate rather than retard initiative, stimulate rather than depress innovation, and encourage rather than destroy a healthy sense of risk-taking.

In the public service, no single personnel action attracts more controversy than the promotion. Constant pressure is applied by employees and their representatives to diminish management's discretion in selecting those who in competition on the basis of merit should be advanced. Absolute seniority, measured to the day and hour, eliminates that type of competition and makes the promotion process automatic. Competitive examination scores as the sole measure of promotability will not please or benefit either the employee or the manager. It will place the basis for measuring relative ability in the hands of the test-maker. In too many employment situations, there is the unsubstantiated expectation that advancement to higher pay rates and more significant assignments can be anticipated by everyone. The fundamental principle of competition for promotion is not adequately explained and demonstrated to the new employee, nor is sufficient attention given to advising the employee what he himself may do to contribute to his future advancement. The promotion, with its tangible features of recognition in the form of additional pay and stature, should be used to engender motivation. It should be the most significant incentive available to the manager in public service. Within broad policy guidelines and assistance from skilled personnel professionals, he should be encouraged to design the promotion system most meaningful as an incentive for employees in the type of work under his direction.

In the federal government, more than fifteen years of experience has been accumulated in the administration of a comprehensive incentive-awards program to reward employees who contribute beneficial suggestions or demonstrate superior performance. Based upon legislation passed in 1954, this program has involved a vast number of employees in an encouraging affirmative effort. In 1968 the suggestion program reached record highs of participation, with a total of 537,000 suggestions received and 146,000 adopted with measurable first-year benefits to the government of $150 million. For these adopted suggestions, the government agencies paid $4,800,000 in cash awards to the employees involved. If these benefits are sustained from year to year, the federal employees who offered them saved the taxpayers a substantial sum and increased the efficiency of government operations. The program is not administered through the traditional suggestion box. Instead, supervisors and foremen are urged to join with the suggesting employee in the development of dollar-saving benefits. It is always difficult to measure the true incentive value of such a program, and almost as difficult to measure the true savings that result from it. At regular intervals the program has been subjected to penetrating criticism to give it new relevance and to eliminate the least beneficial features. For example, for the tenth anniversary a special cost-reduction campaign was announced on a government-wide basis, with the understanding that the most significant recommendations would receive special recognition from the President himself. In a special ceremony at Constitution Hall on December 4, 1964, President Johnson presented Economy Achievement plaques to federal employees before an audience of 3,800 officials, including Cabinet members and heads of independent agencies. He praised the cost consciousness of the award recipients and urged all employees to search for cost-reduction ideas. The award winners had accounted for an estimated first-year savings to the government of $85 million. A motion-picture film of this ceremony was subsequently distributed throughout the government as a means of conveying the President's message to the entire federal work force.

In making awards for superior performance, federal managers were offered another incentive option that they used frequently. In 1968, 97,390 awards were approved for first-year measurable benefits of $99,-460,000. This represented an annual rate of 35 awards per 1,000 employees and netted those employees $14,270,000. These awards were frequently presented at agency awards ceremonies, which since 1954 have become at least an annual occurrence in every department and agency. They have afforded a congenial setting in which to single out those who have performed with particular success and to encourage the entire staff to step up their performance in order to gain similar recognition.

The same statute authorized the President to present annually his own Distinguished Award for Outstanding Civilian Service. Acting upon the recommendations of a designated panel, Presidents Eisenhower, Kennedy, and Johnson selected five or six outstanding career employees for recognition each year. This award has appropriately been viewed as the highest recognition open to those who commit their careers to federal service. The importance of the award was enhanced by the personal participation of the President in the selection and by his presence at the presentation ceremony in the Cabinet Room, the Rose Garden, or the East Room of the White House.

Beyond the government there has been a concern about the failure to recognize excellence when it does appear in the public service. In 1953, in conjunction with Princeton University, John D. Rockefeller 3rd inaugurated a series of Rockefeller Public Service Awards, which have been presented annually ever since to outstanding public servants selected by a distinguished panel from outside government. These awards have enjoyed high prestige, tangibly enhanced in recent years by a cash stipend of $10,000.

A few years later the National Civil Service League, the reforming citizen group that played an active role in the original passage of the Civil Service Act, inaugurated a Career Service Award to be presented annually to ten outstanding men and women selected by the board of directors. The awards banquet of this organization always attracts a large representation from the departments and agencies whose employees win these awards.

In a speech before the Washington Jaycees in 1948, Arthur S. Flemming, then retiring as Civil Service Commissioner, suggested that his audience of live-wire young men place the spotlight on their contemporaries who had recorded significant achievement in government before the age of forty. The Jaycees have carried out the suggestion with verve and drive, and each year since then have presented to crowded Washington luncheons ten young men who had succeeded in government the previous year.

The award-giving process has proliferated with the passage of time without any depreciation of the award currency. There is no doubt that these awards are highly valued by the recipients and that this form of recognition constitutes an encouragement to others who are in the service or are potentially attracted to it. Other elements of government may well emulate this practice in their own way. A number of communities have initiated combined awards programs in recognition of outstanding public servants from city, state, and federal service in their areas. Each program should be designed to fulfill the particular needs of the community involved and to involve a cross section of citizen representatives in recognizing the contribution of the best public servants.

It has been said that the absence of the profit incentive in government will always deflate motivation on the part of public employees. There is little evidence to support this conclusion because the incentive of profit is shared by only a relatively small group of employees in any private enterprise. But there is the occasional conflict in public service between the twin demands of efficiency and service. It may not be efficient to take a little longer time in caring for an ill patient or a retarded child or a beleaguered taxpayer, but it is essential that the citizen receive the service expected. Once again a balance must be secured, this time a balance between cost effectiveness and the rights of the citizen to be served.

There are other areas of management discretion that can constitute incentives. The quality of physical surroundings can be so drab, routine, and uncomfortable that employees are discouraged in improving their work. Locations far removed from the homes of many workers impose transportation problems that lower their job efficiency. Unsanitary washrooms, lack of recreational areas, poor food in the cafeteria, and overemphasis accountability for time are all negative environmental factors that must be eliminated. When the Civil Service Commission moved into a new building in 1963 after eighty years of institutional disadvantage through temporary quarters in structures designed more as national monuments than productive workshops, the morale, productivity, and even appearance of the staff improved. Of course, working conditions were more efficient, desks and equipment were more appropriately located, but the new structure itself became an object of pride and a symbol of the standing of the organization on the physical landscape of Washington.

New incentives may also be shaped through new supervisory attitudes. Behavioral research going all the way back to the Hawthorne study conducted by Western Electric in the 1920s reveals the benefits gained from a more active participation by the employees in the decision making that relates to their work. The departure from rigid hierarchies of supervision and the introduction of a more participative pattern of work assignment and evaluation have paid dividends in satisfaction and productivity. To some extent, public managers have been locked in by an excessive commitment to the principles of span of control, line and staff organizations, and fixed administrative standards. A participative atmosphere need not be a permissive one. Perhaps it can reduce the risk of failure for the employee who has withheld his ideas out of apprehension over the supervisory reaction. Experiments in task setting, performance, and evaluation by the employee with a minimum of supervision may surprise the boss with the capabilities really possessed by his subordinates. Team endeavors for the pooling of individual skills and interests will produce the ultimate result and have frequently proved highly successful in developing group goals and incentives. This mode has been applied with particularly rewarding results in research and development projects where a number of disciplines are necessary in order to design new systems to meet operational specifications. Where there is group achievement, there can always be group recognition to the benefit of everyone involved.

A range of incentives is available. They can be applied at the discretion of the manager, supervisor or foreman in the forum of public service. Public employment, in fact, should take the lead in the testing of these incentives under the most favorable circumstances that can be devised.

The

International

Dimension of

21 Civil Service

For more than half a century, a slow but frequently broken march has advanced toward an international civil service. Since the hopeful days at the birth of the League of Nations to the threatening hours of the early 1970s, a growing number of men and women from a longer and longer list of independent nations have been appointed for service in international organizations. Across ideological walls and cultural barriers, they have come to join talents in support of global missions. Even in the years of World War II, residual staffs in temporary locations preserved the continuity of certain international functions and the evolutionary growth of the international civil service.

But much as the construction of a meaningful and viable national civil service has fallen short of expectations in the United States and other western countries, the international civil service has failed to match the aspiring standards of the charter writers in postwar years. The ideal of an international merit system where individuals would be selected on the basis of relative ability and qualifications, where national origin would be incidental, where total careers would be committed to international service, and where assignments anywhere on the globe might be expected, has not been realized. Nor can it realistically be expected to materialize. Some critics refuse to recognize employment with international agencies as a bona fide form of civil service. They point to the continuing emphasis upon geographical distribution, the inequality of linguistic demands, the preservation of national identification in benefits and allowances, the involvement of national governments in recruitment and placement of individuals, the lack of mobility between organizations and points of duty around the world, the high prevalence of short-term assignments, and the absence of firm personnel policies relating to the entire international community. These criticisms have validity, but they fail to take into account the conflicting policy positions, the complexity of international staffing, and the rapidly changing national composition of international bodies.

With all the seemingly insurmountable problems faced in building an international civil service, it is truly remarkable that a body of employees from more than a hundred nations, in virtually all professions and occupations, are on the job in locations on all continents in support of the missions of the United Nations and its several independent organizations. The management of each agency has secured the services of men and women to accomplish the administrative responsibilities, the technical services, and the support for international conferences, that occur with more than daily frequency throughout the world. Although the forms of coordinated planning and action among the organizations leave much to be desired, there has been agreement on certain basic personnel policies that relate to the entire international community and a continuing effort to broaden that policy base through the difficult process of international discussion. The chief executive officers of international organizations meet at least semiannually to consider common problems in the personnel field, to accept the advice of the International Civil Service Advisory Board, and to determine common objectives. Their deputies with responsibility for administrative decisions and their personnel officers meet with even greater frequency to form a more consistent management position with respect to the human side of international government.

The time has long passed for the world verdict on whether or not there should be an international civil service. There must be a multinational body of men and women to play the parts in the international drama of drawing together the purposes of all mankind. As Dag Hammarskjöld viewed it, it was the task of international administration to form "a center for harmonizing the actions of nations in the attainment of common ends." An international civil service has been recognized as a global imperative. It has become an established fact. The contemporary task of scholars and practitioners, professionals and politicans, must be to develop the means by which this service can effectively and equitably fulfill its mission of human survival.

To achieve this essential progress toward an international civil service, there must be recognition of the fundamental principles forming the foundation for such a service and the inherent problems and conflicts which retard growth and obscure the fundamental objectives. Drawing upon the experience of the League of Nations and the early specialized international agencies, the authors of the United Nations Charter embodied in Articles 100 and 101 the fundamental precepts for the new world organization's human element. These principles formed the foundation upon which this structure of international personnel policy was erected by the recommendations of the preparatory commission of 1946 and later by the advisory observations of the International Civil Service Advisory Board and the administrative interpretations of the Secretaries-General Trygve Lie, Dag Hammarskjöld, and U Thant. In addition, the course of history in international affairs during the ensuing quarter century has brought political pressures which have created obstacles and necessitated new examination of principles in the light of rapidly changing world conditions. The rising tide of national expectation among the newly liberated peoples of Africa and Asia doubled the membership of the United Nations in a relatively short span of time. The peace-keeping activities in Korea, the Middle East, and the Congo injected new stresses and strains in the international organization. The tensions of the cold war and the interaction of the superpowers within the framework of the United Nations tested these principles again and again. The character of the post of Secretary-General itself evolved, gaining and waning in strength, attacked alternately by one or the other of the superpowers, threatened with political triplification and perpetually redefining its scope and powers, and played a vastly significant part in the guidance of the civil service development as well as in the solution of its continuing problems.

Out of this crucible of international political life was forged a doctrine of international civil service that reinforced certain basic principles and aimed at increasing understanding and improving practices. This doctrine is most persuasively set forth in a March 1954 report of the International Civil Service Advisory Board, which prescribed four positive duties for international public servants:

1. Integrity, to be judged on the basis of the individual's total behavior, taking into account personal qualities such as honesty, truthfulness, fidelity, probity and freedom from corrupting influences, bearing in mind that the international civil servant is a public as well as an international official.
2. Loyalty to the international organization, combined with an international outlook flowing from an understanding of and loyalty to the objectives set forth in the charter and involving willingness to try to understand and be tolerant of different points of view, different cultural patterns and different work habits.
3. Independence of any authority outside the international organization.
4. Impartiality in the form of objectivity, lack of bias, tolerance and restraint.

These fundamental standards were supplemented with emphasis upon the need for effort to overcome biased attitudes within the Secretariat, through better understanding and intellectual discipline and through the cultivation of social relationships between members of the staff and between supervisors and subordinates. In terms of external relationships, the standards reiterated the nonrepresentative character of the international official in relation to his own government and to his country's policy, thereby stressing the fundamental principle of independence—which had been and continues to be challenged by national spokesmen.

There was a recognition that the international civil servant must accept special restraints in his public and private life in order to make his positive contribution to the work and ideals of the international organization. In looking forward confidently to the development of a proud tradition, the board set standards for staff members in a genuinely international service.

Beyond these ideals of conduct, the Charter set forth two basic criteria as standards of recruitment and conditions of employment. First, three dominant qualities—efficiency, competence, and integrity—were cited as compulsory features of the personnel system. The second criterion called for subordination of geographical distribution of the nationals selected for service, confining it to recruitment without extension to conditions of employment, without a rigid formula, and with only the condition that it "be given due regard." The geographical basis was to be as wide as possible, which meant that each individual case should be considered on its merits in terms of the principal criteria and the existing circumstances. Both standards were subordinated to the constitutional obligation in Article 1, which called for responsibility to the international organization alone and instituted a prohibition on any action by employees that might reflect on their position as international officials.

These factors of merit and geography, though clearly compatible in the minds of the Charter's authors, created the issue over which continuing controversy has focused ever since. Every year or so as conditions have changed, a new study and a new debate have generated reconsideration of the combined application of these principles. Admittedly, it has become increasingly difficult, with the admission of more and more states from the developing world with fewer and fewer professionals, to sustain geographical balance without sacrificing competence and efficiency. The absence of prescribed standards for the determination of geographical distribution, while permitting administrative flexibility, has been productive of serious political disagreement. Should the predominant standard be national, regional, or continental? Should the determining factor be population, or financial contribution to the international organization? And in view of the increasing divergency in size and resources of the member states, how could reasonable equity be assured both for the very small and the very large?

The search for equitable distribution was further complicated by the predominance of North Americans and Western Europeans in the early period of international agency growth, by periods of studied neglect of these organizations by certain powers, by the unwillingness of many international civil servants or their own governments to accept extended periods of service, and by the relative attractiveness of international service to nationals of different countries. But in the face of these difficulties, administrative devices such as the concept of geographical region and the measure of desirable range have been developed and a remarkable degree of balance and distribution has been achieved. This area of policy will remain a major preoccupation in the further development of the system, but it should not be allowed to submerge or delay the resolution of other problems or the development of other policies. In all likelihood, the pragmatic position will have to be that the standards of true merit will be partially sacrificed in the interest of assuring a reasonable degree of representativeness within the total international work force.

Related to the merit-versus-geography issue has been the threat to career development in the conflict between permanent and temporary appointments. From the outset it has been policy intent to develop a body of career personnel that would possess professional ability, independence from national influence, reasonable employment security, and prospects for individual growth. Many temporary appointments were authorized in the early days in order to meet staffing objectives and because of a natural reluctance on the part of many to accept the permanence of an international organization. But the temporary-assignment device was also utilized to avoid the loss from national service of individuals who accepted international responsibility. The temporary route became a means in achieving the objectives of geographical distribution. Concerted efforts were made to increase the number of permanent appointments in relation to the temporary ones, and the strength of the career system tended to be measured by the rise in that ratio. With the passage of time, temporary appointments assumed greater length and many of the individuals involved became important administrators or professionals in the United Nations family.

With the expansion of technical assistance in a number of different organizations in Asia, Africa and Latin America, the only means for staffing the missions with the required professional skills was to accept a high ratio of temporary appointments. In many instances, these work locations were far removed from the cultural background of the people employed and possessed few of the accustomed amenities to be found in the headquarters cities of the international organizations. Thus the objective of a career service was challenged by the limited availability of required skills for a lifetime of service. The inconvenience of impermanence and the risk of less dissociation from national service had to be accepted if the desired programs were to be conducted on a multilateral basis.

But these compromises should not be viewed as retreat from basic objectives. The international career cannot be expected to follow the prototype of governmental careers within the civil service of western nations. In view of the increasing importance of international organizations in the life of individual nations, a period of international service can be a positive career element for an official in a national civil service and a positive contribution by his nation to the successful accomplishment of the international mission. In short, there can be variations on the career theme in the world of international organizations without an erosion of the basic purpose of the international civil service. The presence of temporary appointees should not be a justification for neglecting the development of affirmative career patterns for those who do commit themselves to a total career in the international arena.

It would be inaccurate to assume that the total staffing of international organizations is influenced by these perplexing problems. Many persons serving on international payrolls are appointed to general service positions in the headquarters or regional offices from the labor market of the host country, so that office and manual workers have been recruited locally regardless of nationality. They do give a local flavor to the headquarters staff. This represents a pragmatic departure from the goal of an exclusively international character for all secretariats. More significantly, it has created relationship problems between the locally recruited and internationally recruited groups working side by side in the same building. The local nationals are compensated on the basis of prevailing rates for their occupations in the host country and do not receive the supplementary benefits that are necessary to compensate for the expatriation of the internationally recruited. These compensation differences frequently create friction, particularly in light of the absence of firm and definitive job distinctions between the two groups. The career of the local national has a low ceiling because he is unlikely to qualify, either through training or because of geographical distribution, for posts on the international staff. Likewise, management tends to concentrate on the international staff, with a resulting neglect of the local group in terms of employee services, training, and other aspects of a sound career-personnel policy. This relationship problem has become increasingly acute in recent years and requires more intensive attention. It is an area in which the staff associations or trade unions of the international organization can rightfully direct pressure and emphasize inequalities. There is no reason that competent local nationals should not be permitted, on the basis of competitive qualifications and performance, to enter the professional ranks of the international career staff in larger numbers than have been permitted to date.

This leads to another perennial problem of international personnel policy: the formulation and maintenance of a competitive and equitable set of professional salaries for global application. This issue was high on the agenda in the early sessions of the League of Nations. But after extensive study in 1923, the so-called Noblemaire principle was adopted as the guiding standard in determining international salaries. This standard called for a level of compensation sufficiently high to attract the personnel of the highest-paid national civil service. Through numerous evaluations during the intervening years, this principle has survived even though World War II moved the national standard from Great Britain to the United States. The use of this standard has placed heavy reliance in recent years on the rate of upward climb in the salaries for United States civil service personnel. The Noblemaire policy continues to stand because it is argued that in order to attract Americans to international service it is necessary to compete with the salary levels in their own government. In view of the fact that these rates are substantially higher than national civil service salaries in most other countries, the pay received by the vast majority of international civil servants is far more attractive than they can expect from service in their own country. In the most recent review of this problem by the International Civil Service Advisory Board, an exploratory excursion was undertaken into the development of a "global market rate" that might be computed on the basis of a composite of salaries paid by a variety of public and private international organizations. But the statistical as well as the political difficulties in formulating such a pay scale forced its abandonment. Still the issue is not closed. More data and more analysis will be necessary to develop a possible improvement over the existing standards.

But even if the issue of base pay is resolved, equality can be assured only if pay rates are based upon common job-classification standards. The pay policy of the United Nations system has been based on the principle of equal pay for equal work, but the job-evaluation framework upon which the administration of such a policy must rest has never been fully matured and there are serious discrepancies within and among organizations in the job classifications assigned. Certain managers and many employees have never fully accepted the job-classification principle. Because certain occupational fields, such as translators and interpreters, have particularly flat career curves, there has been a natural desire to provide career advancement not only in pay but in grade levels over periods of time without substantial changes in duties or responsibilities or even increases in productivity. This conflict in objectives has hampered the intended adherence to job classification and has led to the kind of inequity that undermines morale and promotes grievances. In a move toward greater application of and consistency in job-classification standards, a personnel specialist has been assigned to work across the board with all agencies in improving the system.

Because the international service must function in many different locations with marked variations in cost of living, a system of allowances has been developed to preserve the purchasing power of the basic salary in different markets around the world. Although this system has produced certain anomalies in its place-to-place relationship, it has been economically sound and should be used to foster an underdeveloped aspect of an international career—interorganizational and geographical mobility. Several international officials have served in New York, the Congo, Geneva, the Gaza Strip, Rome, and Paris. But all too many have spent the bulk of their career in one international headquarters. No administrative machinery exists to plan and encourage this type of career development, a unique and positive aspect of international service.

Another underdeveloped phase of the international civil service is that of training and education. There have been a number of moves in this direction in recent times, but none of them have had the urgency or the magnitude to make an appreciable impact. In one area alone, that of language, there is a serious need for training. Mounting pressure has been applied to recruit additional multilingual employees or to give pay premiums to those who already possess ability in more than one language. The appropriate answer, however, is to offer training both in official languages and in other tongues that enhance the capabilities of the international employee.

With the growing scope of multinational operations in development economics, public health, technical assistance, and many other fields, the availability of training programs can provide enrichment that will redound to the benefit of the individual and the organization. A more aggressive and interrelated program of this nature should have the support of the top administrators in the organization and the financial backing of the legislative bodies.

The recruitment of the international force must become better planned, more extensive, and more affirmative. Recruiting campaigns in various parts of the world, particularly in those parts which are underrepresented, should be conducted to find and attract the abilities necessary to replace departing personnel and to augment the staff to meet new program requirements. This type of recruiting can identify sources of persons with a long-term, career-related interest in international organization. It can search for the recent graduates of universities everywhere. Such recruitment will help to overcome reliance on traditional sources and to lower the average age of the professionals, thereby bringing the freshness and initiative of those who see their own future and even their own survival shaped through the success of international organizations.

The advance toward a more fully developed international civil service must be hastened. The progress of the past generation offers few reasons for complacency. The road ahead is hazardous. The reliance of world states upon international cooperation will rise and fall, but the organizations will continue, the scope of their work will expand, the significance of their action on future peace and progress will be continually elevated. The improvement in personnel policy and practice must be applied with wisdom, ingenuity, and courage by those who exercise leadership responsibility in the international world. But the rapidly growing family of member states must be persuaded that their own collective self-interest lies in supporting the development of a high-quality international civil service as a flexible and creative force that will apply ever higher levels of skill to the resolution of problems among nations in the crowded and shrinking neighborhood of mankind.

Futures

in

Public Service

22

The future of American public service will be marked with continuing growth, increasing complexity, spreading diversity in program requirements and occupational demands, and a rising volume of problems demanding solution. Government will not wither away nor will most of its functions be transferred to the private sector. In view of these considerations, the American people must become more aware of the human side of government and have a closer and clearer identity with the men and women who constitute the means by which democratic institutions express themselves in response to the public will.

The growth is obvious. Although the rate of population growth has been slowed and can be slowed even more, the demands for more and better public education, enlarged and enlightened law enforcement, reclamation of the environment, elimination of poverty and disadvantage, evolving relations with other nations, and other forms of public service will propel that growth, particularly at the level of the government nearest the people, that of the city, the town, and the county.

The diversity of public employment will mirror the professional and occupational diversity of the nation at large. Technological change will produce new demands and new opportunities for the development of skills to translate that change into goods and services for the American people. Because of government's prominent place in research and devel-

285

opment, government will continue to stimulate and participate in extending the diverse nature of employment needs. With this diversity will be a reliance upon the educational system of the country to develop the skills. The requirement of more effective interprofessional collaboration in the accomplishment of more complex missions will necessitate more constructive interrelationships among the professions involved. Those who lead the nation's professions must join in attracting a fair share of their colleagues for service in government without insisting upon special conditions or separate identity for them. In its dependence upon professional capacity, the government cannot delegate to the professions its own responsibility for creating policies and conditions relating the services of those professionals in government service.

In meeting future requirements, a public commitment to merit standards as the central policy theme in government will not be enough. The meritocracy cannot be expected to gain the scope or the capacity to match these requirements. The elements of merit must be re-evaluated and redefined through more critical consideration of the true impact of that standard in both operational and human terms. Adherence to the merit principle should not mean an addiction to a process and the abandonment of a purpose. The basic need must be for the most effective performance of public programs in terms of skill, efficiency, and service to the public. The merit employment processes must be so devised that they attract and select from the entire society, with no exclusions whatsoever, those best equipped and motivated for the performance of the public work at hand. The merit principle must not be subverted while all the mechanical steps of announcement, application, competitive examination, register construction, certificate issuance, and the like are duly observed. If the competitors are limited to a narrow segment of the total labor market or to those known to present employees, such silent and subtle subversion may occur. The principle will be blunted if a competitive examination measures skills not required for a particular task or skills substantially superior to the demands of the positions to be filled. The principle can be undermined if the process is so time-consuming that the ablest people in the market are turned away and seek other employment opportunity. The principle may by overburdened if it is applied to short-term noncareer employment in which distinctions of ability among the potentially qualified are minimal. While there must be safeguards to guarantee that the principle is not eroded by partisan political incursions, it must be strengthened in fact and in the eyes of the citizens in such ways as to gain and sustain public confidence in the qualifications, objectivity, and integrity of the public service.

Public managers of the future must strive more diligently to gain a better public understanding of the public service. It has been said that the American citizenry harbors a death wish for its government and consequently accords its public servants little support and low prestige. At times in the past, the public's indifference has contributed significantly to the difficulties in attracting talent to government service. News accounts and editorial opinion have tended to emphasize the least attractive features of the public servant's behavior and have bolstered the belief that any function performed in the public sector can be expected to be deficient, wasteful, and suspect. The vast number of public servants has created a massive, faceless image with an existence all its own and without a direct identification with the daily needs of the citizen.

Obviously, public respect must be earned. An acceptance or an appreciation of public service by the public itself cannot be achieved instantly or through extensive promotional efforts. But those with leadership responsibility must take on a serious obligation to earn that respect through demonstrating interest in the public and through evident achievement in program results.

Much of the criticism of government's performance is justified and can be substantiated. Government institutions have been far too resistant to change. The added investment of public funds and public manpower has not resulted in the desired solution of critical public problems. High hopes raised by legislative action have often fallen far short in actual execution. These disappointments cannot be brushed aside by those with administrative responsibility. The responsiveness of the organizations of government and the people who make up those organizations has not been as innovative as new programs have clearly necessitated. There must be a willingness within government to seek program and institutional change to respond to public needs. There must be a willingness to scale down and ultimately eliminate public programs that have failed to meet their objectives or have accomplished them so completely that there is no need for their continuance. There must be a perpetual demand for quality of performance and increased productivity. New technology and new behavioral findings must be readily available to the public manager in the constant redesign of his organization. Navigational aids must be recalibrated and perfected to assist the manager and those associated with him in charting and maintaining the course of public interest.

An inherent deficiency that must be overcome by public administration is the absence of reliable and meaningful manpower planning. When new programs are designed or the future scope of old programs is forecast, the manpower element has not been formulated far enough in advance and with sufficient precision to avoid the threat of overstaffing or the absence of required skills. The planning process must be designed with a recognition of the most essential factor in program achievement —the people who will make it function. Program objectives in terms of substantive goals and productive output must be translated into organizational patterns, dollar requirements, and manpower needs. Those manpower needs must be expressed not only in numbers but in professions and occupations, levels of skill, and with the time dimension for recruiting and training those skills. These expressions of needs must be evaluated through subsequent experience, and future planning processes must be changed in order to reflect both the reality of experience and the expectation of improved performance. Such planning cannot be performed in a governmental vacuum. The impact and interrelationship of government's manpower demands with the supply and demand of the total labor market and its constantly changing conditions must be considered.

Emphasis on manpower planning can be sustained only if government devotes additional time, attention, and resources to personnel research, which is now distressingly inadequate. Even in the federal government, where nearly 3 million people are employed, the research budget is almost invisible. While large research outlays are authorized for scientific and technical purposes, social-science and behavioral research within the government has been on a perennial starvation diet. The research agenda is long. Back in 1955 a group of public administration scholars and practitioners developed a comprehensive agenda for the guidance of those inside and outside of government who might be interested in this type of research. Few of the items high on that agenda have been explored, but the project list continues to have a challenging validity and now reflects an even greater urgency. The need is not only in the more obvious areas of psychometrics in tests and measurements for employment but also in career patterns, motivation for performance, the behavioral impact of tenure, fringe benefits, pay differentials, employee attitudes toward working conditions, governmental programs, training requirements and evaluation, and myriad other related research objectives. Not all this exploration should be conducted by the government about itself. This is another area where meaningful relationships could be established with the professional world, particularly in the universities, for the benefit of all concerned. Or perhaps the creation of a research institute, similar to the National Institutes of Health, either within the government or as a separate entity, might provide the research talents and the processes for objective analysis of the public service culture and the people that occupy it.

In the future development of public personnel policies and practices, there must be legislative self-restraint to avoid the creation of a statutory strait jacket that would restrict the formulation of new approaches in staffing public programs or hamper the necessary institutional evolution to respond to the forces of change. The basic Civil Service Act of 1883 was a marvel of public policy expression: it enunciated the principles of merit in terms of competition and equal opportunity, it set forth certain broad criteria to govern the administration of the system, and it created the general dimension of organization and administration for the execution of this basic policy, but it refrained from prescribing detailed standards or processes and assigned broad areas of implementation to the President. Legislative enactments in the same field in subsequent years incorporated a mass of statutory specifications, notably the precise formula for the order of reduction in force, the description of the specific benchmark jobs to be used in evaluating postal positions, and the detailed control over the creation and distribution of certain key positions. In certain state jurisdictions there has been a tendency to legislate in such detail that the administrator had to become a Philadelphia lawyer or personnel man in order to steer clear of legal entanglements in the day-to-day direction of the people working for him. The mass of statutes in the federal government expanded geometrically, so that when codification into a single title of the U.S. Code was undertaken the project consumed nearly ten years and covered more than 1,000 pages. A countertrend has been evident in more recent times. Congress has displayed a greater willingness to delegate broader administrative discretion to executive officers, reserving for itself the function of overview and evaluation and ultimately the appropriation of funds after it has provided the statutory framework of public policy. This trend was manifest in the discretions allowed in the Incentive Awards Act and the Training Act in the 1950s and in certain features in the salary-reform legislation of the 1960s. If progress is to be accelerated, this executive flexibility must not only be preserved but extended to permit the responsible official to devise or revise the policy conditions that relate to his staff. He should be encouraged to innovate in relationship patterns, position and qualification combinations, and ladders for career advancement. The risk of failure and the threat of embarrassment or censure should be minimized, while displays of creative innovation, even if not totally successful, should receive affirmative recognition and encouragement to try again.

This emphasis upon the important role of the manager is not casual. Government must develop a more effective breed of managers who will accept responsibility in an arena of spreading discretion. Many of the maladies in the present situation are attributable to managerial failure, more of omission than of commission. In government, those with supervisory responsibility frequently have difficulty in recognizing the significance and scope of that responsibility and are inclined to divorce themselves from institutional management through close identification with their subordinates. Despite counsels of careful selection and intensive training of supervisors, all too many are chosen on the basis of highly subjective judgment and too limited a field of choice. They are often expected to assume new functions and relationships without adequate preparation. There is evidence that it is not always the most skilled or productive employee who can most successfully rise to the different and more demanding role of supervisor. It is at the basic preparatory level of leadership that work attitudes are formed and the climate created where morale will rise or fall.

In the years ahead, more and more managers in American government will advance not from a predominantly administrative experience but from a professional background. Unlike in the civil service systems of Western Europe, American governmental practice has not led to the formation of an administrative corps. Certainly there are, and will continue to be, generalists who are able to move from one program field to another and successfully exercise managerial leadership for a variety of professionals. But it is more likely that the lawyer or doctor, the scientist or engineer, the economist or social worker, will find his governmental career lifting him to responsibilities that involve the direction of the work of others and the management of financial and material resources in the fulfillment of program goals. In this process, selection and training must also assume major importance. There must be evidence that the selected professional possesses the desire and the capability required of a manager. In his earlier experience he must be permitted to develop his capabilities along these lines through understudy assignments, training exposure, and staff leadership.

These affirmative qualities must be prime prerequisites for those who answer the call to the top appointive posts of government. No Chief Executive will be well served unless he gives major attention to the selection of the right people with the right set of qualifications for the key positions available to him in supplementing his own executive leadership. Reliance on the party faithful, the longtime friend, the available job seeker or even the in-line career official can no longer serve as exclusive sources for such posts. The voters who elect Presidents, governors, and mayors should require each candidate to articulate his staffing standards and his search and selection processes before they cast their ballots. The candidate, in turn, needs to give top priority to this function after his election; he cannot launch his administration with any expectation of success without a full crew of talented associates on board. And when the executive's record is presented to the public for electoral evaluation after two or four years, one aspect of performance which should receive critical assessment should be the public performance of his appointees. If the political parties are to meet their obligations in the election ahead, they need to demonstrate to their supporters and their opponents alike their ability not only to select high-quality candidates but to support such candidates if they are successful in manning their organizations with the best person in each post.

It has been popular in recent years to describe government as "a model employer." Each new policy declaration has exhorted government managers, through their implementation of personnel policy goals, to build a showcase for other employers to observe and to emulate. The rhetoric in these statements has been easier to write or to read than to make a reality throughout government. In all too many instances, governmental jurisdictions have allowed their practices to lag behind those of progressive private employers. Pay and working conditions have been permitted to slip below acceptable standards. New equipment and operating systems have been designed and installed without adequate consideration of the human beings who must make them function; the airport control towers and their installed equipment, for example, were constructed without due regard for the operation by air traffic controllers. Outmoded attitudes have been allowed to obstruct the implementation of new programs; the unwillingness of public schools to adopt new curriculum or educational techniques has delayed the utilization of new technology in education. Communication between management and employees and back again has broken down and gaps of misunderstanding have been allowed to widen. Organizational leadership has become isolated from day-to-day operations and is insensitive to conditions that lead to restiveness and dissent. Where performance standards have slackened, mediocrity has prevailed and become the accepted level of performance. Rather than face the disagreeable task of discipline, the manager has brushed his human problems to one side in the belief that the system will not permit him to exercise the discipline he knows he should impose.

Because the mission is the public interest, government must continually strive to become the model employer in full reality. Those who contribute their most important assets, their personal time and talents, to serve their fellow citizens should expect model conditions. Their pay should be equitable in relation with their colleagues' and comparable to that paid to those performing similar tasks in the private sector. They should be free to join or refrain from joining unions of their choosing, and because the strike weapon is not legally available to them as an expression of their collective will, there must be opportunities for affirmative collaboration with management and for prompt and definitive resolution of grievances or disagreements. Penalties for violation of their no-strike pledge should be enforceable and should in all likelihood be imposed upon the union in economic terms through withdrawal of dues-withholding privileges or financial penalties imposed upon responsible leaders rather than upon individual employees.

The role of model employer must be extended with sensitivity and imagination to ensure that equal opportunity truly exists in all parts of the country, in all occupations at all salary levels, and that no segment of the population is excluded from the opportunity to compete for public service. The human component of government should be representative of the pluralistic character of American society; by such means the strength of diversity as well as the sense of justice will build a better government.

Government should be most conscious of the social problems in the American culture. It should be the first institution to identify those who live in conditions of disadvantage, whether economic, educational, or social. While appealing to private employers to contribute the most constructive means for overcoming disadvantage through employment opportunities, government employers should set the pace, should conduct the experimentation, and should provide the demonstrations of success. But no matter how strong the pressure may become for government to "make jobs" for the sole purpose of providing employment, it should be vigorously resisted. In many foreign countries, government performance has been sadly debilitated through the presence of large numbers of employees occupying jobs with no performance requirements. There will always be additional tasks of meaning and substance that can be performed in behalf of the taxpayer if sufficient funds, resources, and supervision are to be invested in those tasks.

As the thousands of American governments, which it is hoped will be reduced through consolidation, move forward toward the third century of American independence, the public service will face the continuing test of balance in serving the public interest. There must be an unremitting quest for balance between efficiency and service, between tenure and risk-taking, between legal rigidity and administrative flexibility, between the need for dissent and the commitment to program, and between individual rights and public obligations. While service to the public remains paramount, the rights and dignity of each individual in public service must be recognized by those who are served. In the growth and diversity of government, a democratic society must not allow the individual and his unique worth to be lost in the service of the state. The American people and the governments they sustain must be both demanding and humane toward those who labor for them and must preserve the essential importance of the human side of government.

Index

Adams, John Quincy, 158
Adams, Sherman, 216
Adult Work Experience, 115
Agency for International Development
    (AID), 148, 234–235, 238
Alcoholism, 107–109
Ambassadors, 226, 234, 237, 246–247
American Civil Liberties Union, 165
American Federation of Government Em-
    ployees, 122
American Federation of Labor, 127
  Metal Trades Council, 122
American Indians, 78
American Society for Public Administra-
    tion, 174
Appropriations, 162–163
Arbitration, impartial, 142
Arthur, Chester Alan, 13–14
Atomic Energy Act of 1946, 29
Atomic Energy Commission, 14, 29, 51,
    199
Authority, limitation of, in government
    leadership, 137–138
  management, 138

Automatic Data Processing Management
    Training Center, 260
Automation, fear of, 261

Behavioral research, 270
Benefits, 211–214
Bernstein, Marver, 215
Bill of Rights for Federal Employees, 154
Birmingham, Alabama, 69–70
Blind, the, employment for, 96
Brookings Institution, 174, 224
  study on student recruitment by, 61
Brownlow Commission, 15, 22
Budget and Accounting Act of 1921, 196
Bundy, McGeorge, 238
Bureaucracy, 2, 169
  federal, 3
  leaders and, 215–216
Bureaucrats, 2
Burns, James MacGregor, 230

California, 157, 167, 193
  employment practices in, 117
  recruiting program in, 61

Canal Zone riots, 152
Career designs, individual, 46
Career developments, 173–175
Career Educational Award program, 177
Career Executive Assignments, 218
Career Service Award, 269
Career systems, relative merit of, 42
  studies of, 44
Census Bureau, 263
Charlottesville, Virginia, 183
Cities (*see* Local governments)
Citizens, attitude of, toward public service, 2
  and quality of public service, 10–11
Civil Aeronautics Board, 255
Civil disorders, participation in, 149–151
Civil rights, 145
  in the South, 69–70
Civil Rights Act of 1964, 75, 92
Civil Rights Commission, 78
Civil-rights leaders, 77
Civil servants, expatriate, 236
  international, duties of, 276
    permanent versus temporary, 278–279
    recruitment of, 277–278
  publicity surrounding performance of, 249–256
  standards of performance for, 249–256
  (*See also* Public employees)
Civil service, ix
  criticism of, 16, 273
  and equal opportunity, 65–66, 70–71
  growth of, 14
  international dimensions of, 273–283
  merit system and, 13–25
  reform of, 145
  and veteran preference, 20–21
  women in, 83–84
Civil Service Act, 13, 20, 67, 159, 269, 289
Civil service agency, functions and location of, 21, 25
Civil Service Commission, 21, 33, 35–36, 53, 55, 58, 60, 68, 75, 84, 97, 103, 107, 125, 129, 157, 159–165, 167–169, 183–184, 216–219, 226–227, 253–255
  appropriations for, 162–163
  Bureau of Training, 181
  Center for Advanced Study, 182
  computers used by, 258–260

Civil Service Commission (*continued*)
  and disability retirement, 155
  equal opportunity program of, 76
  executive inventory made by, 219–221
  Executive Seminar Centers, 182–183
  and federal wage system, 210
  and Foreign Service, 242–243
  state and local governments and, 188
  training program of, 173, 177–178
  twenty-fourth annual report of, 196
Classification Act, 42, 197–202, 205, 209
  overhaul of, 200
  test of, 202–203
Cleveland, Grover, 14
Cold war, the, 275
Collective bargaining, 124–125, 211
College talent, Black recruitment and, 74
  and Foreign Service, 244–246
  government's need for, 49–64
  women and, 88–89
College Work Study, 115
Commission on Political Activity of Government Personnel, 164–169
  members of, 165
Committee on Economic Development, 186
Communication, management-employee, 292
Community Relations Service, 75
Complaints, employee, 155
Computers, use of, in public service, 257–263
  and invasion of privacy, 263
  training in, 260
Conflict of interest, 252–255
Consular service, 233
Consumer Price Index, 299
Contractors, personnel supplied by, 34–37
Contracts, public service and, 27–37
Coolidge, Calvin, 120
Coordinator program, for the mentally retarded, 103
  for the physically handicapped, 97–98
Corson, John, 215
Criminal acts, 149–150, 155

Dallas, Texas, 72
Data processing, 258–263
  training in, 260

Deaf, the, employment for, 96
Defense installations, 6
  (*See also* Military bases)
Democracy, merit system and, 16
  participative, 140
Diplomatic service (*see* Foreign Service)
Disadvantaged, the, employment of, 99–
  109, 111–118
Discrimination, racial, 65–81
  by sex, 83–93
Dismissal, civil service and, 20
Dissent, 145–152
  active, 146
  reasons for, 145
  right of, 145–151
Distinguished Award for Outstanding
  Civilian Service, 268
Doctors, women as, 91
Domestic Council, 192
Dropouts, 88
Dulles, John Foster, 241
Dungan, Ralph, 223–224, 226

Economic Opportunity Act, 164
Economy Achievement, plaques, 268
Economy Act, 197
Education, jobs and, 40–41, 85, 114
  of minority groups, 69, 74
  public, curriculums in, 292
    employment in, 8, 80
  for public service, 171–184
    future of, 286
    international, 282
    mid-career, 175–177
  of women, 88–89, 91–92
  (*See also* College talent)
Education for Public Service Act of 1967,
  189
Educational Testing Service, 75
Efficiency ratings, of mentally retarded,
  104
Eisenhower, Dwight D., 22, 66, 198–199,
  217, 222, 268
Eisenhower administration, 28, 67, 173,
  200, 209
El Paso, Texas, 79
Employee participation, 139–140
Employer-employee relationships, com-
  munication in, 292
  standards for, 36

Employment, compensatory, 72
  equal opportunity in, viii, 65–81
  part-time, 86, 91
  private, 137
  public (*see* Public employment)
  summer, viii, 59–61
Employment experience, 50
Engineers, women as, 90–91
ENIAC (Electronic Numerical Integrator
  and Calculator), 259
Equal Employment Opportunity, Commission, 75, 92
Equal opportunity, realization of, 65–81
Equal Opportunity Employment program,
  23, 76
Ervin, Sam J., 153
Ethical standards, in public service, 249–
  256
  international, 276–277
Executive Assignment System, 217–218
Executives, top, salient characteristics of,
  219–220
Experience, employment, 50
  jobs and, 40, 114

Fact-finding, 142–143
Federal Aviation Administration (FAA),
  132–133
Federal Bureau of Investigation, 14, 230
Federal Executive Boards, 192
Federal Executive Institute, 182–183, 221–
  222
Federal grant-in-aid programs, 7, 15, 44,
  80, 185, 189–190
  (*See also* Government programs)
Federal Salary Reform Act of 1962, 200,
  204
Federal Service Entrance Examination, 55–
  57, 74, 93
Federal Tort Claims Act, 155
Federal wage system, 210–211
  (*See also* Salaries)
Feminists, militant, 83
Fenn, Dan H., 224–226
Firemen, strikes by, 119
Fishkin, Jerome, 157
Flemming, Arthur S., 165, 269
Ford, Henry II, 112
Ford Foundation, 75, 175–176
Fordham, Jefferson B., 250

Foreign aid programs, 234–235
  technical, 278–279
Foreign-policy advisers, 238
Foreign Service, ix, 14, 40, 42, 201, 233–247
  personnel system of, 240–246
  popularity of, 244–245
Foreign Service Act, 234, 240
Freeman, Orville L., 73
Fringe benefits, 211–214

Gardner, John, 227
Garfield, James, 159
General Accounting Office (GAO), 35
General Services Administration, 116
Ghettos, 115–118
Gifts to government personnel, 251–252,
  255–256
Gleason, John, quoted, 73
Glennan, T. Keith, 30
Goldberg, Arthur J., 123, 125
Goods and services, government requirements for, 28–29
Government, as employer, viii, 111–118,
  292–284
  federal, number of statutes in, 290
  and industry, 45
  obligation of, 148
  research and development activities of,
    30–34
  and search for college talent, 49–64
  size of, 2–4
  (*See also entries under* Federal)
Government agencies, 148–149, 180
  and city problems, 192–193
  and equal opportunity, 72–73
  and labor relations, 128
  mentally retarded employed by, 101–103
  personnel of, 34–37, 251–252
  women in, 86–87
  and work training programs, 115–116,
    172, 180
Government appointments, women and,
  92–93
  (*See also* Presidential appointments)
Government Employees Training Act of
  1958, 173–174, 177–178, 181
Government programs, 3
  for career advancement, 178–179
  expansion of, vii
  misuse of funds for, 160

Government programs (*continued*)
  social, 5
  (*See also name of program, as* Foreign
    aid)
Grant, Ulysses S., 158
Grievance machinery, 142, 293
Guiteau, Charles J., 159

Hammarskjöld, Dag, 274–275
Hanford, 29
Harding, Warren G., 197
Hardy, Porter, 36
Hatch, Carl A., 160
Hatch Act, 157, 160–162, 164–167, 170
Health, alcoholism and, 107–109
  occupational, 106–107
Health insurance, 213
Highway construction, 9
Hiring reforms, 116–117
Hobson, Julius, 80
Hollerith, Hermann, 258
Hoover, Herbert, 216
Hoover Commission, 22–24, 215–216
  second, 216
Hopkins, Harry, 160

In-service training, 51
Incentive Awards Act, 290
Incentive Awards Program, 105, 267
Incentives, for improved performance in
  public service, 265–271
  profit, 269–270
  for women, 87–89
Individual, the, development of, 47–48, 174
Intelligence, sex and, 90
Internal Revenue Service, computers used
  by, 261
IBM, 258
International Civil Service Advisory Board,
  274–276, 281
International organizations, 273–283
  staffing of, 279–280
  training and education for, 282

Jackson, Andrew, 158
Jaycees, 105, 269
Jefferson, Thomas, 158
Job ability, 16–17
  tests for, 18
Job classification, 43, 281

Job Corps, 115
Job engineering, 51
Job mobility, 44–45, 47
Job performance, test scores and, 75
Job requirements, 114
Job tenure, 221–222, 266
  merit system and, 19–20
Job turnover, 43, 114
  among women, 84–85
Jobmobiles, 116
Jobs, poverty and, 111–112
  skills and, 113
Johnson, Lyndon B., 60, 68–69, 75–76, 86–
    87, 107, 112, 129, 134, 164, 185, 203,
    206–207, 210, 226–227, 229–231,
    237–239, 243, 246–247, 253–255,
    268
  quoted, 75, 101, 177–178, 181, 204, 217,
    253
Johnson administration, 228, 242, 246

Kappel, Frederick, 207
Kappel Commission, 207–208
Kelly Air Force Base, 78
Kendall, Donald M., 112
Kennedy, John F., 30–31, 52, 60, 66, 68–69,
    83, 86, 98, 100–101, 125–126, 164,
    202–203, 222–226, 237–238, 250–
    252, 268
  quoted, 123
Kennedy, Joseph P., Jr., Foundation, 100
Kennedy administration, 209, 223–224,
    238
Kennedy Library, 226
Kilpatrick, Franklin P., et al., 61
King, Martin Luther, Jr., vii, 69, 119,
    149
Kissinger, Henry, 238
Knowledge, obsolescence of, 179–180
Korean War, 95

Labor force, physically handicapped in,
    98
  women in, 88–89, 92
Labor-management agencies, 24
Labor-management relations, fundamental
    principles in, 141–143
  in public service, vii, 119–144
  task forces on, 123–124, 129–131
Labor market, competition in, 49–50

Landrum-Griffin Act of 1959, 129
Language barriers, 115–116
Law, the, obedience to, 151–152
Lawyers, in government service, 7, 60–61
Leadership, 45
  public employment and, viii-ix, 137
  quest for, in public service, 215–231
League of Nations, 273, 275, 280
Lie, Trygve, 275
Life expectancy of women, 89
Life insurance program, 213
Lloyd–La Follette Act of 1912, 122
Local governments, and civil service,15–16,
    24
  employment in, 7–10
    mobility and, 188
  ethical standards in, 256
  federal employees in, 190–191
  and grants-in-aid, 186, 189–192
  hiring practices in, 118
  and labor relations, 140–141
  political activity in, 168–169
  recruiting programs in, 61
  strengthening administration in, 187–
    188
  training employees for, 187
Los Alamos, 30, 51
Los Angeles, 193

Maas, General Melvin, 101
McNamara, Robert S., 6, 72, 224
Madison, James, quoted, 7
Magruder, Calvert, 250
Management, and authority, 138
  employee participation in, 139–140
  unionism and, 138
  (See also Labor-management relations)
Managers, public, 45–46, 50, 99, 105, 114,
    125, 128, 142, 152, 214, 261, 266,
    270–271
  future, 287–288, 290
  incentives for, 268
Manhattan District, 29
Manning, Bayliss, 250
Manpower, forecasting need for, 53
  increased demand for, vii, 52
  for overseas operations, 239–240
  recruitment programs for, 52–54
  reports on, 37
  waste of, 50

Manpower Act of 1967, 189
Manpower Development and Training Act, 105
Manpower planning, 288–289
Manpower utilization, 171
Marriage, 89
Marshall, Burke, 70
Marshall Plan, 235
Meany, George, 132
Mediation, 142–143
Mediators, 128
Medical Service, 199
Medicare, 260
Meehan case, 152
Memphis, Tennessee, 119
Mental disabilities, examples of job performance and, 105–106
  job placement and, 101–104
  separation rate for, 104
  work and, viii, 99–106
Mental hospitals, 100
Merit system, 13–25, 105, 112, 114
  and collective bargaining, 124
  elements necessary for, 16–17
  equal opportunity and, 67, 80
  in the future, 286
  and job tenure, 19–20
  myths about, 19
  success of, 25
Mexican Americans, 66, 69, 78–79
Michigan, recruiting program in, 61
  University of, Survey Research Center, 165
Militancy, 139
  of feminists, 83
  Negro, 76
  among public employees, 120, 127
Military bases, 236–237
Military service, ix, 42
Minorities, hiring of, 66–81
  number of positions held by, 79–80
MODE (Management Objectives with Dollars through Employees), 259
Morale, 36, 51, 270
Mosher, Frederick, quoted, 39
Municipal Manpower Commission, 9–10, 24, 53

National Aeronautics and Space Administration (NASA), 30–31, 35

National Association of Government Employees (NAGE), 133
National Civil Service League, 117, 165, 269
National Commission on Technology, Automation and Economic Progress, 179
National Council of Technical Service Industries, 35
National Federation of Federal Employees, 122
National Institute of Mental Health, Center for Prevention and Cure of Alcoholism, 108
National Institute of Public Affairs, 175–176
National Labor Relations Board, 122
National Organization for Women (NOW), 83
National Postal Alliance, 136
National Postal Union, 136
Negroes, 56, 136
  equal opportunity for, 65–81
  and merit system, 19
  militancy of, 76
Neighborhood Youth Corps, 115
New Deal, 3, 22, 122, 160, 164, 172
"New federalism," 185
New Frontier, 223
New Jersey, 117, 133
New York City, 24, 78, 133–134
  strikes in, 119, 121, 138
New York State, 24, 121
  recruiting program in, 61
Nixon, Richard M., 118, 130, 132, 134, 184, 192, 222, 238, 255
Noblemaire policy, the, 280
Noncareer Executive Assignments, 218
North, the, equal opportunity in, 71
Nuclear arms contracts, 29–30

Oak Ridge, Tennessee, 29
Occupations, public employment and, 6–7
  women and, 88
  (*See also entries under* Job)
Office of Economic Opportunity, 243
Office of Emergency Preparedness, 228
Office of Management and Budget, 193
Oklahoma v. *U.S. Civil Service Commission*, 167

Ombudsmen, 155
Operation MUST, 113–114
Opportunity, equal, 46, 65–81

Panama Canal Zone, 237
Paper work, freedom from, 261
Patronage, 15, 158
Pay. *See* Salaries
Peace Corps, 47, 59, 224, 237
Peace petition, right to sign, 148
Pennsylvania, University of, 259
Pension plans, federal, 211–214
Personnel research, 288–289
Personnel systems, automated, 262–263
  international, policy of, 280–281
Peter Principle, the, 266
Physical disability, work and, viii, 95–99
Planning, errors in, 51
Police, 8, 40
  Negro, 80
  strikes by, 119–120
Political campaigns, cost of, 163–164
Politics, public employment and, 15–17,
     157–170
  women in, 92
Pollack, Ross, and Paul David, 215
Poor People's March, 150–151
Population growth, 285
Postal employees, 4, 67, 70, 78, 129, 133–
     136
  Negro, 67, 136
  salaries of, 201–202
  women as, 93
Postal Field Service, 199, 205
Postal Service, 201
Postal unions, 205
Postmasters, 136
Poverty, elimination of, 111
  studies of, 115–116
Presidential appointments, 222–231, 246–
     247, 255, 291
Presidential Committee on Equal Employ-
     ment Opportunity, 66
President's Commission on the Status of
     Women, 83
President's Committee on Mental Retarda-
     tion, 101
President's Committee for the Placement of
     the Physically Handicapped, 97,
     101

Princeton University, 172, 175, 177, 269
Privacy, invasion of, 153, 263
Private enterprise, and competition with
     government for personnel, 1
  government employment and, 28
  profit incentive in, 269–270
  and unions, 137–139
Professional Association of Air Traffic
     Controllers (PATCO), 132
Professions, career advancement and, 41
  public employment and, 6–7
  women in, 88, 90–91
Promotion, 46, 266
  of mentally retarded, 104
  of Negroes, 72
  seniority and, 266–267
  standards for, 41
  and take-home pay, 211
  of women, 84–85
Protest, right to, 145–151
Public budgets, vii
  federal, 3
Public careers, ix
  dynamism in, 47
  meaning of, 39–48
  motivations in, 42
Public employees, 2
  and contracts, 27–37
  in foreign countries, 233–247
  fringe benefits for, 211–214
  intergovernmental exchange of, 190–191
  and labor-management relations, 119–
     144
  and politics, 3, 15–17, 157–170
  salaries of, 195–214
  state, 166
  strikes by, 119–120
  tests for, 18
  working conditions for, 138
  (*See also* Civil servants)
Public employers, obligations of, 142
Public employment, authority and leader-
     ship in, viii–ix, 137–138
  in cities and states, 6
  equal opportunity in, 65–81
  growth of, vii, 1, 3
  occupation, professions, and, 6–7
  and private employment, 27
  rights and responsibilities in, viii–ix, 145–
     155

Public employment (*continued*)
size of, 27–28
student reaction to, 55
women in, 83–93
and workers' rights, viii–ix
Public Health Service, 7, 14, 107
Public jurisdictions, multiplicity of, 10
Public opinion, 2
Public payroll, number listed on, 1
size of, vii, 2
Public schools, curriculums of, 292
Public service, compared with private employment, 137–139
computers used in, 257–263
by contract, 27–37
dimensions of, 1–11
diversity in, 40
evolution of, 13
futures in, 285–294
incentives for improvement of, 265–271
intergovernmental cooperation in development of, 185–194
labor-management relations in, 119–134
and public interest, 294
public understanding of, 287
quest for leadership in, 215–231
training and education for, 171–184
(*See also* Public employment)
Public Service Career Awards, 87
Puerto Ricans, 78

Qualification standards, 41

Racial discrimination, 66, 68, 77
Randall, Clarence, 203
Rank-in-man career system, 42, 44, 46, 244
Rank-in-position career system, 42–43, 46
Recruiters and recruiting, 54–55, 57–59, 61
campus response to, 62–64
for international civil service, 282
Rehabilitation services, 97, 103, 105
Responsibilities of public employment, 145–155
Retirement, disability, 98–99, 155
Retirement Act, 213
Retirement systems, 212–213
Retirement Trust Fund, 212
Rights, individual, public employment and, 145–155, 167
Riots, 152

Rockefeller, John D., 3rd, 269
Rockefeller Public Service Awards, 269
Romney, George, 56
Roosevelt, Eleanor, 83, 86, 93
Roosevelt, Franklin D., 14, 66, 122, 160–161
quoted, 123
Roosevelt, Theodore, 14, 22, 159
quoted, 16
Rostow, Walt, 238
Rusk, Dean, 223, 238

Salaries, 34, 37, 57–58, 124, 195–214, 221, 292
deficiencies in system of, 199–200
in industry, 203
in international civil service, 280–282
of postal employees, 135–136
promotion and, 211
reform plan for, 200–205
Salary Reform Act of 1962, 58
San Antonio, Texas, 78
Sanitation workers, strikes by, vii, 119
Schedule C positions, 217–218
Seattle, Washington, 117
Self-expression, right of, 148
Seniority, 43
promotion and, 266–267
Service academies, Negroes in, 68
Sex, discrimination and, 83–93
intelligence and, 90
Sheppard, Morris, 160
Sherwood, Frank, 183
Shriver, Sargent, 223–224
Siciliano, Rocco, 199
Sick leave, 212
Skill requirements, analysis of, 51
new jobs and, 113
Social change, participation in, 153
public employment and, 111–118
Social idealism, 59
Social problems, government and, 293
Social programs, federal, growth of, 5
Social Security Act of 1935, 9, 212
Social Security Administration, computers used by, 260
Social Security benefits, 212–213
Social unrest, 139–140, 153
South, the, and civil rights, 69–71
Southeast, the, 71, 74

Southeast Asia, 146–147
Southwest, the, 78
Space program, manpower for, 52
  women in, 93
Space research, 30–31
Sparling, Rebecca, quoted, 90
Spoils system, 15, 159
Staffing, 51, 53
  (*See also* White House staff)
Stanley, David, 215
State government, civil service in, 15, 24
  employment figures for, 7–9
  ethical standards in, 256
  federal employees in, 6, 190–191
  and grants-in-aid, 186, 189–190
  mobility of public employees in, 188–189
  revised employment practices in, 117–118
  strengthening administration in, 187–188
  training public employees in, 187
State service centers, 193
Stay-in-School campaign, 115
Strikes by public employees, vii-viii, 119–120, 133, 144, 293
  potential, 133
Students, attitude of, toward public employment, 61–64
  idealism of, 59
  recruitment of, 49–64
  (*See also* College talent; Education)
Suggestions, employee, 267–268
Summer Youth Opportunity campaign, 115
Supervisors, 42, 96–97, 103–104, 267
  women as, 85
Support activities, 34
Syracuse University, 172

Teachers, 8, 40
  Negro, 80
  strikes by, 119, 138
Technological changes, public employment and, 285–286, 288
Tennessee Valley Authority, 14, 133, 199
Tests, 41
  bias in, 73–74
  for college students, 55–57
  for the disadvantaged, 113–114
  evaluation of, 75

Tests (*continued*)
  merit system and, 18
  for summer job applicants, 60
  women and, 83–84
Townsend, Lynn, 112
Training Act, 290
Training programs, 51
  for Negroes, 68–69
  for public service, 171–184
  for executives, 221
  international, 282
  intra-agency, 174
Truman, Harry S., 66
Tuthill, John W., 240

U Thant, 275
Unemployment, 112–113, 118
Uniformed Services Pay Act of 1963, 204
Unions, 140, 145, 216
  management and, 138
  in private enterprise, 137–138
  public employee, 3, 35, 120–136, 139, 141–143, 169, 195, 205, 210, 213, 293
  role of, 139
United Nations, 274, 278
  Charter of, 275, 277
  pay policy of, 281
United Public Workers v. *Mitchell,* 167
United States Air Force, 78, 235
United States Army, 235
United States Bureau of the Budget, 36, 192–193, 201, 210, 263
United States Bureau of Executive Manpower, 218
United States Bureau of Labor Statistics, 200–201, 203, 206
United States Cabinet, 5–6, 199, 223–225, 252
  Committee on Mexican-American Affairs, 78–79
  first Negro in, 69
  salaries of, 205
United States Congress, 22–23, 92, 96, 118, 122, 124, 127, 132, 134, 136, 145, 149, 154, 162, 164, 168–169, 173, 189, 191, 196, 198–199, 216, 221–222, 234–235, 290
  and federal programs, 3
  and salary schedules, 201–204, 206–210

United States Congress (*continued*)
(*See also* U.S. House; U.S. Senate)
United States Department of Agriculture, 5, 73, 78
United States Department of Defense, 4, 6, 33, 72–73, 93, 116, 125, 224
overseas employees of, 235–236, 242–243
United States Department of Health, Education, and Welfare, 5, 99
United States Department of Housing and Urban Development, 5–6, 69
United States Department of Labor, 125, 129
United States Department of Transportation, 5–6
United States House of Representatives, Education and Labor Committee, 189
Government Operations Committee, 36
Post Office and Civil Service Committee, 204, 216–217
United States Information Agency (USIA), 235, 238
United States Navy, 235
United States Post Office Department, 5, 67, 116, 122, 125, 129, 134–136
United States Senate, 204, 226
Foreign Relations Committee, 243
Subcommittee on Constitutional Rights, 153
United States State Department, 148, 223, 233–234, 240–241, 245
United States Supreme Court, 167, 170
United States War Department, 259
UNIVAC (Universal Automatic Computer), 259
Universities, and education for public service, 172–175, 180

Vacations, 212
Van Riper, Paul, 215

Veterans, disabled, 95–96
Veterans Administration, 5–7, 70, 73, 99–100, 105, 125, 199, 201
Veterans Preference Act, 21
Veterans' services, 4–5, 20–21
Vietnam war, 4, 146, 237, 245
VISTA, 59
Vocational Work Study, 115
Voting Rights Act, 23

Wagner Act of 1935, 122
Washington State, 117
Weaver, Robert C., 69
White House Executive Biographic Index, 227–229
White House Staff, 224–227, 238
Wilson, Woodrow, 196
Women, discrimination against, 83–93
education of, 87–89
life expectancy of, 89
and part-time employment, 86
public employment and, 83–93
single, 85
Work, participation in supervision of, 270–271
as therapy, viii
understanding of, 113
Work-trainee examining plan, 114
Working conditions, 270, 292
Works Progress Administration (WPA), 160
World War I, 122, 196
World War II, civil service during, 273
employment of physically handicapped during, 95
Negro employment during, 67
salary freeze during, 211
Wriston, Henry, 241

Yarmolinsky, Adam, 223
Youth, disadvantaged, 115

71 72 73 10 9 8 7 6 5 4 3 2 1

DATE DUE			
GAYLORD			PRINTED IN U.S.A.